MINISTERS' MESSAGE

British Columbians, like all Canadians, care deeply about the environment. By any standard, British Columbia offers a rich and spectacular landscape. As stewards of the Province's air, water, and land resources, British Columbians need accurate, timely, and meaningful information on the state of the environment so that informed decisions about the future of the Province can be made. Such information is also needed to help measure our progress in protecting and sustaining the integrity of the environment for present and future generations.

It is with pleasure that we present the "State of the Environment Report for British Columbia".

This State of the Environment Report gives us a snapshot of British Columbia's environment and provides information on a number of environmental benchmarks or indicators which, like measures of economic performance, document current status and trends. This report can be used to make environmentally responsible choices - choices that will reduce or minimize the impact of human activities on ecosystems and promote long term sustainability of the environment.

This State of the Environment Report for British Columbia represents an important step. The public has become familiar with a regular accounting on the economy from government, and should expect, and receive, a similar accounting on the environment. Important first steps, however, should not be confused with definitive last words. While the following pages shed a great deal of light on environmental conditions in British Columbia, there is still much more to learn and document.

This report is the result of cooperative partnerships among many scientists, academics and government officials. The British Columbia Round Table on the Environment and the Economy and members of the public also served in an advisory capacity and helped shape this report. To the many participants and contributors, we extend our warmest thanks. To each of you who will be reading the results of their work, we invite your comments.

John Cashore
Minister of Environment,
 Lands and Parks
Province of British Columbia

Mary Collins
Minister of State (Environment)
Government of Canada

STATE OF THE ENVIRONMENT REPORT FOR BRITISH COLUMBIA

Highlights

This State of Environment Report was prepared to increase understanding of the ecological consequences of human activities in British Columbia. With increased understanding, society can make more informed decisions and more responsible choices; ones which are environmentally sustainable over the long term. Timely and accurate information on environmental conditions and trends is a necessary component of environmentally sound decision making.

The following excerpts from the report provide a sense of some current environmental conditions and trends. But it is not a comprehensive summary. There are nevertheless three overall conclusions. First, considerable progress has been made over the last several decades in protecting and restoring the province's ecosystems. Second, there's lots of room for improvement - many long standing problems remain unresolved, and new problem areas continue to be discovered. Third, human activities and environmental problems in B.C. are closely linked to the rest of the world. Some of our activities have effects which extend far beyond provincial boundaries, and the condition of our local environment is influenced by distant human activities and natural events.

Population growth

- B.C. currently has about 3.3 million people; by the year 2016 it is expected to have 4.9 million - a 50% increase in only 24 years. (pg. 7)

- The Lower Mainland, southeast Vancouver Island and the Gulf Islands make up less than 3% of the area of B.C., but contain two thirds of its people. (pg. 88)

- Between 1981 and 1986, the Vancouver and Victoria urban areas permanently converted over 50 km² of rural land to urban uses. (pg. 93)

Waste generation

- Despite progress in recycling, British Columbians still generate more waste per capita than any developed country - about three times the rate of Sweden. It is estimated that 60% of the province's 236 landfills will be full by the year 2000 if current practices continue. (pg. 64)

- There is no facility in the province for the safe treatment and disposal of hazardous wastes. About 110,000 tonnes are generated each year, and while some are properly stored or recycled, others are disposed of along with ordinary wastes. (pg. 65)

- In the period between 1987 and 1989, a person walking along the 20 km beach of Pacific Rim National Park would on average have seen one piece of debris for every step taken. Most debris is styrofoam and plastics, followed by glass and metal, paper, wood, and fishing gear. (pg. 86)

- Over half the households in B.C. are now using curbside recycling. (pg. 65)

Energy consumption

- B.C. has an energy-intensive industrial base - about half the energy consumed is for industrial use, and a quarter for transportation. (pg. 5)

- British Columbians use about 20% more energy per person than the average Canadian, and about 300% more than the average Japanese.

Rates of energy consumption have remained more or less stable for the last ten years. (pg. 5,8)

- Energy savings gained by B.C. Hydro's Power Smart program for both industrial and domestic customers are enough to supply all the electricity for 70,000 homes for one year. (pg. 8)

Global climate change

- Globally, nine of the ten warmest years since 1881 occurred during the period from 1979 to 1991. In B.C., climate warming appears to be taking place at a rate of around 0.4 - 0.8°C per century. This is indicated by measurements of air and sea-surface temperatures, and studies of shrinking glaciers. These changes may be due to natural climatic variations, or may be a preliminary signal of global warming. (pg. 10)

Stratospheric ozone depletion

- The greatest damage to the ozone layer from B.C. emissions is from bromine-containing halons (used in fire extinguishers). The second largest source of ozone-depleting substances from B.C. was CFC loss from automobile air conditioners. The Province has recently introduced strict regulations to control the use of ozone-depleting gases. (pg. 12)

- Although trends are not yet available for B.C., stratospheric ozone levels over Edmonton have declined since the late 1970s, but are considered to be within the range of natural fluctuation. (pg. 12)

Acidic deposition

- No adverse effects from acidic deposition have been found to date in B.C. forests. (pg. 13)

- Most acid rain concerns focus on sensitive aquatic systems, especially in the Coast Mountains. Sensitive lakes and acidic soils along the Sunshine Coast and the north shore of Burrard Inlet are being subjected to elevated levels of acid inputs. Extensive surveys have turned up no evidence of significant acidification of lakes or streams. (pg. 14)

Air quality

- Smoke is one of the primary air quality issues in many interior B.C. communities, particularly those with active forest products industries. (pg. 14)

- With the elimination of leaded gasoline in 1990, atmospheric lead levels dropped dramatically in downtown Vancouver and most other sampled areas of B.C. (pg. 15)

- Urban air quality in B.C. has shown improvements for some gases (carbon monoxide). For other gases, the situation remains a problem (sulphur dioxide, ozone, hydrogen sulphide). (pg. 15-17)

- Ground-level ozone concentrations in the Lower Mainland have improved over the last decade, but on about 100 days per year one or more locations still exceed Federal standards for desirable levels. Motor vehicles produce more than half of the ozone-forming pollutants. The GVRD aims to reduce total emissions by 50% by the year 2000. (pg. 89-91)

- While improvements in technology and pollution control equipment are generally reducing per capita emissions of air pollutants, these advances may be overtaken by increased population growth in some areas, particularly the Lower Mainland. (pg. 17,89-90)

- Since the late 1970s, atmospheric sulphur dioxide levels have been declining in Trail, partly from zinc smelter modernization, and partially from a control program. (pg. 79)

Water supply

- Data collected around the province over the last 30-70 years suggest average annual streamflows are decreasing at southern sites and increasing at northern sites. Similar patterns have recently been observed in snowpack water storage. The causes of these changes are not known. (pg. 18-19)

- There is currently no indication of large-scale "groundwater mining" in B.C. (pg. 30)

- Seasonal shortages of water have occurred in the Peace-Liard, Cariboo, Kootenays, Central Coast and Sunshine Coast. These shortages may be due to a lack of resources for tapping new supplies, rather than a lack of water. Water supply is a major concern in parts of the Okanagan and Thompson Basins. (pg. 19-21,82,99)

Water quality

- The province has been monitoring water quality since 1987. Established water quality objectives have consistently been met in over 90% of the samples checked. (pg. 26-27)

- A recent study of drinking water sources for communities near pulp mills on the upper Fraser and Thompson rivers showed no evidence of dioxin, furan or other organochlorine contamination. (pg. 28)

- Over 1.5 million people in B.C. live in communities which lack or have minimal sewage treatment. (pg. 24,33)

- Microbiological contamination is the greatest drinking water quality problem in B.C., mostly outside major population centres. The province has the highest incidence of water-borne illness in Canada. (pg. 28)

Contaminants in ecosystems

- Since 1970, there has been a downward trend in PCB levels in eggs of Double-crested cormorants in the Strait of Georgia. (pg. 39)

- Since 1988 dioxin-related fish consumption advisories have been issued for a variety of fish species in areas near pulp mills. These areas include parts of the upper Fraser, Thompson, Quesnel, North Thompson, South Thompson, Kootenay, and Columbia rivers. (pg. 37,48,80)

- Almost 900 km² of coastal marine habitat has been closed to commercial harvest of some shellfish species due to dioxin contamination. (pg. 34,37)

- Dioxin levels in the eggs of Double-crested cormorants in the Strait of Georgia were high during 1983-89 compared with levels detected in the Bay of Fundy, the St. Lawrence estuary, and Lake Ontario. Recent data (1991) indicate a decline in dioxin concentrations in eggs of both cormorants and herons. (pg. 38)

- In 1990, the Province introduced regulations requiring reductions in the discharge of chlorinated organic compounds from pulp mills. Included are dioxins and furans. More stringent regulations were passed in 1992. (pg. 22-24,33)

- Concentrations of the furan TCDF increased in sediments in the Strait of Georgia after pulp mills began chlorine bleaching in the early 1960s. They now appear to be decreasing, probably in response to improved treatment at pulp mills. (pg. 93)

- In 1980/81, the Province ordered improved treatment systems at a copper-lead-zinc mine discharging waste water to Buttle Lake. Since then, heavy metal concentrations have dropped by more than 80%, and some recovery has been observed in the ecosystem. (pg. 85)

Biological diversity and habitat protection

- British Columbia has the greatest diversity of birds and mammals of any province in Canada. (pg. 41)

- At present in B.C., 702 species of plants and animals are candidates for threatened or endangered status. Further research will likely add to this list. Only four species are currently officially designated as endangered. (pg. 42)

- The south Okanagan has more vulnerable, threatened and endangered species (mammals, birds, reptiles and amphibians) than any other area in B.C. Many species found here exist nowhere else in the province, and some are not found anywhere else in Canada. (pg. 83)

- The single most important factor affecting wildlife in B.C. is habitat loss. (pg. 54)

- Each year, about 800 million juvenile salmon and 1.5 million birds use the Fraser Estuary. Up to 70% of the wetlands in the Lower Fraser Valley have been lost, and wastewater discharges are a concern. Actions to restore and protect the Estuary are being taken by the Fraser River Estuary Management Program, the Fraser River Action Plan, and other government and non-government institutions. (pg. 94-96)

- Sea otters, which were extirpated from the B.C. coast by the 1930s, now number about 800. This represents a dramatic recovery following a re-transplant of 89 individuals off the west coast of Vancouver Island during 1969-72. (pg. 55-56)

- The burrowing owl virtually disappeared from B.C., primarily because of habitat loss. A recovery program re-introduced this species into the south Okanagan Valley, transplanting owls from Washington State into artificial burrows. (pg. 42-44)

Protected areas

- B.C. now has about 6.5% of its area in protected status, double the level in 1970, and the second highest among Canadian provinces. A new Protected Areas Strategy is being implemented which calls for the protection of 12% of the province by the year 2000. Nine new coastal provincial parks were recently designated. (pg. 67-70)

- A review of existing protected areas indicates that B.C.'s low elevation, highly productive old growth ecosystems are under-represented, as are wetlands, grasslands, northern boreal ecosystems and marine ecosystems. (pg. 68)

- The Province recently announced the protection of the Khutzeymateen Valley as grizzly bear habitat - the first area in Canada to be protected specifically for grizzly bears. (pg.87)

- The Government of Canada and the Council of the Haida Nation signed an historic agreement allowing for the co-operative management of an area of the Queen Charlotte Islands known as the 'Gwaii Haanas'. (pg. 59)

- The percentage of currently protected area is greatest for the Southern Interior Mountains (13.0%); Georgia Depression (9.4%); and Northern Boreal Mountains (8.7%) ecoprovinces. The Sub-Boreal Interior (less than 2.0%) and Southern Interior (1.8%) ecoprovinces have a small proportion of their areas in protected status. The Taiga Plains and Boreal Interior ecoprovinces have no protected areas. (pg. 68)

Fish

- About 76% of B.C.'s salmon stocks are considered stable or increasing, while 24% have declined. Declines can be largely attributed to overharvesting and habitat damage. (pg. 45)

- Over the past two decades salmon abundance has been sustained largely by enhancement efforts, such as supplementing declining wild stocks with artificially-reared fish. Overall, 'enhanced' salmon represent 15% of the commercial salmon catch. (pg. 45)

- In 1941, there were only 1,100 sockeye salmon spawning on the Horsefly River. By 1989, there were 1.9 million spawners and 8.4 million fish caught. This recovery was due to careful control of harvesting. (pg. 78)

- Since the mid-1980s, there has been a general coast-wide decline in the abundance of steelhead in North America. Reduced steelhead runs are a concern in several Vancouver Island streams and the Skeena River. (pg. 47)

- Fish populations in Okanagan Lake and its tributaries have seriously declined over the past two decades, due to a variety of factors. (pg. 82)

- Since the mid 1970s, populations of kokanee (salmon) in Kootenay Lake have been declining, threatening the population of trophy-sized Gerrard rainbow trout. A lake fertilization program has begun to boost food supplies for the kokanee. (pg. 80)

- Sanitary shellfish closures have increased in recent years with municipal sewage discharges being the largest sole source of closures. (pg. 34)

Forests

- Forests cover about two thirds of the province, and over half of the province is capable of producing timber for commercial purposes. (pg. 48)

- Of the eleven major types of forests in Canada, six are found in British Columbia.. B.C. has a greater diversity of forest ecosystems than any other province. (pg. 48)

- More than half of the province's coastal forests are over 250 years old, whereas only 6% of interior forests are that old. (pg. 48)

- North America has the largest continuous tract of coastal temperate rain forests on Earth. Approximately half of this is in B.C. (pg. 43)

- The amount of timber harvested annually is projected to decline in the near future in many areas of the province. This is due to reassessments of potential long term cutting rates, the need to satisfy non-timber values such as wildlife and aesthetics, and the changing age composition of forests (replacement of old-growth forests with second growth forests). (pg. 50)

- Between 1976 and 1986, the area of land harvested for timber generally exceeded the area that was reforested by planting efforts or natural regeneration. However, since 1986 reforestation has exceeded area harvested, and there has been an increased effort to replant the backlog of harvested areas. (pg. 50)

Agricultural land

- All of the nearly 400,000 ha of grain growing land in the Peace River is classified as high erosion risk, and 15% already shows evidence of erosion. Conservation farming is being encouraged to improve soil management. (pg. 74)

- The Lower Fraser Basin produces about half the gross farm income in the province. Between 1980 and 1987, 750 ha of prime agricultural land in the Lower Fraser Valley was permanently lost to urban uses. The southern third of Vancouver Island faces similar urbanization pressures. (pg. 93)

- In southwestern B.C., the area of farm land in the Agricultural Land Reserve declined by 8.5% between 1973 and 1990. (pg. 93)

Acknowledgements

Development of the first State of the Environment Report for British Columbia was a challenging task. A number of organizational questions had to be answered, considerable information and data had to be gathered and presented in a manner that was accurate and meaningful. More importantly, this report reflects the collective scientific knowledge, perspectives and contributions from a number of individuals and agencies.

Representatives from provincial and federal government agencies developed the structure and focus of the report, provided material to be incorporated, and extensively reviewed a series of drafts for accuracy and balance. The Westland Resource Group assisted government representatives in developing an outline for the report. ESSA Environmental and Social Systems Analysts Ltd. synthesized all government agency contributions and review comments, together with other available literature and informative material, into a cohesive report. The Southern Interior case study was based on material provided by the Centre for Sustainable Regional Development at the University of Victoria. The Secretary of State undertook the French translation. Special acknowledgements are also extended to the B.C. Round Table on the Environment and the Economy and to many other contributors not listed below.

Steering Committee

Ministry of Environment, Lands and Parks
Linda Hannah   Jim van Barneveld   Jamie Alley

Ministry of Economic Development, Small Business and Trade
Louise Arthur

Environment Canada
Don Bernard   Terry Chiasson   Harry Hirvonen
Brian MacDonald

Advisory Committee

Ministry of Aboriginal Affairs
Jacqueline Morgan   Deborah Ainsworth

Ministry of Agriculture, Fisheries and Food
Ron Bertrand   Joe Truscott

Ministry of Energy, Mines and Petroleum Resources
Brian Braidwood   Teresa Morris

Ministry of Environment, Lands and Parks
Wally Bergen	Kul Bindra	Dave Brown
Brian Clark	Hal Coulson	Dan Cronin
Maureen DeHaan	Don Eastman	Elaine Ellison
Glyn Fox	Ron Hall	Andrew Harcombe
Bill Hodge	Greg Jones	Ben Kangasniemi
Al Kohut	Bob Lincoln	Derrick Lowe
Ken Lozoway	Les McDonald	Brian Moen
Ken Morrison	Narender Nagpal	Peter Newroth
Geraldine Parke	Alan Phillips	Larry Pommen
Juanita Ptolemy	Roland Rocchini	Neil Shrimpton
Les Swain	Ron Thomas	Jay van Oostdam
Rick Williams	Barry Willoughby	

Ministry of Finance and Corporate Relations
Thomas Beynon   Gary Weir

Ministry of Forests
Ray Addison   Jim Crover   John Marczyk

Ministry of Health
Ray Copes   Norm Hardy   Andrew Hazlewood

Ministry of Municipal Affairs, Recreation and Housing
Erik Karlsen

Ministry of Tourism and Ministry Responsible for Culture
Jennifer Nichol

Ministry of Transportation and Highways
Mike Kent

Ministry of Women's Equality
Annette Wall   Leah Siebold

Agriculture Canada
Margaret Bancroft	Pat Bowen	Solke De Boer
John Hansen	Gerry Neilsen	Laurens van Vliet
Bernie Zebarth	Sunny Szeto	

Energy Mines and Resources Canada
D.J. Templeman-Kluit

Environment Canada
Victor Bartnik	Bette Beswick	Dick Boak
Duane Brothers	Al Colodey	Alain David
George Derksen	Allen Eade	Joan Eamer
John Elliott	Lee Harding	Gary Kaiser
Dave Lacelle	Adam LaRosic	Hugh Liebscher
Roger McNeill	Kathleen Moore	Hal Nelson
Steve Pond	Dave Scharf	Eric Taylor
Bruce Thomson	Taina Tuominen	Tony Turner
Steve Wetmore	Peggy Ward	Phil Whitehead
Paul Whitfield	Ed Wituschek	

Fisheries and Oceans Canada
Colin MacKinnon   Brian Smiley   Mike Nassichuk

Forestry Canada
Wayne Coombs   Dean Mills

Health and Welfare Canada
Richard Lawrence

Indian and Northern Affairs Canada
John Alexis   Brian Martin

Industry, Science and Technology Canada
John Beveridge

Public Works Canada
Colin Kingman

Supply and Services Canada
Al Shaw

Transport Canada
Alan McKenzie   Boris Pavlov   Robert Sisler

Western Economic Diversification
Frank Eichgruen   Barbara Newton-Vedan

ESSA Environmental and Social Systems Analysts Ltd.
David Marmorek	Pille Bunnell	Trent Berry
Carol Murray	David Bernard	Karen Paulig
Jay Roop	Doug Tait	Jane Wolsak

University of Victoria
Gerry Walter   Orland Wilkerson   Tim Maki
Randy Sunderman

Westland Resource Group
David Harper   Wayne Biggs   Mark Walmsley

Contents

x

Perspectives

The need for a State of the Environment report

Over the past two decades, protection of the environment has become a matter of urgent worldwide attention and concern. There is a growing concern about the environment that is especially pronounced in our province. British Columbians have made it clear that they want to secure for current and future generations both a healthy environment and a healthy economy. This is the essence of sustainable development.

Sustainable development requires that informed choices be based on good environmental information. However, there are often conflicting opinions and a lack of information that is consistent, reliable, and easily accessible.

State of the environment reporting is seen as a step to help chart the course towards a sustainable future. The goal of this report is to inform British Columbians about the state of the environment and to measure our progress towards a sustainable future. State of the environment reporting will allow us to determine whether environmental conditions have improved, are remaining stable, or require efforts to turn around a disturbing trend.

Shaping the report

This State of the Environment Report for British Columbia represents a cooperative effort involving a number of federal and provincial agencies. The British Columbia Round Table on the Environment and the Economy and members of the public also helped to shape this report. This approach has ensured that the report is as comprehensive, objective and relevant as possible.

State of the Environment reporting is not new in Canada. The second National State of the Environment Report was published in 1991 and a number of other provinces (Saskatchewan, Manitoba, Quebec) have prepared reports as well. British Columbia has benefited from the reporting experience in these other jurisdictions and has applied a reporting framework that will enable complementary environmental reporting among jurisdictions over time.

Several criteria guided the selection of issues to be addressed in this report. These included: environmental importance (the risk posed to either human health or to ecosystems); the nature of the risk and whether it is increasing or decreasing, local or widespread; the social and economic importance of the issue; and the degree to which reporting on the issue advances an improved understanding of the relationship between human activities and the environment.

We are still very much at the early stages of reporting comprehensively on the environment. There is much more that could be reported, and should be reported on in the future. For example, it is often difficult to assess the significance of changes, especially

when benchmarks are lacking or information is incomplete. In other cases, the ability to evaluate the significance of information lags behind the ability to generate data. Future reports will address these gaps. It is important, though, that the task of reporting on the environment is started.

The four fundamental questions

The State of the Environment Report for British Columbia is developed around four basic questions: What is happening in the environment? Why is it happening? Why is it significant? and What are we doing about it? (Box 1.1). This framework is designed to inform British Columbians about the current condition of the environment, and to better understand the linkages between human activities and the environment.

Box 1.1

The Four Fundamental Questions

What is happening in the environment?

Why is it happening?

Why is it significant?

What are we doing about it?

Figure 1.1

Sustainable development

Sustainable communities depend on economic prosperity, social equity and environmental values. These can be achieved more fully if they take into account the ecological limits of the world upon which they are grounded.

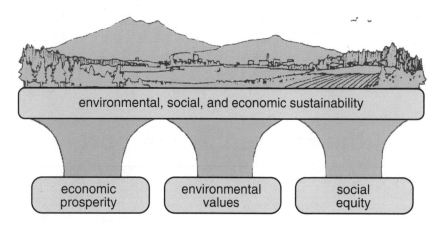

environmental, social, and economic sustainability

economic prosperity

environmental values

social equity

the elements in the system are interdependent. Removing or altering even one, can have serious complications for the entire system.

There is a need to move away from an emphasis on individual elements and move towards a more comprehensive ecological approach. Such an approach would report on the interrelationships and social and economic linkages found in the environment upon which we depend.

The environmental, social and economic processes that support human livelihood are highly interactive. Understanding these processes requires a "systems approach" where society thinks, plans and acts in terms of ecosystems. An ecosystem approach strives to look at how various system

An ecological and sustainable perspective

British Columbia is a mosaic of regions, many possessing unique features of worldwide significance. Each region is part of a larger community, and consequently, each contributes to and is affected by larger scale changes. Our place in this larger community places an obligation on British Columbia to promote economic, social and environmental health at home and abroad.

Traditionally, we have often looked at environmental issues in isolation and not within the context of the larger ecological system within which we find ourselves. An appropriate ecological perspective on sustainability starts with a view of the whole and an understanding that the environment, society and economy are part of a mutually supporting system (Figure 1.1). All of

"What is important is to change our understanding of the world, to focus on ecosystems rather than on individual species and organisms that are a part of them. Such changed understanding of the realities around us will affect fundamentally how we live on our planet home."

Stan Rowe[10]

Figure 1.2

The ecoprovinces of British Columbia

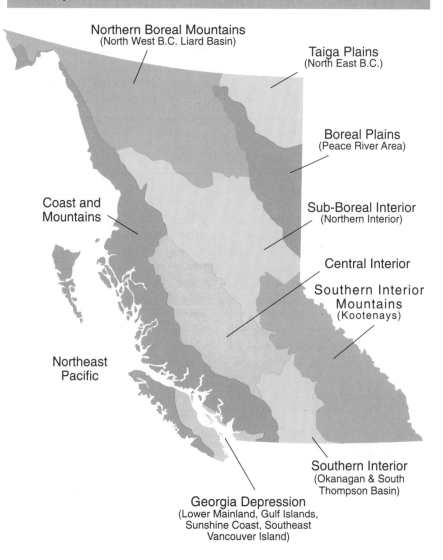

Northern Boreal Mountains
(North West B.C. Liard Basin)

Taiga Plains
(North East B.C.)

Boreal Plains
(Peace River Area)

Coast and Mountains

Sub-Boreal Interior
(Northern Interior)

Central Interior

Southern Interior Mountains
(Kootenays)

Northeast Pacific

Southern Interior
(Okanagan & South Thompson Basin)

Georgia Depression
(Lower Mainland, Gulf Islands, Sunshine Coast, Southeast Vancouver Island)

components - social and natural - interact with one another. Sustainability will be achieved when environmental goals become social and economic goals, and there is a greater degree of integration between environmental, economic and social systems.

For example, when we examine ozone depletion, we must discuss the implications this may have for human health, natural systems, and economic production decisions. An ecological approach requires discussion of the linkages between production of ozone-depleting chemicals, their concentrations in the atmosphere, the impacts this has on stratospheric ozone and levels of ultraviolet radiation at the surface of the earth, and the consequences this may have for crop productivity or cancer rates.

To foster this perspective, an ecological classification system has been adopted for British Columbia. This classification consists of a hierachy of ecological units, ranging from broad to small. The broadest units are the 10 ecoprovinces which are subdivided into ecoregions which, in turn, are divided into ecosections. Most of the information in this report is provided at the ecoprovince level (Figure 1.2). The ecoprovinces of British Columbia are integral components of the ecological classification of Canada. All the nation's ecoprovinces are nested within one of the 15 ecozones of the country.

Each ecoprovince has a unique pattern of biological and physical characteristics that tend to persist over time. The nature of the ecological classification system provides a spatial framework through which provincial, national and global environmental issues can be linked with regional and local ones.

Measuring our progress

In today's world of information overload, there is the need for authoritative, reliable and easy-to-use indicators by which to measure environmental conditions and our progress towards sustainability. Environmental indicators are important tools for translating environmental data into succinct information that can be

Table 1.1

Some potential environmental indicators for British Columbia

Air

Climate change
- Emissions of greenhouse gases
- Atmospheric concentrations of carbon dioxide
- Air temperature, precipitation
- Sea surface temperature

Stratospheric Ozone Depletion
- Atmospheric concentrations of ozone-depleting chemicals
- Thickness of stratospheric ozone layer
- Ultraviolet radiation

Air Toxics
- Lead concentrations in urban air

Water

Fresh and Marine Water Quality
- Discharges to fresh and marine waters
- Compliance with water quality objectives
- Contaminants in ground water
- Contaminant levels in sediments and biota
- Areas closed to shellfish harvesting

Water Supply
- Annual flow of major streams
- Water levels in ground water observation wells

Water Use
- Water use per capita

Plants and Animals

Biodiversity
- Species at risk
- Areas of old-growth forest, riparian, grassland and other habitats

Wildlife and Fisheries
- Population levels of representative wildlife species
- Salmon escapements (returns) and production levels

Bioaccumulation of Toxic Substances
- Mercury, dioxin levels in fish
- Contaminant levels in human tissue
- Contaminant levels in bird eggs

Forestry
- Trends in rates of harvest and reforestation

Land

Protected Areas
- Land under protected status
- Ecosystem representation in protected status

Land Use
- Trends in forest land conversion
- Changes in agricultural land use
- Rates of soil erosion

Solid Waste
- Percentage and amount of waste reduced, recycled and reused

3

readily understood and used in decision-making.

We are all familiar with economic indicators - Gross Domestic Product, interest rates, unemployment rates and consumer price indices that are used to describe the state of the economy. Health experts rely on the rates of birth and mortality, and the incidence of diseases to describe aspects of the physical health of a population. There is, however, no commonly accepted comparable set of indicators to measure the state of the environment. Indicators are essential if we are to improve the capacity to monitor and report on key environmental changes and trends. Indeed, indicators are necessary if environmental considerations are to be integrated with economic and social indicators in personal, public and corporate decision-making.[13]

Developing and selecting environmental indicators is not an easy task. Many conceptual and technical difficulties must be overcome. To be effective, indicators must meet certain tests. They must be scientifically credible, responsive to change, representative and supported by sufficient data to show both regional patterns and trends over time. Moreover, environmental indicators must be relevant to issues of public concern and they must be understandable. Extensive public consultation, research and monitoring will be required before environmental indicators can become a part of our everyday language, culture and activities.

Some of the potential indicators outlined in this report, such as carbon dioxide emissions, document the contribution of particular human activities to global climate change and can be viewed as a measure of *stress* to the environment. Indicators, such as air temperatures or contaminants in sediments, assess the physical and chemical *condition* in the environment. Other indicators, such as salmon productivity and the abundance of wildlife species, represent biological *response* to natural and human-induced stresses. Taken together, these potential indicators provide a profile of the state of the environment in British Columbia. They can be used in documenting trends and measuring progress towards sustainability (Table 1.1).

People are part of the environment

British Columbia is a special place; it has tremendous ecological diversity and richness that is unique in Canada and to most other parts of the world. Humans are very much a part of this environment. It is a communal home that we share with other living things, and our "housekeeping" affects it (Figure 1.3). Human welfare is ultimately dependent on maintaining the environment and its component systems.

Being part of this environment, however, means that we must ultimately look at ourselves. There is growing evidence that we have been neglecting our environmental responsibilities in British Columbia. We are facing a garbage crisis as we run out of landfill sites. The number of threatened and endangered species has been growing. Some fresh water and marine ecosystems are showing signs of stress as contaminants from a variety of activities accumulate. There is growing concern about our ability to prevent and respond to environmental emergencies such as oil or chemical spills.

There is also evidence of positive change. The past decade has seen some improvements in environmental quality. Levels of the chemical DDT have declined in Great Blue Heron eggs, land area under protected status has increased, pulp mill discharges of dioxins and furans show marked declines, and lead emission levels in urban areas have declined. Such positive changes reflect society's ability to tap our environmental knowledge and put our commitment,

Figure 1.3
The environment is our home

The environment is not simply something "out there" that we take care of for ethical reasons. We are part of the environment. We depend on it, and what we do affects it.

Figure 1.4

Energy use by sector

About half the annual energy used in B.C. is for industrial use, and a quarter is for transportation. [4]

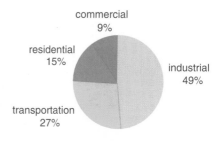

ingenuity and technology to work to improve and protect environmental quality.

Ecological limits

The environment cannot accommodate all the impacts that result from human activities. There are limits. There is a real danger of overfishing, overharvesting, or overstressing our land. In most cases, we do not know exactly what the ecological limits are, but we do know that exceeding them may cause irreversible damage to the environment. If the environment is damaged, our economy will be damaged. Living within environmental limits will allow us to sustain our economy as well as our environment. We have to take these real limits into account when we try to determine our population density, production and consumption patterns, and life style.[1] Various processes are already in place to avoid or minimize the environmental impacts of human activities (Box 1.2).

Our economy depends on the environment

It is easy to appreciate the beauty and richness of British Columbia's natural landscape. It takes a little more thought to recognize how much of our economy is directly tied to the quality of the environment. Fishing, forestry, ranching, mining and other resource based industries provide 20% of the provincial gross domestic product. They also provide most of our exports. Economic analysis shows that resource industries are responsible for 23% of all our jobs. The environment also directly supports tourism, recreation, and other service sectors.[2]

The environment provides British Columbia with one of the world's best energy supplies. Energy has been an important factor in economic growth and industrial development in the province. The province's low energy prices have resulted in an energy-intensive industrial base - about half the energy used in B.C. is for industrial use (Figure 1.4). Production of important B.C. products such as paper and metals requires a large amount of energy. In terms of total energy use, B.C. residents are therefore large consumers of energy, compared to both the average Canadian and citizens in other developed countries (Figure 1.5). As we export these energy intensive products, we are in effect exporting energy.[3]

Figure 1.5

Per capita energy use

Canada as a whole is an energy-intensive society. British Columbia uses even more energy per person than the Canadian average. (One gigajoule is the energy equivalent of 29 litres of gasoline) [3]

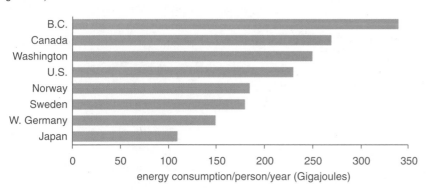

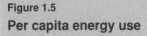

Figure 1.7
How do your choices affect the environment?

This diagram shows how the average Canadian household allocates its disposable income (gross revenue minus taxes and savings). Some of the consumer choices that make an environmental difference are shown for each type of expenditure. The difference we can make is not always proportional to how much we spend.[14]

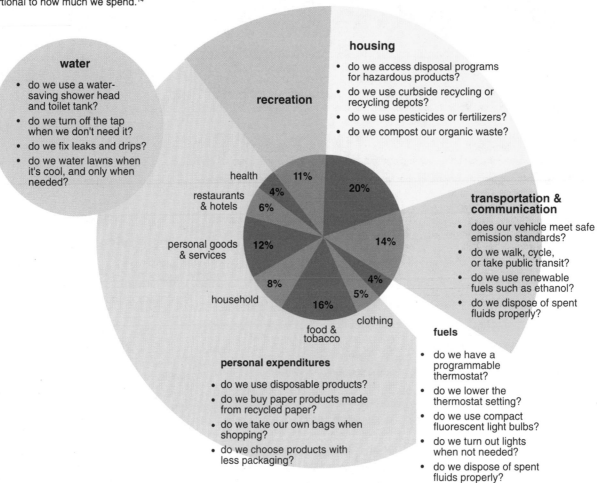

water
- do we use a water-saving shower head and toilet tank?
- do we turn off the tap when we don't need it?
- do we fix leaks and drips?
- do we water lawns when it's cool, and only when needed?

recreation

housing
- do we access disposal programs for hazardous products?
- do we use curbside recycling or recycling depots?
- do we use pesticides or fertilizers?
- do we compost our organic waste?

transportation & communication
- does our vehicle meet safe emission standards?
- do we walk, cycle, or take public transit?
- do we use renewable fuels such as ethanol?
- do we dispose of spent fluids properly?

fuels
- do we have a programmable thermostat?
- do we lower the thermostat setting?
- do we use compact fluorescent light bulbs?
- do we turn out lights when not needed?
- do we dispose of spent fluids properly?

personal expenditures
- do we use disposable products?
- do we buy paper products made from recycled paper?
- do we take our own bags when shopping?
- do we choose products with less packaging?

health 11%
4%
restaurants & hotels 6%
20%
personal goods & services 12%
14%
household 8%
4%
5%
food & tobacco 16%
clothing

Figure 1.6
Energy sources

B.C.'s energy is supplied through imported crude oil, local natural gas and woodwaste, and hydroelectric power.[4]

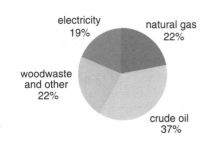

electricity 19%
natural gas 22%
woodwaste and other 22%
crude oil 37%

Most of British Columbia's energy needs are satisfied by domestic supplies of natural gas, hydroelectricity, and residue from wood processing (Figure 1.6). However the province does not have enough oil, and therefore imports 80% of its crude oil requirements, primarily from Alberta.[4]

Our economy affects the environment

The impact people have on the environment is determined by the number of people and by their life style. About 20% of the world's population lives in industrialized countries such as Canada. They consume, however, a disproportionately large share (about 80%) of the world's resources. British Columbians enjoy a standard of living and a range of social amenities far superior to those provided to most of the world's inhabitants. At this time we are a consumer society, and that means that our life style has a high impact on the environment (Figure 1.7).

One of the characteristics of a consumer society is a high level of waste production. The more we consume, the more waste we generate — not only through disposal of packaging and used goods, but also in the process of manufacturing and distributing the goods. Waste may consist of effluents discharged into the water, emissions to the air, or solids disposed on land. Much of the solid waste ends up in landfills, which consume valuable land and produce leachates that can contaminate surface water and ground-

Figure 1.8
Waste production

British Columbians are among the highest per-capita waste producers on earth.[7]

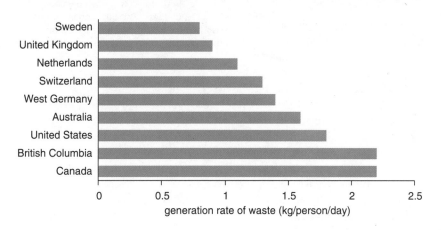

generation rate of waste (kg/person/day)

Figure 1.10
Population growth in B.C.

The population of British Columbia has been growing steadily. This growth is expected to continue so that by 2016 there will be half again as many people.[6]

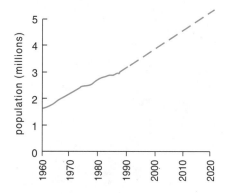

water. Landfills also emit gases suspected of contributing to global climate change. Some kinds of waste have particularly difficult disposal problems, such as toxic materials and other contaminants (see Land chapter).

In 1990, the average British Columbian generated almost 2.2 kilograms of waste every day, for a provincial total of 2.4 million tonnes of garbage per year (Figure 1.8). Approximately half of this waste comes directly from homes. Despite the fact that more than half of the waste

material can be composted or recycled, most of it is currently dumped in landfills or incinerated (Figure 1.9).[7]

More people, more impact

Even if each person has only a small impact, a large population can create a significant stress. When British Columbia joined Canada in 1871, its population was estimated at about 40,000 people, of which about 25,000 were aboriginal.[2] By 1992, the total population had grown to about 3.3 million, of which approximately

158,000 were aboriginal. By 2016 it is expected to reach 4.9 million (Figure 1.10).

B.C. is currently the fastest growing province in Canada. This is not because we have a higher birth rate, but because people like to move here. About half the people moving to B.C. come from other parts of Canada, the rest come from other countries.[6]

Environmental impacts from people are generally greatest where people are most concentrated. The population is not evenly distributed throughout the province. Most of the people live in the

Figure 1.9
Source, composition, and disposal of solid wastes

Most municipal solid waste comes from residential sources. The largest component is organic material, most of which can be composted, and paper, most of which can be recycled. Currently only a very small amount is recycled, and most of the rest goes to landfill. [5,7]

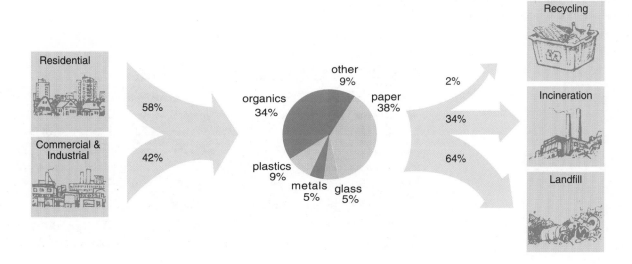

7

Figure 1.11
Population growth rates

The population growth rate between 1986 and 1991 was highest in the Lower Mainland and the Okanagan.[9]

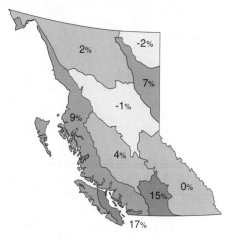

southwest corner of the province, and the north is sparsely populated. The densely populated areas are likely to become even more dense as they are growing much faster than the sparsely settled areas (Figure 1.11).

We can make a difference

As each one of us begins to recognize the environmental implications of our life style — on global climate change, waste, or water quality — we begin to change. Already a number of people are making the decision to switch from cars to public transit, to recycle, and to consciously reduce their overall levels of material and energy consumption (Figure 1.12). This is an encouraging start and a good foundation to build on.

Many initiatives are underway to help British Columbians make the transition to a sustainable society. The following are but a few examples:

- Utilities are helping consumers reduce energy demand. For example, B.C. Hydro's Power Smart program provides information and financial incentives to encourage efficient use of electricity by residential, commercial and industrial users. The energy savings gained by the Power Smart program by August 1992 were enough to supply all the electricity needs for 70,000 homes. Other energy conservation initiatives are underway by B.C. Gas, the provincial government, and various industries.[11]

- An integrated solid waste management strategy has been adopted throughout B.C. The main thrust of the strategy is to facilitate the development of a "Reduce, Reuse, and Recycle" philosophy and infrastructure. This is done through financial assistance programs for local government and non-profit organizations, education programs and a highly effective program targeted at tires and batteries.

- Various measures to improve air quality are being proposed, particularly in the Greater Vancouver Regional District (GVRD) and Capital Regional District (CRD). Several initiatives, including the Air Care program to control vehicle emissions, have already been implemented.

Figure 1.12
How much energy do we need?

Per capita energy use increased steadily during the 1960s and 70s, but has declined somewhat since then. The question is whether we will be able to further reduce the amount each person uses, keep it steady, or let it increase.[11]

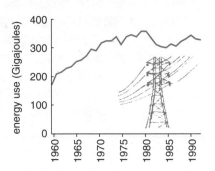

In the long term, the survival of the human race will depend on our ability to see ourselves as an integral part of the environment, and to harmonize our economic systems with natural systems, locally and globally. We must move towards a more sustainable society, one that is in harmony with the environment. We have started moving in this direction through changes in attitudes, policies, and regulations.

"I believe all people started out connected to the land. People like the Gitksan copied nature because they were surrounded by it, not protected from it as we are. They saw the cycle of life, from the very smallest to the very largest, all connected, and saw that the system itself punished any breaking of the cycle... The people saw and understood the checks and balances that were exhibited by the cycle and chose to base their fundamental truths and authority and responsibility on something that has worked for millions of years. They fitted themselves to the full cycle of life."

M. Wilson[8]

Air

Of all the components that are essential to life, air is probably the one most taken for granted. Historically, air quality and climate were periodically modified by natural contaminants, such as those contributed by forest fires and volcanic eruptions. Shifts in global climatic patterns took place slowly, but routinely. Human activities have now added another potent force to those already transforming our atmosphere.

A description of the state of our atmosphere requires that we look far beyond traditional, narrow definitions of air quality. To fully characterize our changing atmosphere we must examine local, regional, and even global atmospheric issues. This helps us to recognize that while some of the many forces shaping our atmosphere are under our direct management as British Columbians, others are beyond our immediate control. Some issues are of immediate concern; others are unlikely to begin affecting our societies and ecosystems until sometime in the next century. Our understanding and awareness of air pollutants is changing, and is becoming much broader and more comprehensive. As a society we must adapt our activities and regulations to meet this improved understanding.

There are over 1,000 climate and weather monitoring stations operating in B.C. Information from these stations, some of which have been in place for over 100 years, is being analysed to detect historical changes in climate. Currently, there are over 50 air quality monitoring stations in operation throughout B.C. In nearly all cases, stations are specifically located in areas that are either known or suspected to have potential air quality problems. Areas expected to have uncontaminated air, or that have contaminants present at background levels, are not routinely monitored. This uneven distribution of monitoring stations makes it extremely difficult to draw provincial-level conclusions regarding overall conditions and trends in the quality of our atmosphere.

This chapter outlines the major atmospheric issues facing British Columbia, starting with those that are most global and distant in time, and working toward those that are more local and immediate (Figure 2.1).

Figure 2.1

Global, regional, and local atmospheric issues

Many atmospheric issues transcend boundaries of both scale and national identity. For example, worldwide emissions of greenhouse gases (e.g. carbon dioxide) and ozone-depleting substances (e.g., CFCs) determine the rate of global warming and stratospheric ozone depletion. Levels of acid deposition are determined by emissions of acid-forming gases within regional "airsheds". Concentrations of ground-level air pollutants (e.g., carbon monoxide) are determined by local emissions. Several gases have effects at multiple levels. For example, sulphur dioxide emissions have both local and regional effects.

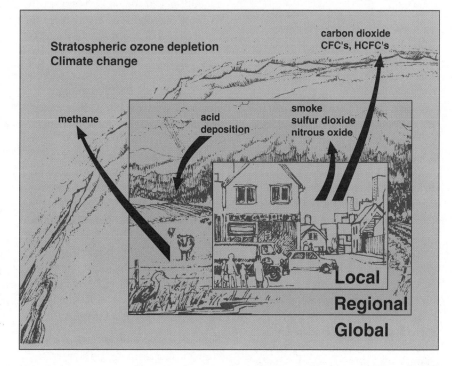

9

Global climate change: adjusting to life in the greenhouse

We live in a kind of natural greenhouse. Although not surrounded by glass, the Earth's atmosphere contains gases that act like glass and help warm the planet. These naturally occurring greenhouse gases - mainly water vapour, carbon dioxide, methane, and nitrous oxide - effectively "trap" solar heat, much as glass traps heat in a greenhouse. Many human activities, such as burning fossil fuels, contribute more of these gases to our atmosphere. When this occurs, there can be an enhanced greenhouse effect, which may result in global warming. Although there is considerable controversy surrounding the possible rate of warming due to human actions, most scientists now agree that our activities could increase global temperatures and change precipitation patterns. Potential effects on British Columbians could be many and significant.

Is the Earth getting warmer? Since 1861 the nine warmest years have been: 1944, 1979, 1980, 1983, 1987, 1988, 1989, 1990, and 1991. How about B.C.? There are several converging lines of evidence for climate warming in our province. A recent study of long-term temperature data from three B.C. regions indicated that warming appears to have been taking place at a rate of between 0.4 and 0.8 °C per century. As an example, figure 2.2 shows that the southern B.C. mountains have warmed slightly over the past 100 years. Likewise, the sea surface at Cape St. James, at the southern tip of the Queen Charlotte Islands, has been slowly warming since the 1930s at a rate of around 1°C per century. Studies of shrinking glaciers in B.C. lend additional evidence and indicate that our climate has been warming at a rate of between 1 and 2 °C during the last century. There is also limited evidence that precipitation amounts have changed slightly at some locations, but these

Figure 2.2

Temperate trends for the southern B.C. mountains

Graph shows differences between annual average temperatures in the southern B.C. mountains and the 1951-1980 average temperature for that area (horizontal line). Although average temperatures have been increasing in the southern B.C. mountains during the past 100 years, the trend is not considered 'significant' when analysed statistically.[1,2]

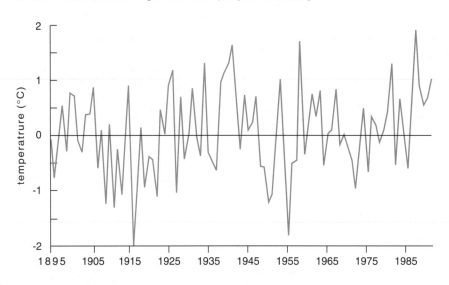

trends are even more difficult to detect than those for temperature. Overall, available evidence suggests that B.C.'s climate is becoming warmer with more precipitation in some locations and less in others. It is certainly too early to announce clear trends, and premature to imply that observed changes are the result of global warming; they may be just part of long-term natural climate cycles.

Small as the reported temperature changes may seem, they are considerably more rapid than those evidenced during our geological past. For instance, over the past 8,000 years, global temperature only varied about 2 °C. A recent report by the Intergovernmental Panel on Climate Change (IPCC) suggests that global warming in the years ahead may occur at a rate of 0.2 to 0.5 °C per decade (Figure 2.3). At that rate, the Earth's temperature will increase in 125 years by an amount equal to the natural changes during the previous 8,000 years!

Some of the possible effects of global climate change on the B.C. environ-

ment are described in a recent report.[3] Global warming could affect most parts of B.C.'s natural and human environment, including forests, wildlife, fisheries, marine mammals, energy consumption, recreation, and water resources. Specific regional-scale implications are difficult to predict, and would be far too numerous to elaborate here. Nevertheless, there are some important general implications. As climate patterns shift, the ability of natural systems to supply food and fibre may be reduced. Forest regeneration may prove to have been based on inappropriate species. Some plant and animal species may be unable to adapt to new temperature and precipitation patterns, and populations may disappear. Protected areas may be in the "wrong place" to serve conservation objectives. Rising sea levels (the IPCC estimates a rise of 21 - 71 cm by the year 2070) may affect coastal communities and ecosystems. Overall, virtually all sectors of B.C. could be affected to some degree if global climate change occurs as rapidly as predicted.

On a per capita basis, Canadians are among the largest contributors in the world of the main greenhouse gas, carbon dioxide. Each year we emit about 4.4 tonnes of carbon per person, with most of this coming from burning fossil fuels. Like all provinces, B.C. contributes not only carbon dioxide (CO_2), but also several other greenhouse gases, including methane (CH_4), chlorofluorocarbons (CFCs and halons), nitrogen oxides (NO_x, N_2O), volatile organic carbon compounds (VOC), and ground level ozone (O_3). The contribution of various gases to the greenhouse effect depends on their molecular structure, as well as their atmospheric concentration. For example, each molecule of methane has 25 times the impact of each molecule of CO_2, while freon molecules are about 10,000 times as powerful as CO_2.

In B.C., carbon dioxide emissions from the combustion of fossil fuels and biomass account for roughly two-thirds of our total greenhouse gas contribution (Figure 2.4). Methane makes up another 25%, mostly from landfills with additional contributions from hydrocarbon extraction and processing. Transportation activities are responsible for most nitrogen oxides, while the majority of CFC emissions escape from automobile air conditioning.

British Columbians can contribute directly to reducing greenhouse gas emissions by modifying behaviour and consumption patterns. Canada and B.C. are committed to a national goal of stabilizing greenhouse gas emissions, at 1990 levels, by the year 2000. The B.C. greenhouse gas emission inventories are helping formulate management options in support of this goal. B.C. is also participating in the National Action Strategy on Global Warming. Finally, maintaining healthy, growing forests in B.C. can help by absorbing carbon dioxide from the atmosphere, thereby reducing this greenhouse gas for some decades.

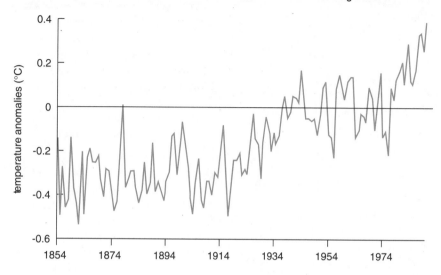

Figure 2.3

Global temperature anomalies: 1854 to 1990

Graph shows differences (anomalies) between annual average global temperatures and the 1950-1979 average global temperature, represented by the horizontal zero line. These data have not been corrected for the El Niño effect. The El Niño is a periodic climatic and oceanic fluctuation. Removal of this effect results in an even more marked warming trend.[4]

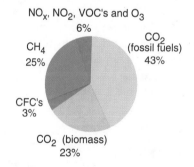

Figure 2.4

Greenhouse gas emissions

Provincial data are for 1990 and only cover gases released into the atmosphere from human activities; natural emissions are not included. Biomass includes pulp liquor, hog fuel and other wood residues.[5]

NO_x, NO_2, VOC's and O_3 6%

CH_4 25%

CFC's 3%

CO_2 (biomass) 23%

CO_2 (fossil fuels) 43%

Stratospheric ozone: our radiation shield

Planet Earth has its own natural sunscreen that shields us from damaging ultraviolet (UV) radiation from the sun. A small amount of ozone, a naturally occurring gas, is located 20-40 km above the earth in a region known as the stratospheric ozone layer. If all the ozone in this layer were compressed it would only form a layer around the Earth's surface about as thick as the sole of your shoe. This important, but thin and fragile layer is now being depleted by certain synthetic chemicals released to the atmosphere by human activities. When these chemicals decompose, they release chlorine and bromine atoms, which convert the ozone to oxygen, which has no ability to filter out harmful UV radiation. If the protective ozone layer is substantially depleted, greater amounts of damaging UV radiation will reach the earth's surface.

Beginning in the summer of 1992, daily ultraviolet levels have been recorded at Saturna Island, in southwestern B.C. Currently there are insufficient data from this station to identify trends. However, an Edmonton station has been conducting measurements to determine the amount of stratospheric ozone since the mid-

11

1950s. Records there show a decline in stratospheric ozone thickness, starting in the late 1970s. The thinning has occurred during the late winter and spring, when ozone thicknesses are normally quite high and the sun-angle relatively low. Consequently, any increase in the intensity of UV radiation reaching the ground due to ozone depletion has probably been small. A number of factors, such as weather and altitude, control the actual UV dose received on the ground.

The largest factor controlling the UV dose received by most humans is their own behaviour. The increase in outdoor leisure activity has already resulted in higher exposure to UV radiation independent of natural increases in UV levels. Human exposure to increased UV levels can result in: more sunburns, premature skin aging, skin cancers, cataracts and other eye diseases, and interference with the human immune system. These effects may represent a considerable cost to the health care system. Using sunscreens and minimizing exposure to intense sunlight can reduce effects. To assist the public in making choices, Environment Canada provides UV Index Values throughout the summer. The index value signifies the degree of risk for people involved in outdoor activities and the lower the index value, the lower the risk. As can be seen in figure 2.5, there are higher

dosages in southern B.C. than in the northern part of the province.

Exposure to higher amounts of UV radiation can also have serious impacts on agriculture, forestry, fisheries, and natural ecosystems. While humans can take protective measures to reduce impacts, managed ecosystems, such as farms and forests, cannot be protected, and may experience decreased yields. Elevated UV levels may also damage natural ecosystems, particularly marine food chains; this could cause impacts on B.C. coastal fish and wildlife resources.

Globally, chlorofluorocarbons (CFC) are the primary ozone-depleting substances released to the atmosphere from human activities. CFCs are used in refrigerants, aerosol cans, foam production, and as solvents. In B.C., emissions of bromine-containing halons (used in fire extinguishers) cause greater damage to the ozone layer than CFC emissions (Figure 2.6). Halons destroy up to 16 times as much ozone as CFCs. In 1990, halons from fire extinguishers accounted for the largest emissions of ozone depleting substances in B.C.; CFC emissions from automobile air conditioners constituted the second largest source.

British Columbians cannot escape some effects of the thinning of the ozone layer even if releases of all such gases were to instantly stop. This is because some ozone-depleting

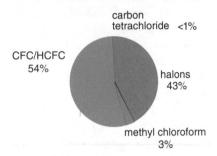

Figure 2.6
Ozone-depleting gases in B.C.

Although combined, the ozone-depleting potential for CFCs and HCFCs are quite different. CFC production and importation will be eliminated by the end of 1995, while HCFCs are not scheduled to be phased out until 2030.[7]

carbon tetrachloride <1%

CFC/HCFC 54%

halons 43%

methyl chloroform 3%

total B.C.1990 production: 1011.8 tonnes

substances remain in the atmosphere for a long time. Moreover, international efforts will be required to control releases of ozone-depleting substances. In the meantime, we - and our ecosystems - may have to adapt to increased UV radiation. But there is much that we can do to reduce B.C.'s contribution to this problem.

Important steps have already been taken to stop stratospheric ozone destruction. Seventy-seven countries signed the Montreal Protocol on Substances that Deplete the Ozone Layer in 1991. By signing this document, Canadians are committed to phasing out ozone-depleting substances according to a schedule recently negotiated in Copenhagen: halons by 1993, CFCs by the end of 1995, and HCFCs by 2030. Environment Canada is training trades-people to recover and reclaim ozone-depleting gases. The Canadian Council of Ministers of the Environment is developing a CFC/Halon Elimination Strategy. In B.C., new regulations to control ozone-depleting substances have recently been introduced. The regulations are the most comprehensive in Canada. The regulations, for example, make B.C. the first province to prohibit, after 1997, the use of CFCs for charging and recharging of motor vehicle air conditioners.

Figure 2.5
UV Index

These are theoretical, clear sky UV Index values for the first week of July, calculated from ozone thicknesses measured from 1979 to 1992. The UV Index scale ranges from 0 to 10 and describes the intensity of damaging ultraviolet-B radiation. A UV Index value of 10 is common in the tropics during the summer.[6]

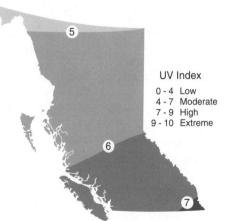

UV Index

0 - 4 Low
4 - 7 Moderate
7 - 9 High
9 - 10 Extreme

Acidic deposition: sins of emission

Acidic deposition is a broader term than acid rain and refers to the fact that acids can be deposited from the atmosphere in a variety of forms (e.g., rain, fog, snow, and particulates). Acid deposition is formed in the atmosphere when sulphur and nitrogen gases combine with moisture to form sulphuric and nitric acids.

Deposition of atmospheric acids is not the main concern. Rather, concerns focus on potential effects to land, water, and biota, as well as to people. When acid deposition levels exceed certain thresholds, biota such as fish and amphibians can no longer inhabit the acidified environment. Damage to surface waters can occur when the pH drops below 6 (lower pH levels mean greater acidity). Productivity of forests and crops can be reduced as acids remove nutrients from the soil. Such problems can occur when large amounts of acid are deposited onto sensitive areas of the environment. So far, no adverse effects have been found on B.C.'s forests, and acid rain concerns focus on sensitive aquatic systems in the province.

Not all regions of B.C. are equally sensitive to acid deposition (Figure 2.7). Those portions of B.C. that are considered vulnerable typically contain

Figure 2.8

Levels of acid deposition in B.C.

Parts of southwestern B.C. receive more total sulphate deposition than allowed by standards set by Sweden or Minnesota for protecting their sensitive surface water ecosystems. Note that the standard set for eastern Canada which is intended to protect moderately sensitive freshwater systems is higher than B.C.'s measured deposition rates. A target value of 8-12kg/ha per year would be required to protect more biologically sensitive waters.[8,14]

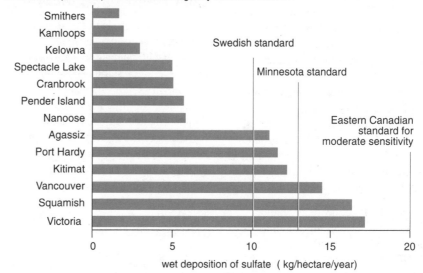

wet deposition of sulfate (kg/hectare/year)

fresh water lakes and streams that are unable to neutralize atmospheric acids. When exposed to acid deposition, such freshwaters become more acidic.

B.C. produces acid-forming sulphur and nitrogen emissions. Major sources of sulphur dioxide (SO_2), in order of importance, are natural-gas processing plants, pulp mills, smelters, oil refineries, and power plants. The major source of nitrogen oxides (NO_x) is motor vehicles.

Acid deposition is not a local phenomenon, since acids formed from these sulphur and nitrogen gases are typically deposited at a considerable distance from the point where they were discharged to the atmosphere. B.C. shares several airsheds with Washington state, so there are some two-way transboundary exchanges of sulphur and nitrogen gases, especially among the Gulf Islands, lower Fraser valley, and in the Kootenays.

Major acid deposition patterns are known for B.C. Figure 2.8 shows sulphate loadings at 13 B.C. locations during 1985. In that year, the highest loadings were recorded at Victoria, and the lowest at Smithers. Some of the acid deposited in Victoria was contributed from a smelter in the Seattle area that has since closed. However, more recent data from five stations on Vancouver Island show little or no change since 1985. Precipitation at Port Hardy is still less acidic than at Victoria, and most rain falling on Vancouver Island has an acidity level that is normal for coastal regions (pH 5.0 - 5.6). Victoria's precipitation, though, is more acidic, with values generally between pH 4.3 and pH 5.3.

Figure 2.7

Vulnerability to acid deposition

The rocks, soils and water of the Coast are less able to neutralize acidity than the B.C. interior. Areas identified as Class 1 have lakes and soils that are least tolerant of increased acidity; those in Class 4 areas are most tolerant.[8]

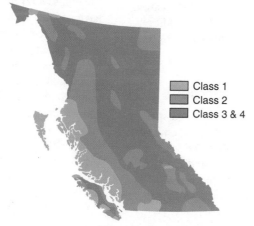

Class 1
Class 2
Class 3 & 4

Risk levels for all sensitive B.C. ecosystems have not yet been determined. It is known that sensitive lakes and soils of low buffering ability along the Sunshine Coast and the north shore of Burrard Inlet are being subjected to elevated levels of acid inputs. The long-term implications of current deposition levels are unknown. However, research has shown that acid levels in Kanaka Creek (near Vancouver) sometimes rise during rainfall events, later returning to normal.[9] This phenomenon results from natural dilution effects (which reduce availability of neutralizing compounds) in addition to acidic rainfall.[10] A province-wide survey of 752 B.C. lakes, between 1977 and 1986, identified only 10 scattered lakes that are high in acidity (less than pH 6) mainly due to natural processes.

What is being done about acidic deposition? Canada signed an international protocol requiring stabilization of NO_x emissions at 1987 levels by 1994. As well, the U.S./Canada Accord requires reductions in NO_x emissions from industrial sources and motor vehicles, and restricts Canadian SO_2 emissions to 3.2 million tonnes per year. Target loadings have been proposed for some areas of B.C. As long as acid deposition inputs do not exceed these target loading levels, sensitive lakes and streams should be protected from adverse effects of acid deposition.

Pollutants in urban and industrial areas

Air quality concerns in B.C. historically focused on urban and industrial areas, and on a limited set of measurement variables (parameters). Emissions from most industrial point sources (e.g. pulp mills, refineries, mines, smelters, saw mills) were inventoried, monitored, and regulated. Starting in the mid-1970s, there has been a shift from an emphasis on emissions to ambient (overall) air quality. This reflects a concern for ecosystem integrity as well as human health. Objectives have been set for key parameters, including total suspended particulates (TSP), sulphur dioxide (SO_2), nitrogen dioxide (NO_2), and ground-level ozone (O_3). Now the B.C. government is addressing more regional, diffuse sources, such as motor vehicles and smoke from open burning. In the future there will likely be an even greater focus on regional-scale air management.

Particulate contaminants

Particulate materials in the atmosphere can reduce visibility, cause harm to human health, and soil the surfaces onto which they settle. These materials, known as total suspended particulates (TSP), can include dust, pollen, ash, and smoke. If inhaled, these materials can be deposited in the human respiratory system and may damage human health. Children, the elderly, smokers, and those suffering from lung disorders may be especially susceptible to this type of air pollution. Total suspended particulates are primarily a local problem, and eventually all of these materials are deposited onto surfaces either locally or downwind.

Province-wide, there have been no significant changes in TSP levels over the past 8-10 years. However, there has been a definite improvement in the Greater Vancouver Regional District (GVRD), with decreased annual TSP concentrations, and fewer 24-hour episodes with high levels of TSP. This decrease has resulted from better control of industrial and vehicular emissions, and reductions in open burning periods. There have also been efforts to control dust and smoke from agricultural and forestry activities. Nonetheless, there are still significant problems with fine particulates and visibility in the GVRD in all seasons of the year when weather conditions are such that particulate materials are not dispersed.

Smoke management

Unlike TSP problems, smoke management is more of a rural, regional issue in B.C. Major smoke sources include burning logging slash and sawmill residues, prescribed burning to improve wildlife habitat or rangelands, burning debris from agriculture and domestic gardening, land clearing, and home heating. Main concerns include visibility impairment and possible impacts on human health. Both suspended particulates and carcinogenic substances are important air pollutants in smoke. There are no quantitative estimates of the amount of smoke generated in B.C.

Three factors influence whether or not wood smoke reaches levels of concern: 1) significant quantities of pollutants must be emitted; 2) local geographic conditions must constrain dispersion; and 3) certain atmospheric and weather conditions must prevail. In mountainous terrain, smoke is often trapped in the valleys. This can result in concentrations of fine particulates rising to levels that may affect human health. More often, though, the greatest impact is on aesthetics or visibility.

Several levels of government are actively addressing smoke management. The Province has prepared regulations to control smoke from waste burning during land clearing and is in the process of developing regulations for wood-burning appliances. This Ministry of Forests has a policy to reduce smoke emissions by 30% through controlled burning. Environment Canada produces a Ventilation Index for 13 smoke-sensitive areas in B.C., which is used by forestry and agricultural managers to help select suitable periods for controlled burning. Regional smoke management plans have been developed for some regions. The GVRD has banned the use of incinerators in apartment buildings, and municipalities in this area are tightening restrictions on open burning. Finally, several B.C. municipalities have adopted voluntary programs to limit the use of wood-burning appliances during periods when meteorological conditions could lead to unacceptable accumulation of smoke. In the future, B.C. may also have to address the issue of transboundary movement of atmospheric contaminants drifting south from B.C. to the U.S.A., where strict air quality and visibility standards are in force for wilderness areas and national parks. As well, B.C. will need to consider the issue of contaminants drifting north from the United States.

Atmospheric lead

Lead is a toxic substance that can be found in particulate form in air, with the major source being leaded gasoline. B.C.'s air quality objective for lead is less than 4 $\mu g/m^3$ over a 24-hour period, and less than 2 $\mu g/m^3$ (average) over a year. Between 1974 and 1990, atmospheric lead concentrations in Victoria, Prince George, Kamloops, Kelowna and most of Vancouver were below 1 $\mu g/m^3$. During this period, concentrations in Trail commonly exceeded 1 $\mu g/m^3$ and sometimes reached over 2 $\mu g/m^3$. B.C.'s air quality objective for lead is to have annual average values at each station less than 2$\mu g/m^3$.

In downtown Vancouver, the highest recorded atmospheric lead concentration occurred in 1976, when the annual mean value was 1.29 $\mu g/m^3$. Since that time values have been steadily dropping (Figure 2.9).

With the elimination of leaded gasoline in 1990, atmospheric lead levels dropped dramatically in downtown Vancouver and most other sampled areas of B.C. Most lead sampling stations show annual average concentrations near background levels, less

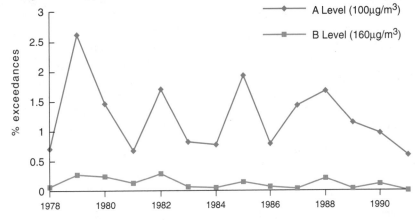

Figure 2.10
Ozone exceedances

Graph shows the province-wide exceedances of 1-hour level A and B objectives for ground-level ozone. There were negligible C level exceedances. There was little change until the early 1990s, when A level exceedances declined. (Note: The configuration of the monitoring network changed during this period, so the influence of different locations on the percent of exceedances changes over time).[12]

than 0.1 $\mu g/m^3$. The Southern Interior Mountains Ecoprovince section contains a description of atmospheric lead concentrations in the Trail area resulting from smelting activities, and a discussion of blood lead levels.

Gaseous contaminants

Concentrations of contaminant gases at ground level are controlled mainly by terrain and prevailing meteorological conditions. Their impacts are local, and are primarily of concern due to human health implications. However, some studies now indicate that even at concentrations acceptable to humans, some air pollutants can adversely affect other biota. For instance, some agricultural crops are much more sensitive to ground-level ozone than most humans. Consequently, to prevent considerable economic damage to agricultural crops, regional air quality objectives may need to be adjusted.

One of the tools used to examine air quality is to compare ambient data obtained from the monitoring stations with predetermined national objectives or provincial standards. In British Columbia, these standards were established in the 1970s and are categorized into three groups. The Maximum Desirable concentration (Level A) is set to provide long term

protection and the Maximum Acceptable concentration (Level B) provides adequate protection against adverse effects on human health, vegetation, and plants. The Maximum Tolerable concentration (Level C) specifies amounts of air contaminants beyond which, due to a diminished margin of safety, appropriate and immediate action is required to protect human health. Ambient air quality at a particular monitoring site may be characterized by describing the number of times these three levels of standards are exceeded.

All available exceedance data from all provincial stations for the fifteen-year period 1978 to 1992 have been compiled and form the basis for Figures 2.10 to 2.13. Provincial average values and trends are provided for five gases: ground-level ozone, nitrogen dioxide, sulphur dioxide, hydrogen sulphide, and carbon monoxide.

Ground level ozone (O_3) is a major component of urban smog. It can cause adverse effects on human health, and is well known to affect most types of vegetation including agricultural crops and forest trees. Unlike stratospheric ozone, which is a problem when it is in short supply high in our atmosphere, ground-level ozone is a problem when it is too abundant. Over the last 15

Figure 2.9
Atmospheric lead in Vancouver

Suspended particulate lead concentrations steadily declined from 1975 to 1990. B.C.'s air quality objective for lead is to have annual average values at each station less than 2 $\mu g/m^3$.[11]

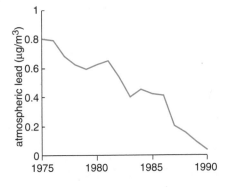

years there has been little change in provincial ozone levels until the early 1990s (Figure 2.10), when there was a drop in the frequency of A Level exceedances. Despite this overall provincial decline, there are areas where ground-level ozone is a significant emerging problem, such as the lower Fraser valley (see Georgia Depression ecoprovince). There are two other regions where ozone may become a problem in the future - the Okanagan and Greater Victoria - and the Province is already monitoring ozone in these areas.

Nitrogen dioxide (NO_2) contributes to ozone (smog) formation and acidic deposition, and can also adversely affect human health. Percentage exceedances at the monitoring stations increased from 1978 to 1985, and then stayed more or less constant. Since 1986, NO_2 concentrations have not exceeded federal ambient air quality objectives.

Sulphur dioxide (SO_2) can have a detrimental effect on plants, building materials, and human health. Furthermore, this gas is a major constituent in acidic deposition. During the 1980s, sulphur dioxide levels were relatively high, and frequently exceeded provincial air quality objectives for both Levels A and B (Figure 2.11). The

most frequent and significant episodes of high SO_2 concentrations occurred at Port Alice, the site of a sulphite pulp mill on Vancouver Island, and at several locations near mining and smelting facilities in the interior. In Port Alice, vegetation has been affected by sulphur dioxide emissions. For example, lichens have been eliminated near the mill, and forest growth has been reduced up to 1.5 km from this site.[13] The situation at Trail is described in the Southern Interior Mountains Ecoprovince section. Starting in 1990, there has been a marked improvement in sulphur dioxide exceedances across all stations (Figure 2.11), but there are still some locations where concentrations frequently exceed provincial objectives.

Some industrial processes, particularly Kraft pulp mills, oil refineries, and natural gas processing plants, release malodorous sulphur compounds to the atmosphere known collectively as total reduced sulphur (TRS) compounds. Perhaps the best known of these is hydrogen sulphide (H_2S), identifiable by its rotten egg smell. Although high concentrations of hydrogen sulphide can adversely affect human health, the main goal of the B.C. ambient air quality objective for this gas is to avoid objectionable nuisance levels in the

atmosphere. Through the 1980s there was little change in the provincial average concentration for this gas (Figure 2.12), and there were frequent episodes when concentrations exceeded maximum acceptable (Level B) concentrations at particular locations. Highest exceedance frequencies were recorded in Prince George and in Castlegar, where major steps have recently been taken by industry to reduce this frequency. The situation at Prince George is described in the Sub-Boreal Interior Ecoprovince.

Carbon monoxide (CO) causes no irritation and has no detectable taste or smell. This gas represents an acute health risk, since the body can become starved for oxygen when the gas is inhaled and absorbed into the bloodstream. The largest human-made source is motor vehicles. Because of high vehicle densities in the Greater Vancouver area, this is the only area of the province where CO is monitored. Average CO concentrations have fluctuated a great deal over the past 15 years and showed no clear trend until the mid 1980s, when the frequency of exceeding Level A concentrations began to decline (Figure 2.13). Problems are now mainly confined to winter months and downtown Vancouver. During recent years there has been an improvement in CO conditions in the GVRD. This trend is probably related to better pollution control devices on new vehicles, but would be reversed in the future if there are substantial increases in numbers or use of motor vehicles.

In summary, gaseous contaminants in B.C. have shown some improvements, particularly in recent years, for some gases (ozone, carbon monoxide). For other gases, the situation remains problematical (sulphur dioxide, hydrogen sulphide). While improvements in technology and pollution control equipment are generally reducing unit emissions, these advances are being overtaken by increased population and development.

To improve air quality throughout B.C., the provincial government has adopted a new policy requiring industries discharging atmospheric

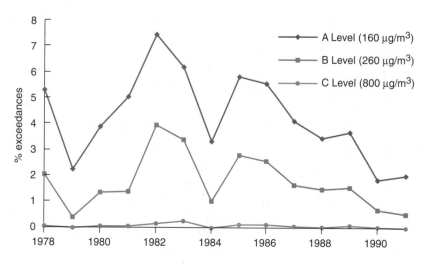

Figure 2.11
Sulphur dioxide exceedances

Graph shows the province-wide exceedances of 24-hour level A, B, and C objectives for sulphur dioxide. Levels were high in the 1980s, but have shown marked improvements in the 1990s. (See note in Figure 2.10).[12]

Total reduced sulphur exceedances

Graph shows the province-wide exceedances of 24-hour level A and B objectives for total reduced sulphur. There was little change throughout the 1980s, but some improvement in 1990-91. (See note in Figure 2.10).[12]

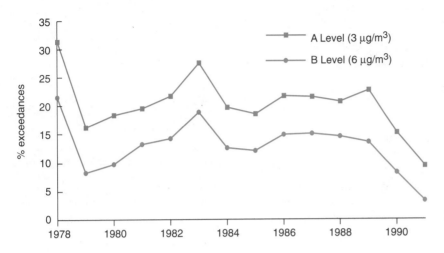

Carbon monoxide exceedances

Graph shows exceedances in the Lower Fraser Valley of 8-hour level A and B objectives for carbon monoxide. There were negligible C level exceedances. There was no clear trend until the mid-1980s, when the frequency of level A exceedances declined. (See note in Figure 2.10)[12]

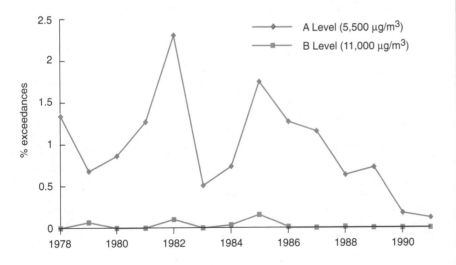

contaminants to use state-of-the-art, Best Available Control Technology (BACT). Other initiatives designed to improve air quality include an international protocol to stabilize nitrogen oxide emissions at 1987 levels by 1994, and the U.S./Canada Accord on Sulphur Dioxide and Nitrogen Oxide Emissions. The federal and provincial governments are also negotiating an

agreement that will implement the Management Plan for Nitrogen Oxides and Volatile Organic Compounds, developed by the Canadian Council of Ministers of the Environment. This is complemented by development of the new provincial AirCare program that requires motor vehicle inspection and maintenance to help reduce smog-forming emissions in the lower Fraser valley.

Emerging issues

In addition to the air quality issues described above, there are several others that are becoming more important in B.C. Of these, perhaps the most pressing is that of air toxics. Included here are hydrocarbons, some of which are carcinogenic (e.g. polynuclear aromatic hydrocarbons - PAH, and volatile organic compounds - VOC), arsenic (another carcinogen), and various toxic compounds (e.g., hydrogen fluoride, ammonia).

Conclusions

One of the reasons why the majority of British Columbians take the air around them for granted is that generally we enjoy good air quality, most of the time, and in most locations. However, with a growing population and increasing level of industrial activity, there is a tendency for air quality to become degraded. While much has already been accomplished in controlling and reducing emissions of atmospheric contaminants, more remains to be done if we are to adequately protect our ecosystems and human residents.

At the same time we must continue redefining what is considered an air pollutant. As a society we must adapt both our activities and our regulations to ensure that we protect our precious air resource. In doing so, we must be aware that we are affected not only by local contaminant sources, but also by regional or global atmospheric factors. Where the forces shaping our regional and global atmosphere are under our direct control, we must exercise our responsibility to manage those factors. Simultaneously, we display wisdom when we begin seeking ways to adapt to longer term changes resulting from forces beyond our immediate control, such as increased UV radiation and global climate change.

Water

Perhaps due to historically abundant and high quality water supplies, British Columbians have not fully appreciated the substantial impacts on water resources. The B.C. Round Table on the Environment and the Economy identified both water quality and quantity as major concerns in the province.[1] The use, and sometimes abuse, of water places more than humans at risk. Water links land, air and plants and animals, and sustains the province's enviable complement of natural ecosystems, which are home to a diversity of wildlife second to none in Canada. Water also transports environmental contaminants within and between ecosystems.

Figure 2.15
Distribution of water.

Only a fraction of the earth's water reserves is located on land and in a form which is appropriate for most human uses. Although B.C. may contain more than an average amount of freshwater, water remains a scarce resource in a global context. [2]

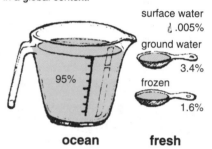

surface water
💧 .005%

ground water
3.4%

frozen
1.6%

95%

ocean   **fresh**

Our fresh surface waters

From one perspective, the supply of water is essentially endless since it is continuously recirculated among different parts of the hydrologic cycle (Figure 2.14). However, only a small portion of this water is available for human use at any time (Figure 2.15). The only reliable measure of regional water supply is annual runoff or stream flow since this represents the fresh water that is continuously renewed through the hydrologic cycle.

Surface water supplies

In British Columbia, it is easy to believe that supplies of freshwater are limitless. Surface waters (streams, rivers, lakes and estuaries) cover 1.2 million hectares, about 1.25% of the province.[3] Runoff from B.C. forms one quarter of all the fresh flowing water in Canada and 1.7% of the total from all land surfaces on earth. However, runoff varies enormously within the province - under 10 centimetres per year in the Southern Interior to over 200 centimetres per year on the west coast of Vancouver Island. This reflects similar variation in precipitation. Much of the water flow is concentrated in a few major rivers (Figure 2.16). Similarly, many areas of the province experience extremes in the seasonal availability of water. Provincial averages for various indicators of water supply (e.g. total runoff volume of water impounded) may disguise these wide ecoprovincial variations.

Water demand in B.C. is typically highest in summer. Unfortunately, this is usually the time of year when runoff is lowest. Seasonal shortages in

Figure 2.14
The hydrologic cycle

Water is in constant motion. It enters the atmosphere through evaporation from land or water surfaces or transpiration from plants and animals. In the atmosphere it condenses and falls to earth as either rain or snow. Once on the surface, it may be stored in ice caps and glaciers, in lakes, in underground aquifers or the oceans. This great recycling process is known as the water, or hydrologic, cycle. The natural quality of surface and groundwaters is largely a function of the composition of the rocks and soils over and through which it passes.

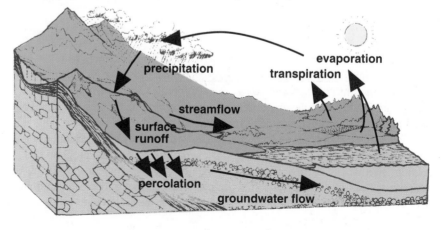

precipitation

evaporation
transpiration

streamflow

surface
runoff

percolation

groundwater flow

domestic supplies have been reported in the Peace-Liard, Kootenay, Cariboo, Thompson-Okanagan, Central Coast and Sunshine Coast regions. Shortages were also experienced in the Greater Vancouver Regional District (GVRD) and Capital Regional District (CRD) in the summer of 1992. This led to some water rationing. One quarter of B.C.'s regional districts cite water availability as a future constraint on economic development.[4] These water shortages, however, may not indicate actual shortfalls in the quantity of available water but rather concerns about the cost of tapping new supplies (e.g. reservoirs, water treatment, and distribution systems). Many water supply concerns in the province probably reflect a lack of resources to bridge the gaps between supply and demand. Even if resources were available to bridge these gaps, diversions and impoundments would carry additional environmental costs that need to be factored into decisions.

There is some evidence, however, of long-term changes in actual water supplies. Long-term data from around the province suggest decreasing average annual streamflows at southern sites and increasing flows at northern sites.[5] Similar trends have been observed in snowpack water storage.[5] Only five of the 17 streamflow stations and four of the 11 snowpack monitoring stations, showed statistically significant trends. Trend detection is made difficult by natural year-to-year variations, a lack of monitoring stations with complete records, inconsistent results among stations, and flow alterations resulting from diversions or dams. Climate models suggest that global warming may further exacerbate this situation by significantly reducing summer precipitation in southern B.C. while increasing summer evapotranspiration.

Figure 2.17 illustrates trends for rainfall, streamflow and snowpack depth of the Fraser River Basin. Streamflow was low in the 1930s and 1940s, high in the 1960s and 1970s and is currently slightly below the long-term average. The causes of these observed variations are not yet known. Changes in streamflow in the

Figure 2.16
River flow

Most of the runoff in B.C. is concentrated in a few rivers. The largest, and one of the most important, is the Fraser River, which drains nearly one quarter of the province.[75]

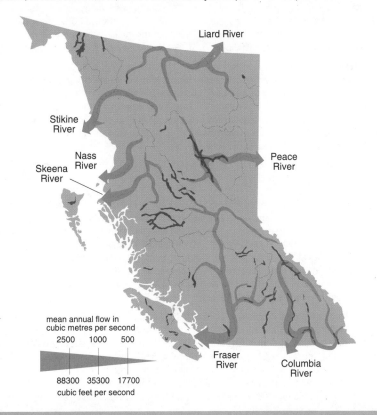

Figure 2.17
Precipitation, snowpack and streamflow

A few stations have been selected to monitor precipitation, snowpack and streamflow in the province and to assess long-term trends. These graphs show representative data from the Fraser River Basin, plotted as 10-year moving averages. The 1920 - 1950 period had light precipitation and low streamflow. Heavier precipitation and greater streamflow were apparent from 1960 to 1980. Maximum snowpack water storage, monitored for a much shorter period, shows a similar pattern between 1960 and 1980, but with a much more pronounced increase. These changes could be due to natural long-term variations, human activities, or some combination of both.[3]

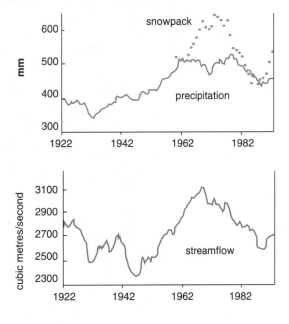

Box 2.1a

The Fraser River Basin

The Fraser River is the fifth longest river in Canada (1,375 km). That's the distance from Vancouver to Regina. It's average annual flow of 3,972 m³/sec is the third largest of any Canadian river. This flow is enough to fill three olympic-size swimming pools in one second. The Fraser also has the fifth largest drainage basin in Canada (234,000 km²), draining almost one-quarter of British Columbia. This vast drainage basin is composed of numerous tributaries, streams and lakes distributed over 13 sub-basins and 6 ecoprovinces.

The Fraser River Basin is recognized internationally for its great biological diversity. For example, it shares top place with the Skeena River in terms of the diversity of native salmon species. It is also the greatest producer of salmon of any river in the world.[6] Equally significant in terms of biological diversity, 21 species of waterfowl breed in the Basin, one of the most diverse waterfowl communities in Canada. The Fraser River Estuary, located at the mouth of the Fraser where it discharges into the Strait of Georgia, contains some of the most productive wildlife habitat in the Basin.

The Fraser River Basin has experienced dramatic changes over the last 100 years, raising questions about the sustainability of development. About two-thirds of the population of B.C. lives within the Basin (over 1.7 million people). The population is increasing rapidly, particularly along the lower Fraser. A recent assessment of water quality in the Basin, judged overall water quality conditions as fairly good in comparison to other drainage Basins in Canada, such as the Lower Great Lakes and the St. Lawrence River.[7] Threats to water quality, however, do exist. The major inputs of wastewater to the Fraser River system occur in its upper reaches at Prince George and Quesnel, from Kamloops through the Thompson River, and in the lower Fraser River from Port Mann to its mouth.[8] Almost 54% of industrial discharges in the Basin come from interior pulp mills, while nearly 93% of municipal waste discharges occur in the lower Fraser Basin.

Many localized or regional problems also exist in the Basin. Ecoprovincial topics discussed in Part 3 of this report include: air quality in Prince George, Williams Lake, and the Lower Mainland; dioxins and furans in fish and sediment in the upper Fraser; problems with introduced plant species in Shuswap Lake; groundwater contamination along the lower Fraser; marine water quality problems at the mouth of the Fraser; land use change in the Lower Mainland; salmon stocks on the Horsefly River; and stresses to the Fraser River Estuary. These problems are being addressed through the Fraser River Action Plan (Box 2.1b).

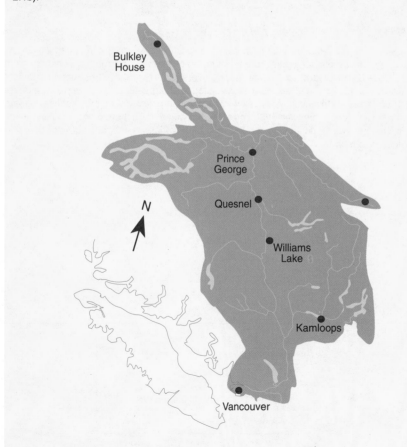

Fraser River can potentially have profound effects. The river basin drains almost one-quarter of B.C., has tremendous biological diversity, and contains two thirds of B.C.'s population (Box 2.1a)

Too many demands or too little water?

Water shortages may also result from excessive or incompatible demands rather than insufficient supplies. Water is used in almost every human activity. Water managers, distinguish between "withdrawal" and "in-stream" uses of water. Withdrawal refers to those uses which actually remove water from lakes or streams such as for agricultural, municipal, and industrial activities. In-stream uses include hydroelectric power generation, navigation, recreation, fish and wildlife. Withdrawal can change stream flows and water levels, which in turn can affect in-stream uses. More data are typically available for withdrawal uses than in-stream uses, so we frequently have an incomplete picture of water demand.

How much water is used in B.C., and how is it used? B.C. accounted for only 6.5% (2,755 million m³) of total water withdrawal in Canada in 1986. Over 60% of the national withdrawal, was used for thermal power generation (conventional and nuclear power stations). Since most of B.C.'s power is generated by hydroelectric plants (an in-stream use), very little water is withdrawn for power generation. This reduces B.C.'s share of the total national water withdrawal. B.C., however, accounted for more than 16% of total manufacturing, 13% of municipal, 17% of agricultural, and 16% of mining water withdrawals in Canada. Manufacturing is the single largest withdrawal use in B.C. (Figure 2.18).

Where does withdrawn water end up? Some water uses are considered to be "consumptive". In consumptive uses some water is incorporated into final products (e.g. soft drinks) or redistributed to the atmosphere or land (e.g. irrigation), making it unavailable for further use downstream. By this

Manufacturing is the largest single water user in B.C., followed by agriculture and municipal use. Thermal power is a very minor user. Hydroelectric generation is not included under withdrawal uses. The data are from 1986.[9]

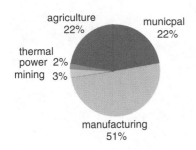

agriculture 22%

municpal 22%

thermal power 2%

mining 3%

manufacturing 51%

total water withdrawal 2,755 million m³

definition of consumptive uses, only 24% (651 million m³) of the water withdrawn in B.C. during 1986 was actually consumed. Non-consumptive uses (e.g. industrial process or cooling waters) remove water from the stream but eventually return it at or near the source. This discharged water, however, is typically of a lower quality than when it was removed, and may affect other in-stream and withdrawal users.

Water licenses are not the only way to control water withdrawal. Water pricing can also be a very effective tool, though currently it is under-utilized. Both the structure and level of water rates influence water usage.[10] Flat rates (a fixed charge regardless of quantity used) provide no incentive for conservation. Declining block rates (i.e. lower rates with increasing quantities) may even encourage consumption. Water utilities frequently do not recover the full cost of supplying or treating municipal water. In 1987, the Federal Water Policy called for realistic water pricing to recover the full cost of water intake, treatment, distribution and wastewater discharge, and to encourage water conservation. In B.C., nearly 78% of municipal water rates do not promote conservation.[11] Although rates have increased substantially in recent years, B.C. still maintains the second lowest water prices in the country.

Water licenses are one means of regulating withdrawal use in B.C. Licenses are sometimes issued for in-stream uses such as storage, hydro-electric generation and sometimes for fisheries (e.g. ensuring adequate flow). At present, other in-stream values such as wildlife, recreation, or aesthetics are not explicitly accounted for in this process. Withdrawal use could also be controlled by an appropriate water pricing system to encourage conservation and improved efficiency (Box 2.2). Recent surveys of per capita domestic water use suggest that there is room for improving the efficiency of our water use.

Monitoring all the various uses of water is a very difficult task. Different uses often present different potential environmental impacts and conflicts between users, and different opportunities for reducing these problems. The Province is currently computerizing information on water licenses (a potential indicator of withdrawal use) and local supply. This should provide some of the necessary information regarding status and trends in water use, and their environmental implications.

Surface water quality

The quality of water varies naturally from place to place and by season. The most important factors influencing natural water quality are the physical and chemical composition of the rock and soils through which the water moves. As water moves over or through these materials, it takes on some of their chemical properties. Natural variations in water quality influence the suitability of surface waters for various human uses, including drinking water.

There are many types of surface water pollutants (Table 2.1). These pollutants can originate from either point sources or non-point (dispersed) sources

Table 2.1
Types of surface water pollutants and some of their effects

Type of Polutant	Examples	Potential negative effects
Biological Contamination	• Micro-organisms • Introduced species	• Threat to human and animal health • Sanitary shellfish closures • Beach closures • Loss of native species
Toxic Compounds	• PCBs • Chlorophenols • Dioxins and Furans • Hydrocarbons (e.g. gasoline, oil, PAHs) • Trace metals (e.g. copper, lead, mercury, zinc)	• Threat to human and animal health • Dioxin shellfish closures • Fish consumption advisories
Physical Pollutants	• Suspended solids • Sediment	• Increased Turbidity • Changed colour • Odour • **Reduced dissolved oxygen** • Loss and reduced quality of fish habitat • Reduced productivity
Chemical Pollutants	• Nutrients (e.g. Nitrogen, Phosphorus) • Manure • Industrial effluents	• Algal blooms • Changed colour • Unpleasant taste and odour • Reduced dissolved oxygen • Fish kills • Reduced biodiversity

(Figure 2.19). In B.C., the main point sources of surface water pollutants are pulp and paper mill discharges, other industrial effluent discharges, municipal sewage and stormwater discharges, acid mine drainage, and, periodically, chemical or petroleum spills. Examples of non-point sources include acid rain from atmospheric deposition, nitrates and pesticides from agriculture activities, sediment from forestry activities, and toxic chemicals in urban runoff. Each type of pollution source has different implications for water quality and ecosystem health, and different requirements for clean-up or control. A selection of these activities and their impacts are discussed below. More information is generally available for point sources than for non-point sources.

Figure 2.19
Sources of surface water pollutants

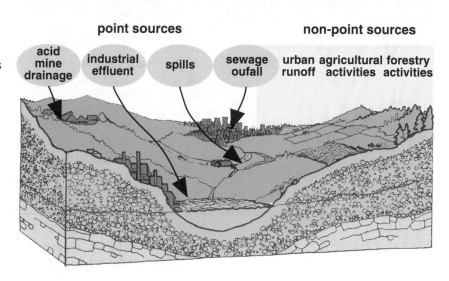

Inland pulp mills

Pulp and paper mill discharges have received the most attention of any industrial effluent discharges in B.C. Effluent from pulp and paper mills contains organic solids, numerous toxic compounds (e.g. certain chlorinated phenolics and resin acids), and nutrients. Some discharged organic solids (such as cellulose fibres) do not degrade very rapidly, forming fibre mats which smother bottom-dwelling communities and reduce fish habitat. This has occurred in the Columbia River downstream of Celgar pulp mill.

Organic solids in effluent are partly consumed by bacteria. Both bacterial breakdown of solids, and oxidation of some of the chemicals, use up oxygen in receiving waters. This demand for oxygen is called the biochemical oxygen demand (BOD) of the effluent. Dissolved oxygen is essential to most aquatic life, so the greater the BOD, the greater the potential negative impact on aquatic life.

Discharges of BOD are regulated under the federal Fisheries Act and provincial Waste Management Act (Box 2.3). Total discharges of BOD from inland pulp mills have generally decreased since the early 1970s, despite increases in pulp production. This is primarily due to on-going

Box 2.3

Discharge management permits

Over the past 30 years, the Provincial government has used a permit system to manage point discharges of waste to air, water and land. Waste Management Permits specify the quantity and quality of wastes which may be discharged. These permits determine the amounts of substances a discharge may contain usually after treatment, such that it will not alter receiving waters or impair their usefulness. The permits also outline the requirements for monitoring and reporting waste discharges to BC Environment. As of October, 1992, there were 3,596 active permits in B.C.[12]

Not complying with these permits can have a number of regulatory consequences. Since July 1990, BC Environment has released lists every six months containing the names of noncomplying or pollution concern industrial operations and municipalities. Since then, over 98% of the permit holders have been in compliance. Of the 259 operations that have been listed on the five Noncompliance Lists since July 1990, only four have remained on the report all five times. Only 12 of the 289 operations which appeared on the Pollution Concern Lists have remained there all five times.[12] Unfortunately, these 'repeat offenders' are among the largest licensed effluent volumes in B.C. It is hoped that such lists will allow public scrutiny and opinion to motivate clean-up. The Province has also stepped up investigations of pollution offences and increased maximum penalties. The number of charges laid under the Waste Management Act increased by 40% between 1989 and 1990 (from 246 to 345 charges).

improvements in secondary treatment of effluents. Secondary treatment systems (e.g. aerated lagoons or activated sludge) are designed to remove 70 to 95% of effluent BOD, and to render the effluent non-toxic to fish, as defined by regulations. All but one inland pulp mill currently have secondary treatment. This mill is expected to have secondary treatment in place by mid-1993, which should greatly reduce overall provincial BOD loadings from inland pulp mills (Figure 2.20). About half of the total provincial inland loading of BOD

occurs within the Fraser River Basin (Box 2.1b).

The discharge of numerous chlorinated organic compounds and other wood extractives from the kraft process remains an on-going concern, and a focus of intensive research.[76,77] Many chlorinated organic compounds discharged to waterbodies can persist and accumulate in aquatic ecosystems, with potentially detrimental impacts on biota.[13] Dioxins and furans are a specific group of highly persistent compounds formed during the chlorine

Figure 2.20

BOD from inland pulp and paper mills

Only one inland mill does not currently have secondary treatment. It is scheduled to start secondary treatment by 1993, which will reduce BOD loadings from inland mills.[15]

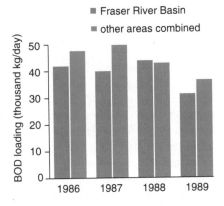

■ Fraser River Basin
■ other areas combined

Box 2.1b

The Fraser River Action Plan (FRAP)

FRAP is a 6-year, $100-million program. Its goals are to reverse environmental degradation in the Fraser River Basin, rehabilitate degraded areas, and develop a management program to achieve sustainable development. Specific objectives include a 30% reduction in the discharge of harmful industrial effluents by 1996, and the virtual elimination of releases of persistent toxic substances by the year 2000. Another objective is to double sockeye salmon stocks within 20 years from an average of 8 million fish in 1975-86 to 16 million. To attain these objectives, FRAP will be forming partnerships among all concerned groups to develop a cooperative management program for the Fraser River Basin. The federal, provincial, and local governments recently signed an agreement establishing a Program Management Board to promote sustainable development in the Basin.

bleaching process. They have been found in all components of the ecosystem.[14] These compounds are of particular concern in animals, plants and sediments. This is because they tend to accumulate in media with higher fat content (such as plants, fish and shellfish) or higher organic matter content (such as sediments). Their persistence and toxicity have potential consequences for both ecosystem and human health.

Since 1988, dioxin-related fish consumption advisories have been issued for parts of the upper Fraser, Thompson, Quesnel, North Thompson, South Thompson, Kootenay, and Columbia rivers for a variety of species. Some sportfish, and fish that are an important part of native peoples' traditional diet, have been included in these advisories. Ongoing monitoring programs are tracking the reduction of these compounds in various parts of the ecosystem.

The concentration of AOX (Adsorbable Organically-bound Halogen) in pulp mill effluent is used to regulate discharges of chlorinated organic compounds in B.C. (Box 2.4). In 1990, the Province passed regulations requiring all mills to incorporate secondary effluent treatment and to reduce AOX discharges below 2.5 kg of AOX per air-dried tonne of pulp produced. Technological changes such as chlorine dioxide substitution have reduced AOX loadings from mills in compliance with these regulations (Figure 2.21). Six of the seven inland bleach kraft mills have already met or surpassed the target of 2.5 kg of AOX per air-dried tonne. The one remaining mill is expected to comply by July, 1993. In early 1992, a new regulation was passed requiring further reductions to 1.5 kg AOX per air-dried tonne by 1995. The Province anticipates eliminating AOX discharges (or the use of chlorine) by Dec. 31, 2002.

Decreases in AOX loadings are also evident in water quality indicators. Chloride is a good tracer of bleached kraft effluent presence and has been demonstrated to closely reflect AOX levels in the receiving environment. Chloride concentrations in the Fraser River have declined since pulp mills curtailed their use of chlorine (Figure 2.22). National regulations have been developed and implemented under the Canadian Environmental Protection Act (CEPA) to regulate the discharge of dioxins and furans from bleach kraft pulp mills. The same process changes implemented to reduce dioxin and furan levels also reduce AOX (Figure 2.21). The Fraser River Action Plan will help to monitor the effects of

Box 2.4

Pulp mill initiatives

Pulp mills using chlorine to bleach pulp also produce hundreds of compounds, many of which are toxic, persistent and/or bioaccumulate (accumulate over time in living tissues). Chlorinated organic compounds, of which dioxins and furans are a small part, are primarily produced through complex reactions between three substances: 1) the wood constituent lignin; 2) lignin breakdown products released during the chemical pulping process; and 3) the chlorine bleaching agent.

Approximately 90% of the chlorine used in the bleaching process is converted to chloride which has relatively little environmental impact. The remaining 10% is bound to organic material. This Adsorbable Organically-bound Halogens (AOX) is used as a measure of the broad group of organochlorine compounds formed during the bleaching process. AOX concentrations in effluent are now used to regulate pulp mill discharges of these compounds.

Proven methods to reduce AOX formation include reducing the amount of chlorine used in the chlorination bleaching stage, changes in the pulping process, and substituting chlorine dioxide for chlorine. Secondary treatment can also lower AOX levels in effluent. The B.C. Ministry of Environment, Lands and Parks is currently researching alternative strategies for regulating pulp mill effluent, (for example, regulating the amount of certain "indicator organic compounds" in addition to AOX). Regulations under the Canadian Environmental Protection Act (CEPA) now require virtual elimination of dioxins and furans.[16] "Virtual elimination" means that amounts are not measurable in the effluent based on current technology.

Figure 2.22

Chloride in water

Chloride is a good tracer of AOX levels in receiving waters. Average chloride concentrations in the upper Fraser River at Marguerite during winter low flow appear to have declined since the implementation of technological changes and chlorine dioxide substitution in bleach kraft mills.[15]

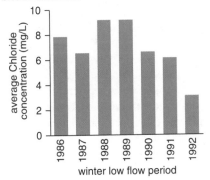

winter low flow period

Figure 2.21
AOX and dioxins from bleached kraft mills

Technological changes and chlorine dioxide substitution at bleach kraft pulp mills have reduced AOX concentrations (kg per air-dried tonne of pulp) and average monthly loadings of AOX, bringing most mills into compliance with new provincial regulations. These changes have also reduced average monthly loadings of dioxins (2,3,7,8 TCDD). The 1995 concentration target for AOX is 1.5 kg/tonne. Data from the upper Fraser are used here to illustrate these reductions.[15]

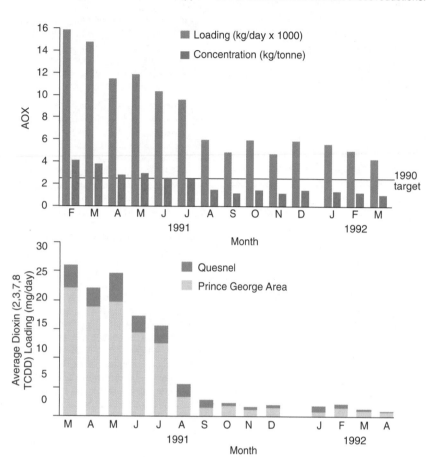

these abatement programs (Box 2.1b).

Nutrients such as nitrogen and phosphorus are also released by pulp mills. While these nutrients are required to sustain aquatic plants, an oversupply combined with light can lead to excessive algal blooms. Algal blooms are a massive "greening" of the water column and lake or river bottom, reducing recreational values, increasing the cost of supplying drinking water and reducing aquatic habitat quality. Dissolved oxygen can be consumed as these algae decompose, and this can affect fish populations. Though some of these effects have been a concern in the Thompson River,[17] they have not been a major concern elsewhere in B.C. For example, the natural turbidity of the Fraser River reduces the amount of light available for plant growth.

Freshwater municipal wastewater discharges

Municipal sewage discharges can consist of residential, commercial and industrial wastewaters. Combined sewer overflows (CSOs) are municipal discharges composed of a mixture of stormwater and municipal sewage; they occur largely in the Lower Mainland. Wastes are partly con-

sumed by bacteria in the receiving environment and therefore exert a biochemical oxygen demand (BOD). They also contain nutrients such as phosphorus and nitrogen which, like pulp mill effluent, may cause algal blooms in nutrient-sensitive waters. Municipal wastewaters also contain suspended solids, disease-causing micro-organisms and toxic contaminants (Table 2.1).

The quality of municipal sewage effluents depends on the level of treatment they receive. There are three common levels of treatment: primary, secondary, and tertiary. Primary treatment involves the removal of large solids and floating substances through settling and screening. Secondary treatment is a biological treatment process used to reduce suspended solids, BOD, and some contaminants. Tertiary treatment is generally used to reduce nutrient concentrations and further reduce toxic contaminants. Disinfection may be used in addition to any one of these treatment levels.

There are currently 64 secondary and 9 tertiary treatment plants discharging to freshwater in B.C. (marine discharges are discussed in the section on Marine Environmental Quality below). Secondary and tertiary treatment serves 550,000 people. Only 6 primary treatment facilities still discharge to freshwaters. The two largest primary treatment plants are at Annacis and Lulu Islands in the Lower Mainland. They serve over 700,000 people and are currently being upgraded to secondary treatment (see Georgia Depression Ecoprovince). The remaining four primary treatment plants, serving 26,000 people, are located at Trail, Nelson, Lillooet and Lytton.[18] They each discharge into large water volumes.

In B.C., municipal and industrial wastewater discharges require a Waste Management Permit or a Liquid Waste Management Plan with operational certificates under the Waste Management Act (Box 2.3). Permit requirements consider the ecological sensitivity of the environment receiving the waste, such as its ability to accommodate a given level of BOD. In early 1992, the Province adopted a policy of Best Achievable Control Technology (BACT). Consequently, at least secondary treatment will probably be required at most locations, with further nutrient removal required at sensitive sites (e.g. the Cheakamus River and lakes in the Okanagan area).

The provincial government plans to work with local governments to provide secondary wastewater treatment throughout the province. Both technical assistance and new options for financing facilities may be provided.[19] These improvements should address concerns regarding BOD loadings. The release of nutrients is a concern in some areas, but existing or planned tertiary treatment is expected to address this problem.

Microbiological and toxic chemical contamination remain the greatest threats from municipal discharges. The ability of treatment to remove toxic contaminants changes with the type of contaminant and level of treatment. Toxic substances, however, may simply become concentrated in the sludge. This reduces the beneficial uses of sludge as fertilizer and poses another disposal problem on land. The Province is currently revising interim guidelines for the disposal of domestic sludge under the Waste Management Act. Control of contaminant sources is the best method of controlling toxic substances in municipal wastewater and sludge.

Urban runoff (stormwater) is a potentially larger source of toxic contaminants than sewage treatment plants. In most large urban centres, stormwater is typically collected separately from wastes destined for sewage treatment plants. Storm sewers and ditches discharge urban runoff at numerous points in the lower Fraser River Basin. There are 22 combined sewer overflow points on the Main Stem and North Arm with average annual flows of 22 million m[3].

Urban stormwater often contains a wide variety of contaminants, (including solids such as plastics), from roads, parking lots, industrial and commercial areas, and residences. The quantities of contaminants vary but many are persistent, potentially toxic, and a threat to aquatic organisms. This problem has not been monitored systematically. British Columbia, like other Canadian jurisdictions, currently has few regulations controlling stormwater discharges. Though stormwater discharged via outfalls comes under the Waste Management Act, few permits have been issued for such discharges. The Province has also developed urban runoff quality control guidelines.[20]

Mining - acid rock drainage

The main environmental impacts of mining are site disturbance from exploration activities and mine development, contaminated tailings, pond effluents, groundwater seepage, alkaline rock drainage and acid rock drainage. Acid rock drainage (ARD), if uncontrolled, has the most significant impact on water quality. It occurs when sulphide minerals contained in rock are exposed to air and water, forming sulphuric acid. The sources of ARD in metal and coal mines include underground workings, open pit mine faces, waste rock dumps, tailing deposits and ore stockpiles.

ARD is not necessarily confined to mining activities. ARD can occur wherever sulphide-bearing rock is exposed, such as in highway and railroad rock cuts. Some natural springs are acidic, usually near outcrops of sulphide-bearing rocks. However, not all exposed sulphide-bearing rock results in acid drainage. Acid drainage does not occur if either the sulphide minerals are non-reactive or if the rock contains sufficient alkaline material to neutralize the acid.

When drainage water is acidic, it can dissolve metals contained in the rock. Uncontrolled and untreated ARD, typically containing elevated levels of metals and sulphates, can have severe environmental and economic consequences for aquatic ecosystems. These include elevated metal levels in fish tissue and changes in the biodiversity and abundance of plankton communities.

How extensive is the ARD problem in British Columbia? There are eight operating coal mines in B.C., none of which is presently generating ARD. There are 16 operating metal mines in B.C., of which six generate ARD and several others have the potential to do so.[21] These six mines are currently collecting and treating all acidic drainage. There are approximately 72 million tonnes of acid generating mine tailings and 250 million tonnes of acid generating waste rock in B.C. (4% and 8% of the Canadian total). This amount is increasing by 25 million tonnes per year.[22] The strongest acid mine drainage is produced from a waste rock dump at Equity Silver in the Central Interior Ecoprovince. The mine is scheduled to close in 1993.[23]

Good planning can prevent or minimize ARD in new mining developments. However, a larger problem is that ARD can persist for hundreds of years at closed and abandoned mine sites. At least 5 abandoned mines in B.C. are known to generate ARD. One example is the Britannia mine adjacent to Howe Sound.[21]

Remediation is underway at a number of abandoned sites, including the Mount Washington mine on Vancouver Island and the Union mine near Greenwood.[24] In 1987, the B.C. Mining Association, mining companies and the federal and provincial governments together established the B.C. Acid Mine Drainage Task force, which will coordinate and help fund research on ARD. Under the provincial Mine Development Review Process, approval of mine development requires companies to conduct detailed studies which demonstrate that potential ARD problems can be technically and economically managed.[25] Companies are also required to post bonds so that ARD from closed mines can be managed in perpetuity. The most preferable long-term form of control is prevention of acid generation reactions, such as through exclusion of oxygen by flooding.

Spills of hazardous materials to freshwater

Spills of hazardous materials represent a potentially important impact on environmental quality. They are difficult to monitor since they must be reported either by those involved or by a witness. The Province has recently developed a Dangerous Goods Incident Database designed for assessing data on reported hazardous chemical spills. The Federal government also has a role in assessing and recording hazardous spills.

The transportation industry (truck, rail, shipping) accounts for the largest number of known spills of hazardous material. However, a much larger number of spills are of unknown origin. Possible sources include road service runoff and storm sewer inputs, leaking storage tanks and illegal dumping to sewers or freshwater. Although these incidents frequently involve smaller quantities of material, many such spills can add up to a significant environmental impact.

Figure 2.23
Hazardous material spills

A total of 506 hazardous material spills to freshwater were reported between April 1991 and March 1992. Hydrocarbon fuels (oil and gasoline) were involved in the largest number of spills. Materials in the "other" category included acid, anti-freeze, base, various industrial materials (e.g. adhesives, dry cleaning fluid, fire retardant), silt, paints and solvents, PCB/transformer oil, pesticides and many unknown substances.[26]

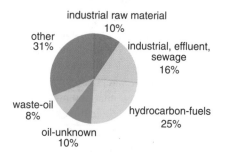

industrial raw material 10%

other 31%

industrial, effluent, sewage 16%

waste-oil 8%

oil-unknown 10%

hydrocarbon-fuels 25%

Petrochemicals (oil and other hydrocarbon fuels) represent the material most often accidentally spilled or released to freshwater (Figure 2.23). Other spilled materials include organic and industrial effluents (e.g. sewage, landfill leachate, mine tailings and industrial wastewater), industrial raw materials (e.g. ammonia, chlorine, creosote, crude oil and wood chips), and non-fuel oil.

The environmental impacts of these spills varies with the quantity and type of material spilled, and the characteristics of the receiving environment. Spills affect water quality, the plants and animals living in aquatic ecosystems, and in some cases human health. Petrochemicals in particular have a tendency to biomagnify (increase in concentration) as they move through the food chain and are known to negatively affect reproduction in bald eagles, seals and sea otters. They are also extremely toxic to certain species of fish such as salmon.

The majority of incidents occur due to human error, equipment failures and vehicle accidents. Recent increases in the number of reported incidents may be the result of new provincial spill reporting regulations. They may also reflect heightened public awareness due to information campaigns (such as the B.C. Handle with Care and Recycling programs). The Province has released guidelines for developing response plans in the event of an industrial emergency, improved its own emergency response capability, and provided marina operators with minimum performance standards and response capability requirements.[27]

Forestry

Forests, water, fisheries, wildlife and human activities are linked together by the hydrologic cycle. This cycle can be significantly changed by forestry activities such as road construction, logging, slashburning and post-logging operations. These changes may include increased summer water temperatures, modified stream flow, soil erosion, and nutrient leaching. All of these changes potentially affect both fish and wildlife

habitat and the attractiveness of a stream or lake for recreation. Soil erosion can have a marked impact on water quality and fish habitat, particularly in areas with steep slopes and high rainfall.

Fish-forestry guidelines have been jointly developed by the federal and provincial governments and the forest industry. These guidelines are intended to address potential negative effects on fish habitat. These guidelines, however, have not always been followed by logging companies (see Plants and Animals, section on salmon). The Ministry of Forests is also developing watershed sensitivity rating and terrain management guidelines for coastal watersheds based on 10 years of federal/provincial research in the Queen Charlotte Islands.[28] Finally, the provincial government and forest industry are developing a Forest Practices Code to address environmental concerns.

Water quality objectives

Over the past eight years, B.C. has been developing water quality criteria and objectives to protect water quality for a variety of uses.

Water quality criteria are recommended safe conditions or limits, applicable province-wide, to protect each type of water use, such as drinking, recreation, irrigation or use by fish and wildlife. Ambient water quality criteria have been set for 15 measures of water quality based on an assessment of current scientific information. These include: conditions that have a direct effect (pH), substances that degrade water quality (nutrients, algae and particulate matter), substances that are toxic at low levels (cyanide, PCBs), substances that are toxic at higher levels (various forms of nitrogen, chlorine, fluoride), metals (aluminum, copper, lead, mercury, molybdenum), and microbiological indicators of risks to human health (fecal coliforms).

Setting water quality objectives involves taking the set of water quality criteria and adapting them to a specific body of water. The aim is to protect its

Figure 2.24
Water bodies with water quality objectives[29]

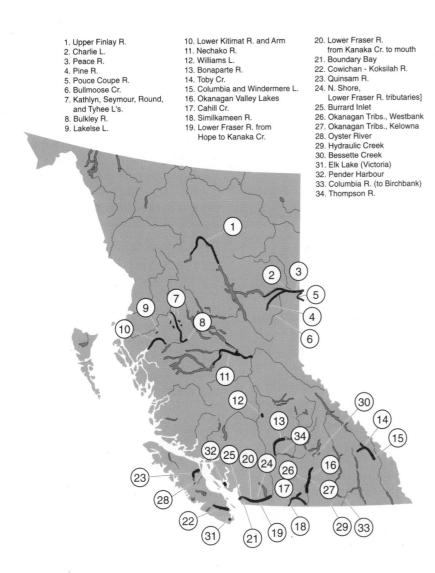

1. Upper Finlay R.
2. Charlie L.
3. Peace R.
4. Pine R.
5. Pouce Coupe R.
6. Bullmoose Cr.
7. Kathlyn, Seymour, Round, and Tyhee L's.
8. Bulkley R.
9. Lakelse L.
10. Lower Kitimat R. and Arm
11. Nechako R.
12. Williams L.
13. Bonaparte R.
14. Toby Cr.
15. Columbia and Windermere L.
16. Okanagan Valley Lakes
17. Cahill Cr.
18. Similkameen R.
19. Lower Fraser R. from Hope to Kanaka Cr.
20. Lower Fraser R. from Kanaka Cr. to mouth
21. Boundary Bay
22. Cowichan - Koksilah R.
23. Quinsam R.
24. N. Shore, Lower Fraser R. tributaries]
25. Burrard Inlet
26. Okanagan Tribs., Westbank
27. Okanagan Tribs., Kelowna
28. Oyster River
29. Hydraulic Creek
30. Bessette Creek
31. Elk Lake (Victoria)
32. Pender Harbour
33. Columbia R. (to Birchbank)
34. Thompson R.

most sensitive use. While they are not legally enforceable, the objectives form a reference point for judging water quality at a particular site. Water quality objectives have been set in 34 bodies of water in the province (Figure 2.24). These include large rivers such as the lower Fraser, Thompson, Columbia and Peace rivers, the Okanagan Valley lakes, and a few major marine areas such as Boundary Bay, Burrard Inlet and Kitimat Arm. Objectives for several other important basins are currently being developed.

Monitoring of basins to check for attainment of water quality objectives has been carried out annually since 1987. Objectives have consistently been met in over 90% of the samples checked. Measures for which objectives were sometimes exceeded in more than one basin included: measures of general water quality (suspended solids, turbidity, pH, dissolved oxygen), nutrients (phosphorus, nitrogen, and, chlorophyll-a, an indicator of excess nutrients), metals (copper, iron, lead, mercury, zinc), and organics (chlorophenols). This program is used as a screening device. Objectives which are exceeded are often followed up by regional B.C. Ministry of Environment, Lands and Parks staff.

Information on objectives attainment is one means of describing the state of water quality. However, there are four limitations to the data collected so far. First, objectives are set for a limited number of basins where problems are expected to occur. This gives an overly pessimistic view when used to report the province-wide state of water quality. Second, only limited resources are available to monitor whether objectives are being met. Confidence in the results from monitoring will be increased through more complete and more frequent coverage. Third, objectives need to be set for more substances of concern than has been the case so far, especially toxic organics. Fourth, although some objectives related to sediments, fish and other ecosystem-level phenomena have been developed, more are needed in order to give more direct measures of aquatic ecosystem health.

Water quality trends

In 1985, the provincial and federal governments began a cooperative water quality monitoring program. Its goal is to collect long-term data suitable for detecting regional trends in ambient water quality. Over 40 water quality variables are being monitored at 25 joint federal/provincial stations and 15 federal stations. Since many of these variables vary naturally from year to year, detecting trends typically requires at least five years of consistent, regular data collection. Sometimes more than a decade of data are needed to detect subtle trends.

The effects of changes in regulations or effluent loadings can be immediately apparent in some monitoring data (Figure 2.22). To date only data for the Flathead and Similkameen Rivers have been assessed. No trends are apparent except those due to declining streamflows. Other data are currently being assessed - these include nine stations in the Fraser Basin (monitored for overall water quality) and six small lakes in southwestern B.C. (monitored for the effects of atmospheric deposition of pollutants).

27

Drinking water quality

Surface waters supply almost half the municipal waterworks in B.C., serving 85% of the population. Many natural factors influence the suitability of these drinking water supplies. For example, soil and rainfall patterns affect water turbidity, hardness and metal concentrations. Naturally high turbidity (such as in the North Thompson River upstream from Kamloops) influences the ability of municipal systems to collect and treat water. Municipal and industrial waste discharges, forestry, urban development and agricultural activities can also influence drinking water quality.

Toxic contaminants in drinking water are a major public concern. However, most of the chemicals detected in surveys of drinking water quality across Canada are at concentrations hundreds or even thousands of times below Canadian Drinking Water Quality Guidelines. Drinking water is not believed to be a significant source of human exposure to contaminants.[31] In B.C., a recent study of drinking water from communities near pulp mills on the upper Fraser and Thompson rivers showed no evidence of dioxin, furan or other organochlorine contamination - compounds which are of particular concern at the moment in B.C.[33]

Microbiological contamination is the greatest drinking water quality problem in B.C. The incidence of intestinal infections in B.C. is much higher than in the rest of Canada. Moreover, rates of intestinal infection have generally increased over the past eight years (Figure 2.25). The cause of these increases is not yet known. The primary sources of intestinal infections are contaminated food (70%) and water (30%). Since 1980, there have been 16 outbreaks of waterborne disease throughout the province as well as two suspected outbreaks in 1991.[34] Sixty percent of these outbreaks have been caused by Giardiasis (Box 2.5). Boil-water advisories, which provide

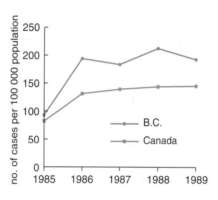

an immediate corrective measure for suspected microbiological contamination of drinking water, have increased 6-fold since 1986 (Figure 2.26).

Most water in B.C. requires only the minimal level of treatment (chlorination and some settling) to meet Canadian Drinking Water Quality Guidelines. In 1992, compliance with

bacterial standards became a legislated requirement in B.C. Chlorination and other processes of disinfection being investigated include ultraviolet treatment, ozonation and chloramination. Chloramination, which uses both ammonia and chlorine, generally produces better disinfection at lower cost than chlorination. Chloramine and chlorine have comparable toxicity to fish. However, chloramine is more persistent, increasing the risk to fish, particularly in the event of a spill or water main break in the vicinity of fish habitat.

Some microbiological threats are resistant to chlorination. Filtration is extremely expensive, but has the added benefit of improving clarity. Five communities in B.C. currently take water treatment beyond chlorination.[4] Integrated management of community watersheds is the best means of preventing contamination of drinking water supplies (Box 2.6).

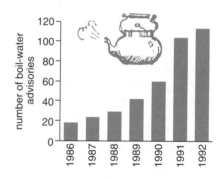

Community watersheds in B.C.

About 300 watersheds provide the primary water supply for B.C. municipalities, regional districts, water districts, water utilities and water improvement districts. Resource development in watersheds sometimes conflicts with the objective of providing safe, clean and abundant supplies of domestic water. In a recent survey, the majority of regional districts identified human activity in community watersheds as the major threat to drinking water quality. These conflicts included logging, livestock grazing, public access for recreation, industrial accidents, hydroelectric generation and transmission, residential development, the exploration and development of oil, gas and minerals, and fisheries. The reported problems included increases in turbidity since the onset of logging, microbiological contamination from recreation, and contamination from agricultural runoff.[4]

A number of initiatives have been undertaken in the province to resolve these conflicts. In 1980 a provincial interagency task force produced guidelines for forestry, agriculture, grazing and recreation in community watersheds.[35] The guidelines are currently being revised in response to public input. In 1985, the Province also began "integrated watershed management planning". This process brings all concerned groups together to reach a consensus on the management of their watersheds. Plans have been completed for 9 community watersheds and plans for 13 more watersheds are underway. Water quality monitoring is currently being undertaken in 12 community watersheds to support this process, evaluate existing water quality objectives, and develop new objectives.

Figure 2.30
Well-interference

A large well may "draw-down" the local water table, thus interfering with nearby, smaller wells.

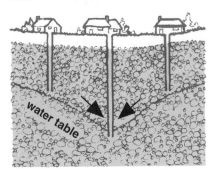

Groundwater - our hidden treasure

Groundwater represents over 68% of the world's freshwater, and is a major invisible link in the hydrologic cycle. Part of the precipitation falling to the earth's surface percolates into underground aquifers (Figure 2.27). While groundwater movement is generally quite slow, it eventually reappears to augment surface runoff as a source of water in streams, rivers, marshes, lakes and ultimately the ocean. In some areas (e.g. parts of the Lower Mainland), groundwater discharging into streams provides the primary source of summer streamflow.

Figure 2.27
Aquifers

Groundwater exists almost everywhere underground. Water is found in soil pores, rock fractures, faults and joints. The level below which all of these spaces are entirely filled with water is called the water table. This is also the level to which water will rise in a shallow well. An aquifer is a geological formation of permeable rock or loose material which may be developed to yield useful quantities of water. Aquifers range in size from a few hectares to thousands of square kilometres and thicknesses of a few metres to hundreds of metres.

Confined aquifers are located beneath a layer of impermeable materials. Confined aquifers can be susceptible to draw-down (declines in volume) since they are poorly connected to surface recharge areas. There is, however, no evidence of draw-down in B.C. Unconfined aquifers rise up as far as the water table. Though easier to recharge, they are more susceptible to contamination from pollution sources such as agriculture, industry and urbanization.

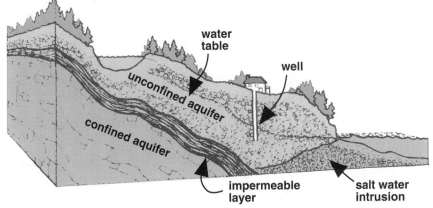

Figure 2.28
Groundwater use

Industry is the largest single user of groundwater in B.C., followed by agriculture and municipal use. Figures for industrial use refer to groundwater which is self-supplied for either commercial or industrial purposes. Agricultural uses includes both irrigation and water extracted for livestock. Municipal use includes any use served by a municipal distribution network. Rural use includes only domestic uses. The data are estimates made for 1981 consumption.[37]

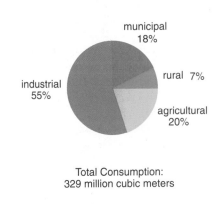

Total Consumption:
329 million cubic meters

Groundwater may also discharge as springs and free-flowing artesian wells. In B.C., groundwater supplies water to over half of the people living outside of Greater Victoria and Greater Vancouver.

Groundwater use

The extraction of groundwater is not regulated in B.C. There are no water licences issued, as there are for surface waters. Consequently, there is very little information regarding provincial trends in use. Because its extraction is not regulated, groundwater is also not priced, except to the extent that users must pay the actual cost of developing the resource.

B.C. relies on groundwater for about 9% of its total water use.[37] This volume (an estimated 329 million m^3 in 1981) represents 25% of all the groundwater extracted in Canada. The largest groundwater user in the province is industry, followed by agriculture, municipalities (composed of domestic, commercial and industrial urban users) and rural domestic users (Figure 2.28).

Groundwater supplies

The provincial government's Water Management Program operates a network of 150 groundwater observation wells. Information on water levels and various groundwater quality parameters is used in groundwater evaluation. Based on observations from these wells, there is at present no indication of large-scale "groundwater mining" in B.C. (Figure 2.29). "Groundwater mining" refers to a situation where extraction exceeds aquifer recharge from infiltration of precipitation and surface water sources. In most areas of B.C., aquifers are connected with the surface, and recharge areas experience high rates of annual precipitation. Well levels, however, fluctuate seasonally, reflecting seasonal changes in recharge (precipitation) and extraction. Concern about groundwater mining has been expressed by residents in some areas of the province (e.g. Cache Creek valley).

Figure 2.29
Water levels in observation wells

Though there are natural seasonal fluctuations, there has been no overall lowering trend in the average levels of observation wells in major provincial aquifers.[38]

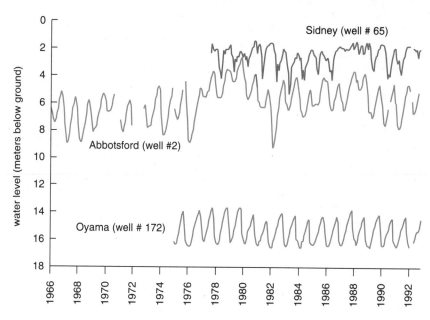

Localized supply concerns often occur because of uncontrolled, large-scale extraction by individual users. This phenomenon, known as well-interference, may reduce water supplies and/or quality in smaller surrounding wells (Figure 2.30). This has been observed in the Lower Mainland (Surrey and Abbotsford), on some Gulf Islands, and on Vancouver Island. Well interference can also affect observation wells, making it difficult to discern aquifer-wide trends in groundwater supplies.

Conflicts between groundwater and surface water occur where surface water withdrawal is fully allocated and groundwater extraction is uncontrolled. This has occurred in Cherry Creek (Kamloops), Chimney Creek (Williams Lake), and Kalamalka Lake.[39] These conflicts may increase in the future if interest continues to grow in using groundwater as a source of freshwater (Figure 2.31). Groundwater supplies become attractive when the costs of engineering surface water supplies rise (i.e. dams, reservoirs, and treatment facilities). They also receive more consideration with increased chemical or microbiological contamination of surface supplies.

Figure 2.31
Groundwater inquiries

Groundwater inquiries have increased dramatically in recent years suggesting a growing interest in groundwater supplies.[38]

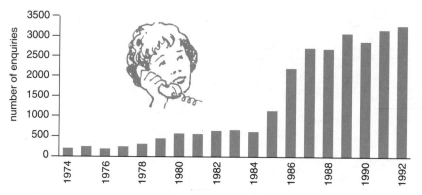

Figure 2.32
Sources of groundwater contamination

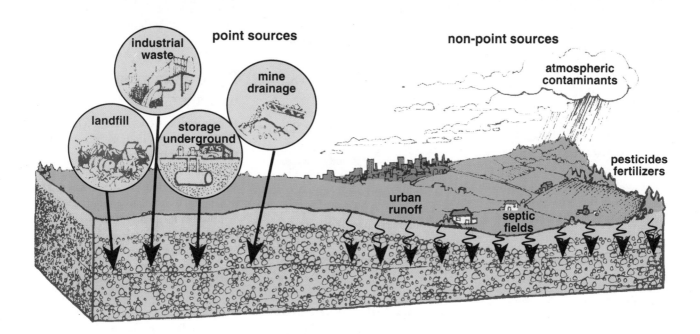

Groundwater quality

Groundwater quality varies naturally with local geological conditions. Human activities also influence groundwater quality. The main sources of chemical threats to groundwater quality include industrial discharges of solid or liquid waste to land, chemical spills, urban runoff, landfills, leaking underground storage tanks (primarily gasoline and diesel), agriculture (manure, fertilizer and pesticide storage or application), septic fields and mine drainage (Figure 2.32). Groundwater contamination can occur very slowly and is often difficult, expensive or impossible to clean up once it has occurred. Shallow aquifers in highly permeable soils are more susceptible to contamination than deeper, more confined aquifers (Figure 2.27). While contamination may be localized, groundwater frequently transports contaminants to nearby lakes and streams.

Microbiological contamination is generally not a problem in groundwater because of natural filtration provided by soil and rock, and long underground residence times. However, local microbiological contamination has occurred due to poor well and septic tank construction and maintenance, and improper well abandonment.

Nitrate and pesticide contamination

The B.C. Water Management Program has identified nitrate contamination near Abbotsford, Osoyoos, Grand Forks, Armstrong, and Oliver.[39] In some instances, nitrate concentrations exceed Canadian Drinking Water Quality Guidelines (e.g. Abbotsford aquifer). Nitrates can reduce the ability of blood to carry oxygen. Infants are particularly at risk from drinking well-water with high concentrations of nitrates. Contamination of groundwater with nitrates may result from intense agricultural activities (e.g. fertilizer overapplication or improper manure management) and land disposal of domestic sewage effluent (e.g. poorly sited or functioning septic fields). Agricultural activities are also a source of pesticides in groundwater. Pesticides have been detected in low concentrations in some areas (see Georgia Depression Ecoprovince). However, the health implications of those low concentrations are not well-understood.

In 1992, the provincial government passed the Agricultural Waste Control Regulation under the Waste Management Act. A Code of Agricultural Practice for Waste Management is attached to this regulation. The code describes practices for using, storing and managing agricultural waste in an environmentally sound manner. In 1992, the provincial government, B.C. Federation of Agriculture and the Poultry Industry of B.C. together released Environmental Guidelines for Poultry Producers.[40] Guidelines for other types of producers are currently being developed. As with other sets of environmental guidelines, proper implementation is required.

Leaking storage tanks, landfills and spills

Leakage from aboveground and underground storage tanks, such as those used by gas stations to store petroleum products, has led to pollution of soil and groundwater for many years. In 1989 the Canadian Council of Ministers of the Environment (CCME) developed an environmental code of practice for underground storage tank systems containing petroleum prod-

31

ucts. The code is currently being amended, and a code is being developed for aboveground storage tanks. In keeping with the code, the Province released draft provincial regulations for comment. The regulations will set standards for new tanks, requirements for monitoring, and criteria for upgrading or replacing existing tanks.[41] Similarly, the federal government has drafted guidelines under the Canadian Environmental Protection Act (CEPA) for underground tanks on federal lands. Until these provincial regulations and federal guidelines have been legislated, tank owners in B.C. are encouraged to follow the applicable drafts.

Landfills and industrial sites, particularly older and abandoned ones, also pose a threat to groundwater quality. These older sites are not generally regulated or managed, and are often poorly constructed. They have also received less study.

Spills represent a less frequent but potentially important source of contaminants in groundwater. During the period from April 1991 to March 1992, spills to groundwater represented only 2% of total reported spills to water (both fresh and marine). Most of the 34 spills to groundwater reported to the B.C. Ministry of Environment, Lands and Parks over that period involved hydrocarbon fuels (e.g. oil and gas) and organic effluents (e.g. sewage).[27]

Saltwater intrusion and cross-contamination

Saltwater intrusion can also reduce groundwater quality. This is a problem in some coastal areas where high rates of groundwater extraction, particularly during periods of low precipitation such as May to October, causes seawater to move into freshwater aquifers. This has been identified as a problem in the Gulf Islands, the Saanich Peninsula, and Belcarra Park. This problem can be avoided by better wellfield design near the ocean.

Unlined wells can also cross-contaminate aquifers by introducing older and highly saline water in deep aquifers to

younger and less saline water in shallower aquifers (Figure 2.33). This impact is often confused with seawater intrusion, particularly on the Gulf Islands where both types of problem occur.[42]

Reforming groundwater management

The Province is considering a number of important new initiatives to protect and manage groundwater. These include increased monitoring (particularly of community wells) and new legislation to regulate groundwater use and protect its quality. Proposed initiatives may include legislative authority to certify well drillers, establish standards for well construction and license groundwater use.[19]

Figure 2.33
Well cross-contamination

Cross-contamination refers to the movement of salt water from deep aquifers into shallow freshwater aquifers along improperly sealed well casings.

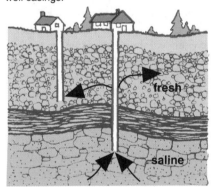

Figure 2.34
The B.C. Coast

Three ecoprovinces (Coast and Mountains, Georgia Depression and Northeast Pacific) make up the marine environment of British Columbia.

Marine environmental quality

The coastline of B.C. is composed of 27,000 km of shoreline, islands, estuaries, fjords and bays, containing a rich abundance of wildlife, fish, and forests (Figure 2.34). These resources depend on an abundant supply of high quality water. There are, however, no data on long-term, coast-wide trends in marine environmental quality. Previous assessments and reviews have

generally focused on site-specific issues, for the most part considering only potential threats to marine environmental quality.[43,44] Indeed, data on marine environmental quality, both status and trends, are largely absent. The exceptions to this general rule are bacterial contaminants in shellfish growing waters, and chemical contaminant levels (e.g. dioxins) in fish and shellfish destined for human consumption and in bird tissue. Although marine waters are currently not governed by any comprehensive water quality legislation, they are subject to general provisions of the federal Fisheries Act and the provincial Waste Management Act. Provincial water quality objectives, which are not enforceable, have been set in a limited number of areas including Boundary Bay, Burrard Inlet, Kitimat Arm and Pender Harbour. Objectives are currently being developed for Sechelt Inlet, Malaspina Strait and Howe Sound.

Potential threats to marine environmental quality include pulp and paper discharges, other industrial discharges, toxic and persistent organics (e.g. PAHs, oil), rural runoff, municipal wastewater discharges, dumping of dredged material, mine tailing releases, spills or related environmental accidents, and aquaculture. The nature of these threats encompasses microbiological contamination (e.g. viruses and bacteria); toxic contaminants (e.g. dioxins, furans, PCBs, heavy metals, and petrochemicals); nutrients (e.g. nitrogen and phosphorus); and physical contaminants (e.g. suspended solids, sediment, and persistent debris) (Table 2.1). Some of these potential threats are discussed below.

Coastal pulp and paper mill discharges

There are ten pulp and paper mills which discharge effluent into marine or estuarine waters along the B.C. coast. These effluents contain large quantities of organic waste and numerous toxic compounds. The impact of pulp and paper mills on Canadian marine and estuarine ecosystems was recently reviewed by Environment Canada.[45]

Coastal pulp mills can damage intertidal communities through effluent toxicity and log-booming. Releases of settleable wood chips, bark and cellulose fibres also smother bottom-dwelling habitat. Approximately 3,400 ha (34 km^2) of the seafloor have been affected by wood fibre discharged from coastal mills. These mills have traditionally only had primary treatment. As a result of more stringent regulations, many coastal mills

installed long outfalls and diffusers in the late 1970s and early 1980s. This resulted in significant recovery of intertidal communities.[44]

Despite increases in pulp production, both BOD (biochemical oxygen demand) loadings and effluent toxicity have been reduced by coastal pulp mills through the installation of primary and secondary treatment works. As of the end of 1992, six of the ten coastal pulp mills had full secondary treatment. By the end of 1993, three of the four remaining mills will have implemented full secondary treatment (two already have partial secondary treatment). The remaining mill should have secondary treatment by the end of 1995. Expanded secondary treatment should significantly reduce effluent BOD and toxicity (Figure 2.35).

Coastal bleach kraft pulp mills are the major source of the dioxins and furans which have been detected in shellfish and have resulted in coastal dioxin closures (see below). Under CEPA, discharge limits for dioxins and furans are used to regulate releases of these persistent organochlorines. In cases where technological changes have

been implemented at mills to control dioxins and furans, AOX loadings (tonnes/day) declined 45 to 90% between 1989 and 1991.[45] Eight coastal mills have already met or surpassed the provincial target of 2.5 kg AOX per air-dried tonne of pulp. This has been achieved through technological changes such as chlorine dioxide substitution, which also reduces discharges of dioxins and furans. The provincial government anticipates eliminating AOX discharges by the end of 2002.

Marine municipal wastewater discharges

Municipal wastewater can consist of residential, commercial and industrial wastewaters. Like pulp mills, it also exerts a biochemical oxygen demand (BOD) on receiving waters. Discharges to calm, poorly mixed marine environments such as shallow estuaries may deplete oxygen, causing fish kills. These same discharges are also important sources of suspended solids, microbiological contamination and toxic contaminants. Toxic contaminants (e.g. heavy metals) may persist and accumulate in sediments or biota, regardless of where they are discharged. Microbiological contamination is a widespread concern, as reflected in coastal shellfish closures (see below).

The quality of sewage discharges is dependent on their level of treatment (see discussion in freshwater section above). There are 9 untreated discharges to marine waters in B.C., serving some 204,000 people. From largest to smallest, these are Victoria, Prince Rupert, Masset, North Cowichan, Port Alice, Port McNeill, Port Edward, Queen Charlotte City and Tofino. There are also 7 primary sewage treatment plants on the B.C. coast, serving over 660,000 people. The largest is Iona Island in the Lower Mainland, followed by Lion's Gate, Nanaimo, Ladysmith, North Cowichan, Zeballos and Alert Bay. Twenty-one secondary sewage treatment plants, serving just over 110,000 people, also discharge to coastal waters.[18]

Figure 2.35
Marine BOD from pulp and paper mills

Six out of ten coastal pulp and paper mills have full secondary treatment. Two additional mills have partial secondary treatment. By the end of 1993, nine out of ten of the mills will have full secondary treatment, with the remaining mill expected to implement secondary treatment by the end of 1995. Increased secondary treatment will significantly reduce BOD loadings to coastal waters.[15]

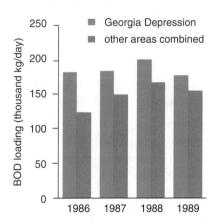

BOD loading (thousand kg/day)

- Georgia Depression
- other areas combined

1986　1987　1988　1989

Heavy metals and the toxic organics that associate with particulate matter are largely removed by secondary treatment. These contaminants, however, accumulate in the sludge, reducing the number of potential uses of sludge and posing another type of disposal problem. Effective source control is the best means of controlling toxic contaminants in both treated sewage and sludge.

Shellfish closures

The B.C. Coast yields an abundance of shellfish (e.g. crab, prawn, clam, mussel, scallop and oyster) for human consumption. To be safely eaten, these must be harvested from areas without sewage contamination or dangerous levels of toxins and pathogens, both natural and human-produced. Fecal coliform counts are typically used to assess sewage contamination. These are intestinal bacteria originating from warm-blooded animals. There are currently about 160 sanitary closures in B.C. per year, encompassing 72,000 hectares of coastline.[15] The total area of closures has increased since 1972 (Figure 2.36). This increase is not thought to be due solely to an increase in sampling effort but may reflect an actual worsening of the problem. Multiple pollution sources account for the largest area of closures. Municipal sewage discharges are the largest sole source of closures. Other sources of contamination include agricultural runoff, boat sewage discharges and non-point source urban runoff (including septic seepage). Additional shellfish closures have occurred as a result of dioxin contamination (see below).

Ocean dumping

There are 20 active ocean dump sites in British Columbia, most of which are rarely used. The greatest quantities of material have been dumped at the Point Grey and Sandheads dump sites at the mouth of the Fraser River. The total amount of material dumped off B.C.'s coast increased from 1986 to 1990, and then dropped significantly in 1991 (Figure 2.37). Dredge and

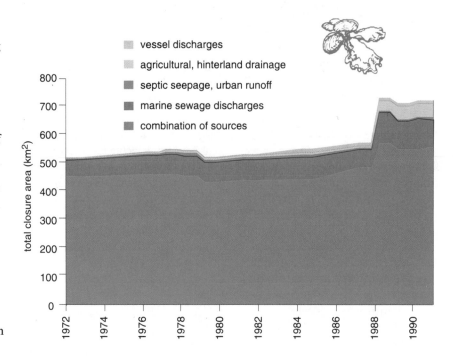

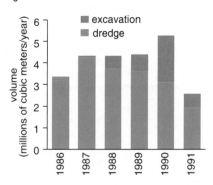

excavation spoils represent the largest proportion of material being dumped.

Under the Canadian Environmental Protection Act (CEPA), Environment Canada is responsible for controlling ocean dumping. The Regional Ocean Dumping Advisory Committee (RODAC), composed of representatives from both federal and provincial agencies, reviews all dumping permits. Regulations developed under CEPA outline substances which are prohibited or restricted from ocean disposal. All material destined for ocean disposal must meet stringent Contaminant Testing Guidelines. RODAC has developed regional guidelines for both dioxins and polynuclear aromatic hydrocarbons (PAHs) which have been detected in dredge materials from areas near pulp mills and in industrial harbours.

Monitoring is conducted at active dump sites. Results from 1979 to 1987 have been published[46] and an update of this information is being compiled by Environment Canada. There is no evidence of increases in contaminants to levels of concern at any active dump site.[15] Funding has been provided through the Green Plan to allow increased dump site monitoring and research.

Oil and chemical spills

Oil and chemical spills are random stresses on coastal ecosystems. These spills, however, may have significant short- and long-term impacts. The actual impacts depend on the volume and type of material spilled, the location, weather conditions and the proximity to sensitive environments. The most common impact of oil spills is bird kills. Oil and chemical spills are toxic and can kill fish in the receiving environment.

While large oil spills may occur virtually anywhere along the coast, they are more likely in areas with higher navigation risk. In addition, some areas are more ecologically sensitive to these spills, increasing the chances of negative environmental impacts. In B.C., the area of greatest navigation risk is the waters surrounding the southern third of Vancouver Island from the entrance to Juan de Fuca Strait to the southern portions of the Strait of Georgia. This is also a region of great ecological sensitivity to spills.

Between 1972 and 1992 the federal government recorded 437 significant marine spills (i.e. greater than one tonne or affecting sensitive habitat)

(Figure 2.38). The number of spills decreased dramatically in 1976 due to changes in tanker technology, stiffer penalties and a new vessel management system for harbour traffic. Recent increases may be due to increased tanker traffic. The provincial Dangerous Goods Incident Database recorded a total of 901 spills of all sizes to marine ecosystems between April 1991 and March 1992. The largest number of spills involved oil and other hydrocarbon fuels and industrial or organic effluents (Figure 2.39).

Figure 2.39
Marine hazardous material spills

A total of 901 spills to marine waters were reported from April 1991 to March 1992. The majority of these spills involved oil in some form or another, followed by other types of hydrocarbon fuels (gasoline), and organic or industrial effluents (sewage, mine tailings and industrial wastewater).[26]

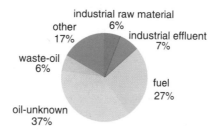

industrial raw material 6%
other 17%
industrial effluent 7%
waste-oil 6%
fuel 27%
oil-unknown 37%

The federal and provincial governments have developed an Oil Spill Response Information System in order to address concerns about oil spills. The system provides information on sensitive shorelines that require protection or clean-up, as well as suggestions regarding appropriate countermeasures in the event of an actual spill. In addition, the provincial and federal governments have implemented a number of recommendations from the Joint States/British Columbia Oil Spill Task Force set up in 1989 following the Nestucca oil spill (see Coast & Mountains/Northeast Pacific Ecoprovinces). The Province is currently evaluating procedures at oil handling facilities and the Canadian Coast Guard is evaluating offshore transportation by the oil industry. These actions are expected to greatly reduce the risk of major spills.

Aquaculture

Several species of shellfish and finfish, including salmon, are commercially cultured along the B.C. coast. The public has expressed concern about some aspects of marine salmon farms which have increased in numbers from about ten farms in the early 1980s to about 135 farms in 1989/90. Due to a recent industry consolidation, 105 farms currently operate on the coast. Public concerns include impacts on water and sediment quality around salmon farms, the use of chemicals, improper management and disposal of fish mortalities, disease transmission to wild stocks and general siting conflicts. These concerns are being addressed by the industry and the provincial government through regulations, licensing, guidelines and codes of practice. Uncertainties regarding behavioural and genetic effects of escaped fish on wild salmon stocks are still being investigated.

The main water quality impact from marine salmon farming is deposition of uneaten fish food and fecal material on the sea floor, possibly smothering important habitat for bottom-dwelling organisms. Recent studies to investigate this effect have concluded that such impacts are largely confined to

Figure 2.38
Significant marine spills

Marine spills are considered significant when the quantity spilled exceeds 1 tonne, or when sensitive habitats are affected. The number of significant spills decreased dramatically in 1976 due to changes in tanker technology, stiffer penalties and a new vessel management system for harbour traffic. Increases since 1976 may be due to increased tanker traffic. Significant spills make up one sixth of all spills reported to Environmental Protection.[47]

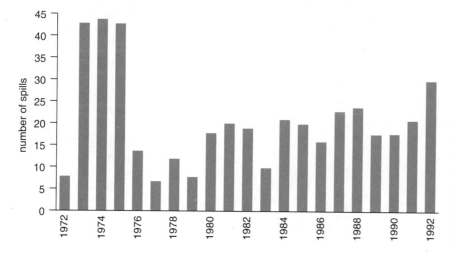

35

areas directly beneath seacages.[48] Another recent study, indicates that bottom-dwelling communities at well-flushed sites may recover completely within 2-3 months after a farm has been moved, whereas recovery may take several years in areas of low currents.[49] Similarly, the provincial government has recently completed a 5-year study of the Sechelt Inlet, an area that has been heavily used by the fish farming industry. Preliminary conclusions are that no significant water quality impacts have occurred.

The provincial government has developed guidelines for both the siting and operation of fish farms.[50,51] Based on recommendations of the 1986 Gillespie Inquiry on Finfish Aquaculture, the provincial government imposed a mandatory environmental monitoring program on salmon farmers. This program requires quarterly data reports from salmon farmers on water quality, solid waste handling and sewage disposal. The

data from this program are currently under review and will be used to modify or revise the program, if necessary. The provincial government licenses farms on the basis of a thorough analysis of farm size, site-suitability and plan feasibility.

There are also some trout rearing facilities on lakes and streams. Three commercial lake cage facilities and 20 upland hatcheries rear salmon smolts (young fish) on two lakes. Some members of the public have voiced concerns about potential environmental impacts from lake cage smolt rearing. The Province is supporting a comprehensive 3-year study of environmental effects at existing lake cage fish farms.

Toxic contaminants

A vast number of pollutants are released to the marine environment from human activities (Table 2.1). Those pollutants capable of causing harm to the environment or human life

Figure 2.41
Bioaccumulation and biomagnification

Bioaccumulation refers to the increase in levels of toxic substances in an organism over time, due to continued exposure. This can only happen if the substances do not break down quickly, and are essentially "stored" in some part of an organism. Biomagnification refers to the increase in the concentration of contaminants as they move up the food chain. A predator unknowingly "collects" whatever toxic substances happen to be in the food that it consumes. These two processes are also sometimes referred to as bioconcentration.[53]

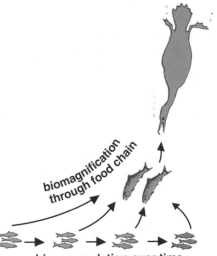

Figure 2.40
Movement of toxic substances

Contaminants such as heavy metals and organochlorines enter the marine environment from a variety of sources. These include atmospheric fallout, precipitation, river discharge, runoff from land surfaces, and discharges directly to the ocean (e.g. industrial and municipal outfalls or spills and dumping). Many of these contaminants adhere to silt or other particles, which eventually fall to the seabottom and become buried by newer sediments. Fish and other aquatic organisms, may take in and accumulate these substances. This occurs through either direct contact with contaminated sediments or sources, or by eating other organisms (e.g. plankton and invertebrates) living near these sources.

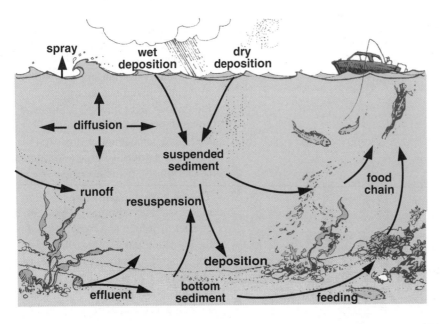

are considered toxic under the 1988 Canadian Environmental Protection Act (CEPA). Toxic substances may be persistent or non-persistent in the environment depending on how long they take to break down and what they break down into. Toxic substances may be taken up by aquatic organisms either directly (e.g. gills) or through their food. If an organism is unable to breakdown or eliminate a substance, it may bioaccumulate. These substances may subsequently become biomagnified in the food-chain, making "predators" good potential indicators of environmental contaminants (Figures 2.40 and 2.41). Even low-level concentrations of many contaminants are known to affect long-term marine environmental quality.[52] The following sections provide a brief summary of some of the information available on substances of concern in B.C.'s marine environment.

Heavy metals

Trace metals such as lead, mercury, cadmium, arsenic and copper occur naturally in the water, sediment, and biota. Elevated levels of these metals are frequently found in sediments around such sources of contamination as industrial and municipal effluent outfalls and ocean dumping sites. These metals are usually in a form that is not readily taken up by organisms and so pose little direct threat to marine life. However, in some circumstances not fully understood, heavy metals can change into forms available to organisms, making them highly toxic. Contaminated sediments may persist as sources of metals, particularly to bottom-dwelling organisms and their predators, causing deterioration in marine environmental quality.

Environment Canada has detected trace metal concentrations in sediments, fish, and invertebrates at some 75 locations along the B.C. coast, at varying distances from pollution sources and ocean dump sites.[54,55,56,57] Studies in these areas, have revealed relatively uncontaminated sediments, with no evidence of wide-spread accumulation in marine food webs. There has been localized contamination of both sediments and biota, particularly invertebrates living in sediments containing high metal concentrations. Continuous sampling over several years and a variety of sites has generally not been undertaken to provide data regarding trends. However, sediment monitoring near municipal outfalls has revealed trends of increasing trace metals. The levels are lower than those found near harbours, pulp mills and coastal mining sites.

Health and Welfare Canada has established acceptable limits for mercury in fish and shellfish intended for human consumption. In most areas, average concentrations are below the guidelines of 0.5 mg/kg (0.5 parts per million) wet weight. The highest shellfish tissue concentrations of mercury in B.C. (as high as 13.4 mg/kg) were detected in the early 1970s in

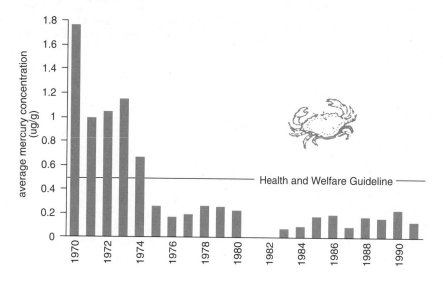

Figure 2.42
Mercury in crabs

Average mercury levels in edible crab tissue and in other fish in the vicinity of a mercury-cell chlor-alkali plant in Howe Sound decreased following imposition of stricter environmental controls in the early 1970s. The plant recently closed.[58]

Howe Sound, near a mercury-cell chlor-alkali plant. Stricter environmental controls have essentially eliminated mercury contamination of shellfish at this site (Figure 2.42).

Dioxins and furans

Dioxins and furans are chlorinated organic compounds. They may be formed as by-products of combustion processes such as incinerators and power boilers, or chemical processes such as bleach kraft pulp mills and chemically treated lumber. Both dioxins and furans persist in the environment and may be extremely toxic. Of the 210 known forms of these contaminants, 2,3,7,8-TCDD (tetrachlorodibenzo-p-dioxin) is the most toxic. Health and Welfare Canada has published a maximum residue guideline for this form of 20 parts per trillion (ng/kg) in fish for human consumption. This is equivalent to about twenty grains of sugar in an Olympic-sized swimming pool. Long-term exposures to 2,3,7,8-TCDD in mammals have resulted in immune system damage, liver dysfunction, impaired reproduction, birth defects and cancer. However, chloracne (a temporary skin condition) is the most

common health effect to date that has been conclusively linked to dioxin exposures in people.

In 1987, Environment Canada analysed samples of marine sediments, fish and invertebrates obtained near coastal pulp mills and other industries for dioxins and furans. The majority of fish samples contained no detectable residues of the most toxic form of dioxin (2,3,7,8-TCDD). However, some shellfish samples of oysters and crab were near or well above Health and Welfare Canada guideline of 20 parts per trillion (ng/kg). Less toxic forms of dioxins and furans were detected at some sites. Scientists identified the chlorinated bleaching process in kraft pulp mills as the major source of these contaminants.

Subsequent sampling revealed elevated levels in three locations: Port Mellon, Woodfibre and Prince Rupert.[59] This led to closures of crab, prawn and shrimp fisheries in these areas in November 1988. Further monitoring led to additional closures of shellfish fisheries in November 1989 in the vicinity of Kitimat, Gold River, Crofton, Nanaimo, Powell River, Campbell River, and Cowichan Bay. Five of these closures were extended in

1990 on the basis of new data supplied by the companies involved. Today, almost 900 km² of coastal area is closed to harvesting of certain species (Figure 2.43). Some of these closures have been in the vicinity of sawmills which formerly used pentachlorophenol (heavily contaminated with dioxins and furans) for antisapstain control.

Great blue heron and double-crested cormorant eggs are valuable indicators of persistent chemicals such as dioxins and furans in coastal waters.[60] In the 1980s, eggs analysed from 20 heron colonies and 12 cormorant colonies throughout the Strait of Georgia showed dioxin and furan contamination.[61] Dioxin levels in eggs of double-crested cormorants in the Strait of Georgia were high compared with levels detected in the Bay of Fundy, the St. Lawrence estuary, and Lake Ontario.[53] Studies have shown that elevated levels of dioxin in heron eggs were associated with effects on developing embryos.[62,63,64]

Data from 1991 show a downturn in dioxin concentrations in herons and cormorants (Figure 2.44). In 1989,

Figure 2.43
B.C. coastal dioxin closures

As of May 1992, about 1% of the total potential shellfish (crab) harvesting area in B.C. was closed as a result of dioxin contamination. In almost all cases, the primary source of dioxins is believed to be pulp and paper mills. Potential sources in Cowichan Bay and Kitimat include pentachlorophenol (formerly used as a wood preservative by sawmills) and contaminated wood chips. The sources in Victoria are not known. There is substantial overlap between these dioxin closures and sanitary shellfish closures (Figure 2.36).[65] The total area available for harvest is calculated as the area between the low water line and the 200m contour along B.C.'s coast.

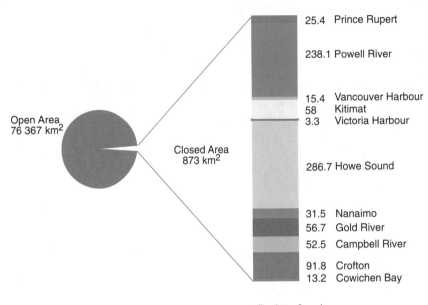

Open Area 76 367 km²

Closed Area 873 km²

25.4	Prince Rupert
238.1	Powell River
15.4	Vancouver Harbour
58	Kitimat
3.3	Victoria Harbour
286.7	Howe Sound
31.5	Nanaimo
56.7	Gold River
52.5	Campbell River
91.8	Crofton
13.2	Cowichen Bay

contribution of each closure to total (km²)

Figure 2.44
Dioxins in sea bird eggs

Dioxin (2,3,7,8-TCDD) levels in the eggs of great blue herons and double-crested cormorants have declined in recent years. The data below are from colonies at Crofton, one of the most contaminated sites where eggs were sampled. Recent declines may reflect efforts by the nearby bleach kraft pulp mill to reduce dioxin emissions.[61]

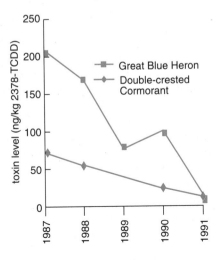

government regulation and the demand for alternative pesticides eliminated the use of chlorophenols (heavily contaminated with dioxins and furans) for antisapstain control by the B.C. lumber industry. Chlorophenols, however, are still used for heavy duty processing of poles. Since 1988 many pulp mills in the Strait of Georgia have reduced or eliminated dioxins and furans in discharges into marine waters in response to new CEPA regulations (Figure 2.21).[61] The decline in dioxin levels in herons and cormorants may indicate a rapid cleansing of these substances from the food chain, Continued monitoring is being conducted to verify this.

The Province supported a recent study of organochlorine levels in seven harbour porpoises and one killer whale from the Strait of Georgia. Dioxin (2,3,7,8-TCDD) concentrations were lower in these mammals than in marine mammals from the Arctic or the St. Lawrence River. Furan concentrations (2,3,7,8 TCDF), however, were higher in the B.C. mammals. The sample size was too small to provide definitive conclusions.[66]

The Province also undertook an extensive two year monitoring study of organochlorines in various components of the ecosystem, including soils, sediments, foliage, shellfish and fish, sludge, ash, runoff and leachate. Preliminary results show that levels of dioxins and furans in B.C. vary a great deal from place to place. Concentrations appear to fall within the range found in comparable sites from other parts of the world.[67] However, a detailed inventory of the number and extent of contaminated sites, and more information on the rate of contaminant discharges, is required to assess the significance of these observations.

Figure 2.45

PCBs in cormorant eggs

Seabirds are good indicators of contaminants in marine environments. PCB concentrations in double-crested cormorant eggs on the Pacific and Atlantic coasts have generally declined since the early 1970s due to stricter controls on the use, transportation, storage and disposal of PCBs. Data are from colonies at Mandarte Island, B.C; Ile aux Pommes, QB; and Manawagonish, N.B.[78]

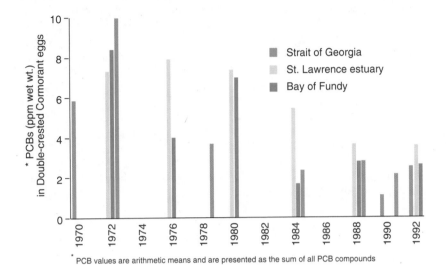

* PCB values are arithmetic means and are presented as the sum of all PCB compounds

Due to the variety of toxic effects seen in animals and the various dioxin sources in B.C., concern has been raised about increased human exposure in the province. Researchers at the University of British Columbia recently undertook a study for the B.C. Ministry of Environment, Lands and Parks and Ministry of Health to assess the levels of dioxins and furans in human tissues. Dioxin and furan levels in British Columbia residents were found to be similar to those of residents in other parts of Canada, as well as to those of industrial populations with no known exposure to dioxins and furans.[68] Populations from agricultural economies tended to have lower levels, and groups with known exposures tended to have higher tissue concentrations.

PCBs

Polychlorinated biphenyls (PCBs) are another type of chlorinated organic compound. PCBs used to be incorporated in a variety of products including plastics, inks, carbonless paper, paints, casting waxes and electrical transformers. They are highly persistent in the environment and accumulate in living tissues following ingestion of even minute quantities. Although their effects on human health are not completely known, there is evidence that they cause cancer and birth defects in some mammals, and reduced reproduction in fish.

Concerns regarding impacts on both human health and the environment led to widespread controls of this substance in many parts of the world. In North America, their manufacture was ended in the early 1970s. All non-electrical uses of PCBs in Canada were banned in 1977 under the federal Environmental Contaminants Act. Subsequent federal and provincial regulations were developed to control the use, transportation, storage and disposal of PCBs in B.C. Safe incineration technologies are being applied to the destruction of those in storage in certain regions of Canada.

PCBs have low solubility in water and tend to concentrate in sediments. Sediment data collected in areas away from industrial activities generally have PCB concentrations ranging from non-detectable to about 0.1 mg/kg (or parts per million). Though concentrations are quite variable, higher levels have been observed in areas around various industrial sites and in a number of harbours including Victoria and Vancouver (ranging from 2.2 to 17.0 mg/kg).[44] A recent survey of organochlorine levels in various ecosystem components in B.C., found contamination to be highly site-specific. PCBs were generally present in higher concentrations than other contaminants.[67]

Although few studies of PCBs in biota have been undertaken in B.C., scientists have identified PCBs in some marine species.[53,66,69,71] The recent study of one killer whale and seven harbour porpoises in the Strait of Georgia (described above) found lower levels of PCBs than in marine mammals from the St. Lawrence River. These levels were also lower than concentrations found in previous studies on six killer whales and two false killer whales in the Strait of Georgia.[73,74] Again, the sample size was too small to draw definitive conclusions.[66]

Concentrations of PCBs in certain seabird species have been monitored since the early 1970s. Seabirds are good biological indicators of toxic contaminants which biomagnify up the food chain (Figure 2.41). For example, double-crested cormorants feed near the shore and do not migrate, thereby 'sampling' local pollution. Since 1970, there has been a declining trend in the level of PCBs in eggs of the double-crested cormorant in both the Strait of Georgia and the Atlantic coast (Figure 2.45). Other seabird species along the BC coast have been sampled for PCBs but levels were relatively lower.[53] Levels of PCBs at these sites are currently below concentrations known to threaten the health of seabirds.[72] This trend follows a decline in PCB use due to voluntary and regulatory actions in Canada and other countries since 1977.[70] However, PCBs continue to persist even though strict controls are in effect, suggesting that large amounts remain in the marine environment. The federal government plans to continue research and monitoring efforts related to PCBs and other organochlorines in seabirds and mammals.

Conclusions

B.C. is blessed with a greater than average share of the world's water. Overall, both water supplies and water quality appear to be in good shape. There are, however, some localized concerns.

Seasonal shortages of surface water are a problem in some areas. Many of these shortages reflect a lack of resources and infrastructure for tapping supplies. There is currently no indication of large-scale groundwater mining in the province, but concern for groundwater depletion has been expressed by residents in some areas. Pressures on groundwater are likely to increase with growing interest in this largely invisible, and currently unregulated, resource. Water supply concerns may also reflect excessive or incompatible demands. More information on actual use of both surface water and groundwater is required to fully assess options for reducing demand and resolving user conflicts.

Much of the information regarding both surface and ground water quality is related to specific human activities. The largest single public concern regarding water quality is toxic contaminants. Levels in drinking water are generally well below Health and Welfare guidelines. Contamination of groundwater with nitrates and pesticides remains a concern in some very localized areas. The greatest threat to drinking water in B.C. is microbiological contamination. While improved treatment will reduce this threat, prevention remains the best solution.

Toxic contaminants in sediments, fish, shellfish, and birds have been observed in both freshwater and marine ecosystems. Fish and shellfish consumption advisories and closures have been issued in some areas in order to protect human health. Existing or planned regulations on contaminant discharges from some sources (e.g. dioxin and furan from pulp mills) are expected to reduce contaminant levels in the environment. Guidelines have been developed for controlling other contaminant sources (e.g. urban stormwater, agriculture and storage tanks).

There is a limited amount of information from which to draw province-wide conclusions concerning the state of water. In some cases, long-term data are available only on a site-specific basis or at a limited number of locations, such as groundwater observation wells or streamflow gauging stations. Given limited resources, environmental agencies tend to focus monitoring efforts in problem areas. In other cases, data are available over a wider area but for a shorter period of time, limiting the ability to detect trends.

Interpretation is limited by the types of indicators monitored. More information is typically available for stresses on water rather than the actual state of water. The Fraser River Action Plan is developing a set of integrated monitoring stations to assess the condition of the Fraser River's aquatic ecosystems. This will help to provide a template for the design of future monitoring on the actual state of water.

Plants and Animals

Biodiversity

Biodiversity is the variety of life on the planet. It is important for a number of reasons. First, we have an ethical stewardship responsibility for other living things with which we share the planet. Second, high species diversity contributes to ecosystem stability.[61] Third, biodiversity has immeasurable aesthetic value; provides food, medicine and other products of enormous economic value; and generates critical ecosystem services essential to all life (Box 2.7). Biodiversity can be described at three different levels: genetic diversity (variations among individuals or populations of the same species), species diversity (the variety of species in an area), and ecosystem diversity (the variety of ecosystems across the landscape).

Species diversity - B.C.'s rich inheritance

British Columbia has the greatest diversity of birds and mammals of any province in Canada.[1] B.C. comprises about 10% of Canada's land area, but has over half of its vascular plant and vertebrate animal species (Table 2.2). It is estimated that 1,000 species of moss and liverwort, 1,000 lichen species, 10,000 species of fungi and 35,000 insect species are also present in B.C. Of species native to Canada, 9% of the breeding birds, 12% of the reptiles, 17% of the mammals (excluding marine mammals) and 27% of the

amphibians are exclusive to B.C.[2] Over 25% of the freshwater fish native to B.C. are found nowhere else in Canada.

In addition to their diversity, the population sizes of a number of species in B.C. have global significance. The province has 75% of the world's stone sheep, 60% of the world's mountain goats, 50% of the world's blue grouse, at least 50% of the world's trumpeter swans, and 25% of the world's grizzly bears and bald eagles.[3,4]

Box 2.7

Ecosystem services

Biodiversity is essential to maintain ecosystem processes that support all life. These include: maintaining the gaseous composition of the atmosphere, climate control, regulating the hydrological cycle, generating and maintaining soils, cycling nutrients necessary for the growth of living things, and decomposing waste materials.[5]

Table 2.2

Plants and animals in Canada and British Columbia

This table presents numbers of species for selected plant and animal groups in Canada and B.C., and number of species introduced to B.C.[6,7,8,9,10]

	Number of Species		
	Canada	B.C.[b]	introduced to B.C.
vascular plants[a]	4153	~2579	557
freshwater fish	181	83	15
marine fish	~900	~387[c]	3
amphibians	41	20	2
reptiles	41	19	4
birds	580	454	14
mammals	199	143	12

Note: These numbers come from a variety of sources and are not necessarily fully comparable because of differences in date of reference and taxonomic treatment. They provide a general picture of the species diversity in B.C. and Canada, and the proportion of B.C.'s species that are native. Additional species are regularly recorded due to the expansion of home ranges and more intensive searches by professional biologists and naturalists.

[a] The numbers for vascular plants include some subspecies as well as species.
[b] Includes native and introduced species.
[c] 22 of these are also freshwater fish.

The total number of species is only one aspect of species diversity. The number of individuals of a species is also important. The province's Red List contains species that are candidates for legal designation as endangered or threatened, while the Blue List contains sensitive or vulnerable species. The number of species on these lists roughly indicates the number of species at risk. Over time these lists illustrate the general success or failure of wildlife management and conservation efforts. Table 2.3 presents a snapshot of the current situation in B.C. This can be compared with future lists to evaluate the success of current efforts to maintain biodiversity in the province.

Introduced Species

Introduced species are species that are not native, or do not naturally "belong". They can seriously affect an area's biodiversity by displacing or replacing native species. Lacking natural predators, parasites, and other natural controls, species not native to an area can increase in numbers and take over enough of the available habitat to limit the populations or habitat of native species. This can reduce both the stability and the productivity of an ecosystem. Also, imported animals bring in their own parasites and diseases. Table 2.2 lists the numbers of introduced species within selected plant and animal groups in B.C.

Purple loosestrife is an aquatic weed that has recently invaded at least 37 wetland sites in B.C. The problem is suspected to be much larger, but this is difficult to document because of inaccessible terrain. Eurasian watermilfoil is another introduced aquatic plant that is fouling aquatic ecosystems of British Columbia (see Box 3.1, Southern Interior section, Ecoprovinces chapter). Knapweed is a substantial problem for southern B.C. grasslands, and its invasion into burrowing owl range was one of the many factors that contributed to the decline in burrowing owl numbers in the province. Knapweed has also significantly displaced forage vegetation for grazing livestock and wildlife in southern B.C. grasslands. Introduced rats and racoons pose serious threats to ground-nesting seabirds on offshore islands, some of which are globally significant populations. For example, 75% of the known world population of ancient murrelets breed in B.C., as do 80% of the known world population of Cassin's auklets.[12]

Genetic diversity

Individual plants and animals within the same species still differ from each other as a result of genetic variation. This variation within species is an important aspect of biological diversity. For example, much of the diversity among freshwater fish in B.C. is due to subspecies, groups of populations and unique populations.

Genetic diversity enables species to adapt to changes in their environment over time. It is difficult and costly to measure genetic diversity, and therefore difficult to assess its current state in B.C. Changes, such as the conversion of natural forests to managed stands and the enhancement of wild fish stocks with hatchery-reared fish, reduce genetic variation in natural ecosystems.

Maintaining genetic diversity is difficult. It requires conservation of wild species across a wide range of natural habitats and protecting areas in which plants and animals can evolve.

Ecosystem diversity

B.C. is Canada's most ecologically diverse province or territory. It has four of the world's five major types of climate. It encompasses 10 ecoprovinces and has more distinct ecosystems than any other province in Canada, from coastal rain forests, to dry interior grasslands, to alpine tundra and northern boreal forest. Some of these ecosystems occur nowhere else in Canada, such as Garry oak woodlands and coastal temperate rainforest.

Garry oak woodlands

Garry oaks are the dominant tree species in one of B.C.'s rarest types of forest. The Garry oak woodlands are found on Vancouver Island, the Gulf Islands, and at two known sites on the mainland. Less than 5% of their original range exists on the Saanich Peninsula and the rest is found in widely scattered fragments resulting from continued urban expansion.[13] Urbanization and agriculture have reduced Garry oak woodlands in other areas as well as has the control of fire. Natural fires and fires set by aboriginal peoples helped to maintain the structure of these woodlands.[14,15] Finally, the introduction of exotic species such as Scotch broom has significantly changed these areas.[16]

Table 2.3
Species and subspecies at risk in British Columbia

			Number of Taxa			
	vascular plants	freshwater fish	amphibians	reptiles	birds	mammals
Red List	638	28	4	4	33	25
Blue List	217	7	2	5	55	27
Extirpated	29	1	0	2	4	7

Red-listed species are candidates for legal designation as endangered or threatened under the B.C. Wildlife Act. Of the candidates on the Red List, only four species have been legally designated as endangered under the B.C. Wildlife Act: burrowing owl, white pelican, sea otter, and Vancouver Island marmot. No species have yet been legally designated as threatened. Sensitive or vulnerable species and subspecies appear on the Blue List. The Committee on the Status of Endangered Wildlife in Canada (COSEWIC) produces similar lists of species at risk, but use slightly different criteria. Since this table includes subspecies, the numbers at risk cannot be compared to the total numbers of species in Table 2.2.[6,7,11]

Grasslands

Unforested dry grasslands cover less than 0.5% of B.C.'s land area. The pristine natural, unaltered grasslands that existed in south central B.C. prior to European settlement have essentially vanished.[17] Much of the grasslands in the Okanagan Valley have been completely replaced by settlement, orchards and crops. The structure and species composition of the non-cultivated grasslands in this area have been significantly altered by fire suppression, introduced species, and grazing by cattle.[18] Many of the low elevation grasslands of the southern interior are considered to be fire-induced ecosystems. This means that they depend on periodic fires to maintain proper species composition. Historically, fires occurred as often as every 6.4 years in grassland sites in the Kootenay Trench.[19] Modern fire suppression and subsequent tree growth have substantially reduced the amount and productivity of these grasslands, affecting both wild and domestic animals.

Today, many grasslands are dominated by introduced species. Cattle and horse grazing pressures are high in the bunch grasslands of the Okanagan, parts of the Fraser Valley and the East Kootenays. Some grasslands in these areas have also been taken over by cultivation for agriculture. Grasslands most closely resembling conditions prior to European settlement are found only in areas inaccessible to cattle, or areas without a year-long water supply.[17,20] Only some alpine grasslands remain relatively unaffected either by human activity or introduced species.

Grasslands also provide habitat for a large number of diverse species, many of which are now rare or endangered. The southern grasslands contain most of the vertebrate species at risk in the province.[18]

Wetlands

Wetlands are waterlogged areas in which the water table is at or just below the surface, such as bogs, fens, swamps, and marshes. These productive wetlands provide for a great deal of biological diversity, and are vital to migratory birds. Just over 6% of B.C. is covered by wetlands. Figure 2.46 shows a breakdown of this value by ecoprovince. The northeast corner of B.C. has the highest percentage of its area covered by wetlands. There are no good estimates of the past or current changes in wetland area across the province. However, conversion of wetlands to agricultural, reservoir and urban uses are known to have caused significant wetland loss and alteration.[22]

Coastal temperate rain forests

Trees in coastal temperate rain forests grow to very large sizes and exceptionally old ages. Such ecosystems have the highest standing biomass of any ecosystem on earth, and provide for tremendous biodiversity.[23] Coastal temperate rain forests occur in a few scattered spots around the world, and are considered rare on a global scale. North America has the largest continuous tract of coastal temperate rain forests on earth, approximately half of which is in B.C.

A study of 354 primary watersheds (land draining into a stream system that flows into the ocean) in the coastal temperate rainforests in B.C. found that 20% of them are undisturbed by industrial activity, 13% are slightly modified, and 67% have had some level of development (Table 2.4). Ten of the 354 watersheds are protected in their entirety, and 14 are partially protected. Six of the fully protected watersheds are pristine (in a natural, unaltered state). Most of the fully protected watersheds are relatively small.

Only 30 to 50 hectares of the 275,000 ha (2,750 km²) Kitlope River watershed have been modified (by logging) and the rest of the watershed is pristine. This may be the only coastal temperate rain forest watershed of this size, in nearly pristine condition, left in the world.[23] The Kitlope River watershed is consequently an area of major conflict as it has the potential to

Figure 2.46
Wetland habitat

Wetlands are not evenly distributed. Some ecoprovinces may have small wetlands scattered across the landscape; others may have only a few large wetland areas.[21]

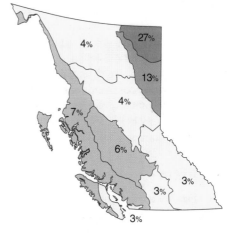

Table 2.4
Rainforest watersheds

Watershed Size (hectares)	Pristine		Modified		Developed		Total	
5,000-20,000	61	[6]	37	[2]	143	(4)	241	[8](4)
20,000-100,000	11	(1)	8	[2]	69	(2)	88	[2](3)
>100,000	0		1		24	(7)	25	(7)
Total	72		46		236		354	

This table presents the development status and protected status of primary watersheds in B.C.'s coastal temperate rainforests. Pristine watersheds show virtually no evidence of past human activities, and any past removal of trees covers less than 5 hectares. Modified watersheds have less than 2% of their area — or for watersheds larger than 10,000 hectares, less than 250 hectares — affected by development activity. Protected watersheds have their entire area within a National Park, Provincial Park, Park Reserve, Ecological Reserve, Recreation Area or Wilderness Area.[24] [ ] = protected, ( ) = partially protected provide for a number of uses. The area provides a unique opportunity for preservation or, alternatively, an important opportunity for economic development.

Conserving biodiversity

Conservation of habitat is often much easier than restoring it. For example, burrowing owls are presently designated as endangered in B.C., and at one time virtually disappeared from the province. This was due to a combination of factors, which included the destruction and loss of habitat. Ten years ago, a recovery program was begun that involved bringing families of owls from Washington State to the south Okanagan Valley, and "transplanting" them into artificial burrows. The goal was to re-establish enough owls to sustain a provincial population. The burrowing owl recovery program was sponsored by the Habitat Conservation Fund. The fund is administered by the Province and receives funding from, among other sources, surcharges on hunting, angling, guiding and trapping licences. Though successful in re-establishing a limited number of breeding pairs in B.C., it is still unclear if the program will result in a self-sustaining population. The transplant program was very expensive, and was replaced in 1992 with a captive breeding and release program aimed at broadening the number of release sites in suitable locations in the province.

The B.C. Conservation Data Centre has begun to locate, document and map the last remaining natural stands of Garry oak woodlands. Volunteers and advocacy groups are increasing public awareness of how important this community is to biological diversity. However, management practices designed to simulate the natural processes and disturbances which historically maintained these communities must be implemented if the endangered Garry oak woodlands are to survive in the province.

The South Okanagan Critical Areas Program (SOCAP) is one initiative aimed at protecting B.C.'s grasslands. SOCAP has identified and mapped high concentrations of threatened communities and species. Many of these represent the northern-most populations in their ranges and are therefore potentially vulnerable to climate change.

A number of government agencies and non-government organizations in B.C. are working on research and inventory projects to identify, map and conserve biodiversity. For example, the B.C. Conservation Data Centre is compiling information on rare and endangered plants, animals and habitats; the Endangered Spaces Project is involved in mapping the distribution of important species and habitat; a Corporate Resource Inventory Initiative has been undertaken by several provincial ministries to fund biodiversity inventory studies and other research; gap analysis is being done as part of the interagency Protected Areas Strategy to identify high biodiversity areas that are not already sufficiently protected; and several non-profit organizations, working in partnership with governments, are purchasing lands with critical ecosystems.

At the United Nations Earth Summit in Rio de Janeiro, Brazil in 1992, Canada was one of the first of many countries that signed a Convention on Biological Diversity. The objective of the Convention is to conserve biological diversity, to ensure that it is used in a sustainable manner and that the benefits arising from the use of genetic resources are shared.[25] British Columbia is preparing a B.C. Biological Diversity Strategy, and a member of a national group that is preparing a Canadian Strategy, due to be completed near the end of 1994.

Fish and aquatic invertebrates

 B.C. has an abundance of freshwater and marine life. Many species provide unique, world-class opportunities for recreational and commercial uses, and have sustained aboriginal peoples for centuries. Fish and invertebrates are also essential to B.C.'s natural ecosystems and are the major food source for top predators such as grizzly bears, killer whales, seals, sea lions and bald eagles.

Salmon

Salmon are anadromous fish (fish that hatch in fresh water but grow up in the ocean). They are of particular economic importance in B.C. Five species of salmon (sockeye, pink, chum, coho and chinook) spawn in over 3,900 streams and rivers in the province, and their young swim and feed hundreds of kilometres offshore in the Pacific Ocean. The status of salmon stocks is difficult to determine. The best available indicators are sustained harvests and spawning stock estimates. Province-wide, about three quarters of the salmon stocks are considered stable or increasing based on those representative salmon streams for which biologists have sufficient information on spawning trends. (Figure 2.47). However, over the past two decades salmon abundance has been sustained largely by enhancement efforts (Box 2.8), such as supplementing declining wild stocks with artificially-reared fish. Despite this and other enhancement measures, some commercially-important stocks have declined, such as the coho and chinook in the Strait of Georgia. Sockeye and pink salmon in the Fraser River have significantly re-built their numbers since the Fraser Canyon slide in 1913.

Biologists estimate that the present salmon harvest taken by commercial, recreational and aboriginal fisheries together account for approximately 75% of all salmon offspring which survive to adulthood. Commercial enterprises catch most of these salmon, although a growing proportion,

Figure 2.47

Salmon stocks

Based on available trend data for representative salmon stocks between 1976 and 1990, 76% of B.C. salmon stocks are considered stable or increasing, and 24% have declined. An unknown number of stocks have been lost from small coastal streams. Salmon enhancement has made a significant contribution in sustaining stocks classified as stable or increasing.[26]

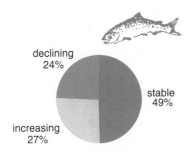

declining 24%

stable 49%

increasing 27%

especially of the chinook and coho, are taken by recreational fishers and aboriginal people. More salmon have been caught commercially in B.C. during the past ten years than in any comparable period over the past 40 years. Scientists attribute this to high fish production resulting from favourable climatic and ocean conditions. In 1991 over 4,300 commercial vessels harvested over 80 thousand tonnes of salmon, with a landed value (the value of the fish when they are caught) of nearly $170 million. This represents about 9% of the world's supply of wild salmon.[28]

In addition to fishing pressures, destruction of fish habitat from chemical spills, stream blockages and other impairments poses risks to salmon populations, especially in their vital spawning streams. For example, a recent survey of selected forest cut blocks on Vancouver Island found that logging has had some adverse effect on 34% of the 53 surveyed streams. Impacts judged as major (23%) and moderate (17%) were found mainly in streams with the highest potential to support fish, including salmon species.[29]

Clearly, governments and all fishing groups must work together to manage salmon. The need to protect salmon for human uses must be balanced against the need to protect them as part of

Box 2.8

Salmon enhancement

The Salmonid Enhancement Program was started by the Department of Fisheries and Oceans in 1977 to maintain and increase the abundance of anadromous salmon stocks in B.C., and the public is actively involved in hundreds of Enhancement projects. Water storage, bank stabilization, fishways and side channel construction are some of the projects through which fish habitat is restored or improved. Hatcheries are also used to rear fish. Biologists assess the outcome of these projects in order to distinguish between enhanced and wild stocks in the fisheries. In particular, care and attention must be given to the genetic and ecological interactions between and within stocks.

Overall, enhanced salmon now contribute about 15% of the salmon caught in B.C. commercial fisheries. In some areas such as the Strait of Georgia, enhanced coho salmon account for almost half of the catch.

marine and freshwater ecosystems. B.C.'s increasing fishing pressure is resulting in shorter fishing seasons, reduced bag limits, lower allocations, limited participation in the fisheries, and restricted fishing gear. A number of initiatives support salmon management: the Pacific Salmon Treaty, signed with the United States in 1985; Salmon Stock Management Plans, prepared since 1986; the Salmonid Enhancement Program (Box 2.8); annual evaluations carried out by the Pacific Stock Assessment Review Committee (PSARC); the 1988 B.C. Coastal Fisheries Forestry Guidelines; and the Aboriginal Fisheries Strategy implemented in 1992. In 1992 the Department of Fisheries and Oceans announced a plan to reform the allocation and licencing process on the west coast. The new process will lead to a more independent review and

allocation system. B.C. also supports a growing aquaculture industry. Salmon, along with trout and shellfish, are cultured along B.C.'s coast, and provide an opportunity to reduce harvest pressure on wild stocks.

Pacific herring

Pacific herring is a small, silver-coloured fish which, because of its migratory and nearshore spawning concentrations, is vital food for other fish, birds and mammals, including people. In the 1950s and 1960s, Pacific herring populations were wrongly believed to be large enough to sustain intensive harvesting. The biomass of B.C.'s herring (a measure of stock size) soon plummeted to a few thousand tonnes (Figure 2.48), in part due to a simultaneous decline in natural survival of eggs and young

Figure 2.48

Herring catch and stock

The trend in the commercial catch and the stock biomass of Pacific herring in B.C. has fluctuated greatly during the past 40 years. This is believed to be a result of both natural factors and harvest pressure.[27]

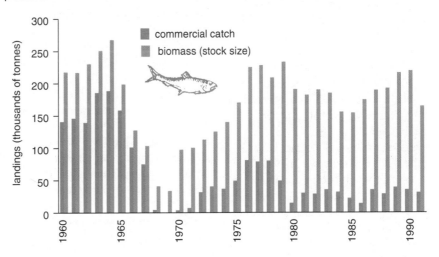

fish. The fishery collapsed and closed in 1968. The herring populations began to recover, enough to allow cautious resumption of fisheries in the late 1970s for the herring's roe (ripe eggs) and its spawned eggs on kelp. In recent years, about 150 seine vessels and 1,327 gill net vessels have annually landed from 30 to 45 thousand tonnes of herring worth up to $80 million. Since 1983, commercial fishing of herring has been tightly managed.

Variations in oceanic conditions off the west coast of Vancouver Island strongly affect the survival of herring and their principal predator, Pacific hake. Both fishes have exhibited marked 16-year variations in abundance over the past 50 years or so, which is believed to be a result of El Niño (a periodic change in circulation of the equatorial Pacific that results in warmer temperatures along the B.C. coast).

Pacific halibut and other groundfish

The halibut fishery is one of the oldest commercial fisheries on the Pacific coast. Halibut has always been highly valued by consumers, and the landed value is often over $5 per kilogram, compared with $3 for salmon. Over the past 15 years, the amount of halibut in B.C. waters has ranged between about 15 to 20 thousand tonnes of biomass (Figure 2.49). In the early 1900s, halibut populations throughout the Northeast Pacific were severely depleted, primarily due to overfishing. The Canada-United States Convention for the Preservation of the Halibut Fisheries began to address this in 1923, and halibut populations gradually rebuilt. Halibut populations again declined in the late 1960s to early 1970s, due mainly to accidental catches (by-catch) of halibut by foreign high-seas trawlers. This affected halibut numbers in B.C.'s waters. Canada and the U.S. declared a 200 mile fishing jurisdiction in 1979, stopping foreign fishing and its by-catch. This contributed to a short recovery of B.C.'s halibut populations in the mid 1980s. Once again, how-

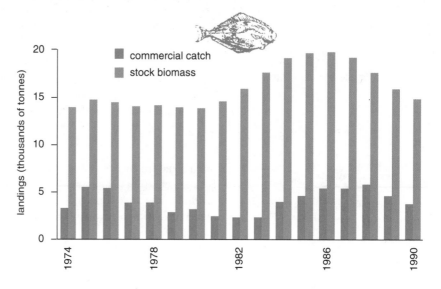

Figure 2.49
Halibut catch and stock

The commercial catch and stock biomass of Pacific halibut in B.C. has declined over the past few years, likely due to by-catch in Alaskan waters.[32,33]

ever, the by-catch of juvenile halibut has increased in Alaskan waters, and B.C.'s halibut stocks are again declining. The International Pacific Halibut Commission and the Canadian government have recently persuaded U.S. harvesters to reduce the by-catch by 25% by 1993. The Department of Fisheries and Oceans has begun an observer program on Canadian trawlers to reduce domestic bycatch of halibut, now presently about 5% of the halibut biomass.

While the commercial catch of halibut has decreased in the last 5 years, the commercial harvest of other groundfish populations has increased. Most groundfish populations, such as the sablefish, Pacific hake and Pacific cod, are known to be in good shape. However, the lingcod of the Strait of Georgia, inshore rockfish and Pacific ocean perch along the whole coast are suffering from overfishing. Today the catching capacity of the commercial fleet far exceeds the sustainable yield of these stocks. This calls for strict control by limiting Total Allowable Catches, using shorter seasons, closing areas, reducing trip limits and other measures. As well, an expanding sports fishing industry for groundfish is placing further pressures on these stocks.

Marine invertebrates

B.C.'s ocean waters house about 3,800 species of marine invertebrates, representing about 3.5% of the world's marine invertebrates.[30] However, there are little or no data on their condition and trends. Their status must be inferred from survey and harvest statistics. Trends from province-wide records of commercial catches of shellfish (crabs, shrimp, prawns, clams, oysters and so on) indicate that the amount harvested has increased about 400% since 1960. The harvest has also broadened from 15 species in 1981 to over 30 species in 1992. These changes reflect a demand among international markets for more varied seafood, and may also result from new harvest techniques and approaches.

Harvest rates, pollution and natural fluctuations all play a role in determining population numbers. Some marine invertebrate communities change dramatically from year to year because of climate or ocean fluctuations, whereas others gradually change over a longer period. Some species have naturally small, restricted populations due to their slow and sporadic reproduction, long lifespan or space limitations. Overharvesting of such species is easy, and can lead to their complete removal from an area. This happened to B.C.'s abalone (a large edible grazing snail with a mother-of-pearl shell). In 1991, much of B.C.'s abalone fishery was closed to commercial and recreational divers because the animals were getting smaller and more scarce.[31] Many invertebrate populations are fully-exploited by commercial, recreational and aboriginal users, and increased levels of harvest may affect their sustainability.

Other anadromous and freshwater fishes

British Columbia's diverse natural landscape provides a wide variety of ecosystems and creates the conditions for species and genetic diversity. The freshwater fish fauna of B.C. contains 83 named species, plus another three or four species that have not yet received formal scientific names. If subspecies, groups of populations and unique populations are included, the numbers more than double. Like all species and populations, each is suited to a specific set of conditions. These conditions include such things as oxygen and other chemical tolerances, temperature limits, food items, predation, competition with other species and with fish of the same species, and many others.

While many species are generally small and known to most people simply as "minnows", 38 species are much larger and well known. Besides the five species of pacific salmon, the most valued species are anadromous steelhead and its freshwater form (rainbow trout), cutthroat trout and Dolly Varden. These fish are the basis for B.C.'s world renowned freshwater sport fisheries, and many traditional aboriginal fisheries. However, the public values fish for other reasons besides their direct use for food and angling. They enjoy watching fish or just knowing they are alive in our waters and will continue to be there in the future.

B.C. is the third largest province in Canada, yet Saskatchewan, Manitoba, Ontario and Quebec each have four to ten times B.C.'s surface area of freshwater. Although there are not many species of freshwater fish in B.C., discovery of new subspecies and unique populations is not uncommon.

Factors affecting freshwater fish

There has been little recent change in the status of most populations of freshwater fish in the province. There is a great deal of fishing pressure in some areas; more people in southern B.C. want to fish than can be supported by the existing water and biota. This has caused reductions in some populations of fish sought by anglers in certain areas at certain times. Most fish populations in the northern half of the province are not experiencing the same levels of fishing pressure. Aboriginal fisheries for freshwater fish take place throughout the province but rarely affect the overall status of most species.

Many areas of the province experience factors other than fishing which threaten or reduce fish populations, such as reductions in the quantity and quality of water, and the removal or reduction of riparian habitat. Habitat disruptions from a wide variety of human activities remain the major environmental problem facing most anadromous and freshwater fish species and populations.

Fish are good indicators of environmental health and have been described as miner's canaries for ecological change. Thirty six species or subspecies are presently listed and tracked by the British Columbia Conservation Data Centre due to their status as endangered, threatened or vulnerable, as defined by the B.C. Wildlife Act. There are serious concerns about the survival of some populations of these fish (e.g. Salish sucker, white sturgeon and the Enos Lake sticklebacks).

In some cases, a number of factors contribute to the decline of freshwater fish populations. Since the mid-1980s there has been a general coast-wide decline in the abundance of steelhead in North America. Summer steelhead, which enter rivers in late summer but do not actually spawn until the following spring, are known to occur in 25-30 streams on Vancouver Island. Recent stock monitoring of these fish suggest that the numbers of fish currently returning to these streams are only 50-60% of the potential (Figure 2.50). Reasons for this decline include reduced marine survival, commercial and native fishery interception (accidental or incidental catches), widespread freshwater habitat deterioration mainly related to logging, and poaching losses.[34] Some populations may deserve "vulnerable" or "threatened" status if current trends continue or worsen.

The Skeena River system produces an internationally famous summer steelhead run of large, aggressive fish which has attracted recreational anglers worldwide. In most years approximately 50% of these fish are intercepted by Alaskan and Canadian commercial fishing vessels. This,

Figure 2.50
Steelhead on Vancouver Island

Summer steelhead counts on two rivers on Vancouver Island illustrate the decline in steelhead populations that is evident along the B.C. coast.[34]

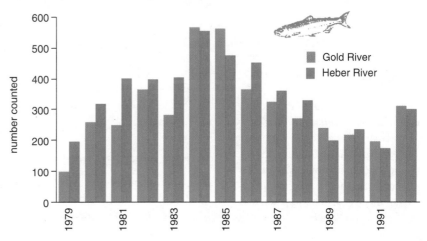

combined with incidental catch and by habitat alterations (logging, highway and railway construction, mining and settlement) have contributed to significant reductions in stocks of summer steelhead.

The quality of freshwater fish in B.C. is generally very good, with some site-specific exceptions. Public health advisories, due to elevated levels of mercury contamination, have been issued on consumption of walleye in the Columbia River at Trail, lake trout (char) in Pinchi Lake in northern B.C., and Dolly Varden in Williston Lake. An advisory has also been issued on the consumption of the liver of any fish from Atlin Lake due to toxaphene contamination. Advisories have also been issued on certain species of fish in areas of the Columbia and Fraser rivers adjacent to and downstream of pulp mills because of dioxin and furan concentrations. Tissue samples of six species of fish from 54 B.C. lakes considered relatively unaffected by human pollution were recently analysed for the presence of 14 heavy metals. All metal concentrations were considerably below acceptable levels of contamination and only mercury gave any indication of bioaccumulation.[35] Very few cases of tissue abnormalities are reported from the nearly 10 million fish taken each year from fresh water, an indication that such growths are rare in our freshwater fish populations. The percentage of angler-caught fish that are actually eaten is the highest of any province in Canada, which suggests

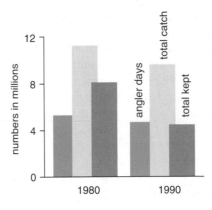

Figure 2.51
Recreational freshwater fishing

Although fishing effort (angler days) and catch has decreased slightly from 1980 to 1990, the number of fish kept have decreased dramatically. To conserve fish populations, anglers have adopted a catch and release ethic, and currently return over half of their catch.[7]

high confidence in the quality of B.C. fish.

B.C. supports the third largest freshwater sport fishery in Canada, as well as the largest saltwater sport fishery. In 1990, 390,000 people spent 4.5 million days angling and caught 9.6 million fish (Figure 2.51). That is an average of over two fish per day. They spent $457 million: $187 for direct angling-related expenses, $13 million for guided fishing trips, and $257 million on major purchases such as boats, special vehicles and property wholly attributable to sport fishing.[38] This level of expenditures is estimated to support 5300 person years of employment in various segments of the sport fishing and tourist industries.

Actually catching fish may not be the most important factor in sportfishing enjoyment. In a 1990 survey to determine what motivates an angler's desire to fish, relaxation and the surroundings rated higher among B.C. anglers than reasons relating to actually catching fish. Lack of pollutants in fish and the quality of the water are ranked by anglers as the two most important factors determining their choice of fishing destinations.[38]

The Fisheries Program Strategic Plan 1991-1995 has two primary objectives to achieve sustainable fish populations: conservation of wild stocks, and protection and management of fish habitat.[39] Conservative catch limits, angling regulations and a modern effective fish culture system (Box 2.9) are combined to modify angling pressure on wild native stocks in areas of high fishing pressure, while at the same time satisfying the demand for quality angling opportunities.

Box 2.9
Stocking freshwater with fish

Approximately 11,000,000 fish are raised and released in over 1000 B.C. waters each year. With a few exceptions, they are the progeny of wild fish populations. Managers do not use perpetually captive brood stock selected for fast growth and high egg production. Lakes are stocked with hatchery raised fish if there is no natural reproduction, or if the natural reproduction rate is not high enough to take full advantage of the productivity of the lake.

Forests

Forests cover nearly two-thirds of British Columbia (63.7%).[36] In addition to this abundance of forests, the province has an unusual diversity of forest ecosystems. Of the eleven major forest regions of Canada, six are found in B.C., more than any other province.[37] Each forest region has distinct differences in the species composition and age of trees. For example, the forests

on B.C.'s coast are much older than forests in the interior. More than half of coastal forests are over 250 years old (55%), whereas only 6% of interior forests are that old (Figure 2.52). Over half of the interior forests are 120 years old or younger (54%).

Forest disturbances

B.C.'s forests are susceptible to a number of natural disturbances, including fire, wind storms, freeze

damage, droughts, landslides, insects, and disease. They are also subject to human disturbances, such as logging, and to a lesser degree, land clearing for urban development and agriculture. Of these disturbances, insects, wildfires and logging have disturbed the largest area of British Columbia's forest since the beginning of the century (Figure 2.53).

Figure 2.52
Forest age

The age distribution of trees in B.C.'s interior differs from coastal forests. A much greater proportion of coastal forests are over 250 years old.[40]

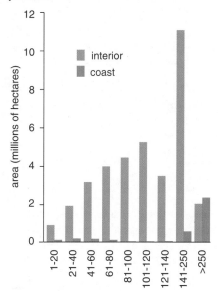

Note: Includes only stocked, productive forest land inside Timber Supply Areas (TSA). Excludes tree farm licences, Crown forest land in timber licences, private and federal lands outside TSAs, and non-stocked, non-productive and non-forested lands inside TSAs.

Figure 2.53
Forest disturbances

Disturbances affect forests in different ways and to different degrees. Logging typically removes 50-80% of the biomass of a forest, fire removes 20-60%, and insects remove 5-10%.[41]

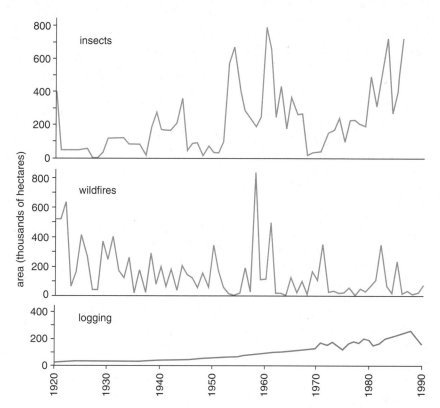

Insects

Insects can have major impacts on forests. During the past year, joint federal-provincial insect disease surveys found that 98,000 hectares of B.C. forest were affected by bark beetles (particularly mountain pine beetle in lodgepole pine forests). Another 690,000 hectares were affected by defoliating insects (insects that strip off the leaves and needles), such as western spruce budworm in Douglas fir forests east of the Cascade Mountains. This area adds up to 1% of the province's forested area. Figure 2.54 shows the total area of B.C.'s forests affected by these two insects over the past 20 years. During the past year about 1.7 million cubic metres of timber were destroyed by bark beetles, 1.6 million by defoliating insects, and 1.4 million by root disease.[43] Insect damage has led to salvage logging of some very large areas. Salvage logging involves harvesting the timber before it's wood value is further damaged or destroyed

Figure 2.54
Area affected by pine beetles and spruce budworms

"Affected" means that over 10% of the trees have been killed by these pests. In 1987, the area affected by spruce budworm equalled 1.5% of B.C.'s productive forest.[42]

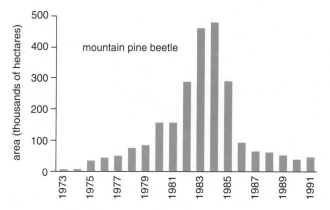

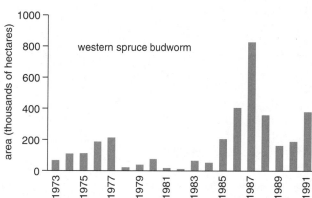

by the insects, and also aims to remove the threat of further insect spread.

Diseases are also significant factors affecting forest health. Root rot and white pine blister rust are just two examples. Blister rust was introduced to B.C. and has virtually wiped out the use of white pine as a commercial tree species.

Fire

The annual area disturbed by wildfires has decreased over the last 30 years. The largest annual area disturbed occurred in 1958, during which over 800,000 hectares burned. Since the mid-1960s, the average area of forest land affected by wildfires has dropped well below pre-1965 numbers. The annual average for the last ten years is just under 95,000 hectares, which is less than 0.2% of the productive forest land in B.C.[44] The ecological implications of these changes vary by ecosystem. It is generally believed that fire suppression has resulted in forests that are at greater risk to insects and disease, especially in the southern interior.

Timber harvest

The Ministry of Forests considers 51.8 million hectares (54.5% of the province) to be "productive forest land", land that is biologically capable of producing commercial timber. When economic viability or environmental sensitivity is considered, about one half of this area is available for timber harvesting. The quality of forested land is highly variable, with the most productive forest lands generally found on valley bottoms along the coast and in the interior wet belt.

Figure 2.55 shows the annual timber harvest over the past decade. The amount of timber harvested annually in B.C. is projected to decline in the near future in many areas of the province. Past and current timber harvesting activities are changing the composition of B.C.'s forests. Existing forests with high volumes of timber are being harvested and replaced with younger, smaller trees, and in the future an increasing proportion of the timber harvest will come from these "second growth" forests. These future forest

stands are expected to be harvested at an earlier age and will therefore contain a lower volume of timber per unit area than the original forest. Changing public values and a consequent increase in demand for non-timber resources will also likely result in a decrease in timber harvest in the future.

The Ministry of Forests is reviewing all Timber Supply Areas to decide whether to maintain, increase or decrease the volume of timber harvested. For example, the Ministry has already reduced the timber harvest volumes on British Columbia's Mid-

Coast by 34 percent to account for revised estimates of commercially operable area, as well as other forest values such as aesthetics and wildlife.

To maintain productive forest land and sustain the forest industry, harvested areas must be reforested (Figure 2.56). Since 1987, industry has been required by provincial law to reforest harvested areas. The Ministry of Forests has begun an audit of all reforestation plans filed in B.C. since 1987 to investigate the degree of compliance. In 1989, it was estimated that there were 3.8 million hectares of Not Satisfactorily Restocked (NSR) forest

Figure 2.55
Area harvested for timber

The total area harvested in B.C. each year increased throughout most of the 1980s but has started to drop off in the last few years. Most of this area is clearcut.[46,47,48,49]

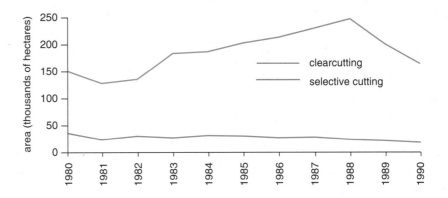

Figure 2.56
Reforestation

The rate of reforestation has increased dramatically in the last five years, as a result of replanting on recently harvested sites as well as efforts to replant the backlog of Not Satisfactorily Restocked (NSR) sites. Net harvest = harvested area - roads. Net reforestation = planting + natural regeneration - failure. An 80 - 120 year time lag is expected between the time a forest is replanted and the time it is ready to be harvested.[50]

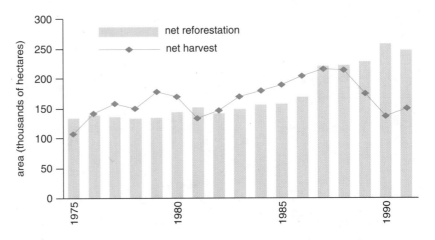

land in B.C., that is land not growing trees to its full potential.[45] Harvesting, wildfires, and pest outbreaks occurring between 1982 and 1989 accounted for approximately 1.1 million hectares of this NSR (29%). The British Columbia Ministry of Forests has plans in place to reforest these areas. The remaining 2.7 million hectares (71%) originated from harvesting, fires, pests and other causes prior to 1982. Much of this land is considered inaccessible, uneconomic or is classified as poor or low site quality. Approximately 440,000 hectares are considered good or medium site quality. The remaining areas are expected to regenerate naturally over time.

Forest values

In 1991, exports of all forest products from B.C. were valued at $8.4 billion. This represented 55.4% of the value of all products exported from the province that year.[51,52] This includes both raw materials and fabricated products. That same year, the forest industry supported approximately 84,000 direct and 126,000 indirect jobs.[51,53] Forestry is vital to many towns in B.C.

Public values have changed over the years, and people no longer consider forests as simply a timber resource. In addition to performing a wide variety of ecological functions (Box 2.10), forests are valued for their beauty, recreational opportunities, and spiritual significance.

Recreation is a major use of B.C.'s forests. Annual recreational use of provincial forests administered by the British Columbia Ministry of Forests is over 40 million user-days, twice that for provincial parks. Nature study, including scenic viewing, is the most common activity in these forests (Figure 2.57).[54] The Forest Service manages 1,300 recreation sites and 5,000 kilometres of trails. About 42% of B.C. residents have used a Forest Service recreation site in the past five years.[55] Considerable commercial recreation activity also occurs in the province's back country areas. Adventure tourism is one of the fastest growing industries in B.C.

Old-growth forests

Old-growth forests in B.C. have become a very high profile topic both within and outside of the province. A great deal of attention has been focused on how much old-growth is left and how they should be managed (Box 2.11).

Old-growth forests have a number of distinct features: large trees, wide variation in tree spacing, a full range of tree sizes, large dead trees (both standing and fallen), multiple canopy (tree-top) layers, canopy gaps and

understory patches; and broken or deformed tree-tops, boles and root decay. The age at which a forest develops these old-growth characteristics varies significantly across the province, depending on the forest type, climate, site characteristics, and the history of disturbances in the area.

In B.C. there is no agreed-upon single definition of old-growth, although most definitions specify a stand age greater than 150 years. Ministry of Forests current inventory information necessitates that 140 years be the minimum age for depicting old-growth forests. Figure 2.52 indicates the size of the areas where old-growth attributes may be found. Note that only some of these areas will possess all the attributes necessary for designation as old-growth (Figure 2.58).

The on-going debate over how old-growth forests should be managed is a reflection of conflicting values (Box 2.12). Some values require the preservation of old-growth while others require its harvest. The complexity of managing for old-growth is further complicated by not being able to compare all values in the same terms. For example, tourism and timber values

Figure 2.57

Recreation use of provincial forests

British Columbians use the provincial forests for a number of recreation activities. Participation is measured by the number of adult user days. On the average each adult participates in 2.4 activities per day of use.[54]

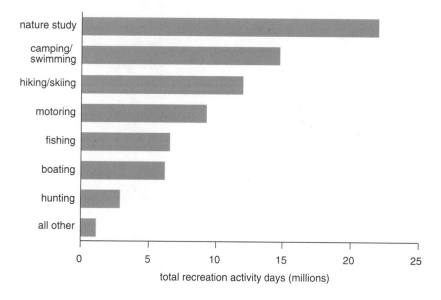

total recreation activity days (millions)

Box 2.11

Coastal old-growth forest

Nowhere in British Columbia is the issue of the future of old-growth forests as contentious as on the coast. The majority of forest growth greater than 250 years old is found in coastal areas. At the crux of the debate over the future management direction for coastal old-growth forests is the dilemma of mutually exclusive societal values. Many old-growth forests provide a unique opportunity for preservation or, alternatively, an important opportunity for economic development. Making a sound choice based on insightful views on both short and long term implications is a key societal challenge.

Highlights

- 5.1 million hectares (almost 65 percent) of the 7.9 million hectares of the productive coastal forest land base are over 120 years old.

- 2 million hectares of mature, coastal forest are considered operable for timber harvesting.

- 3 million hectares of mature coastal forest are considered inaccessible for harvesting and will remain indefinitely as coastal old-growth forests. A large proportion of this area is at higher elevations.

- about 200,000 hectares of coastal old-growth forests are protected in parks and wilderness areas. More than half of this total is protected on Vancouver Island.

- low elevation, highly productive old-growth forests are under-represented in existing protected areas.

- an additional 400,000 hectares of coastal old-growth forests have been identified for possible protection in British Columbia's Protected Areas Strategy.[54]

Figure 2.58
Coastal old-growth

This figure shows the portion of productive coastal forest land that has trees older than 120 years of age. Old-growth forests can be found in this age group, but not all forests in this category possess the required attributes to be considered old-growth. [40]

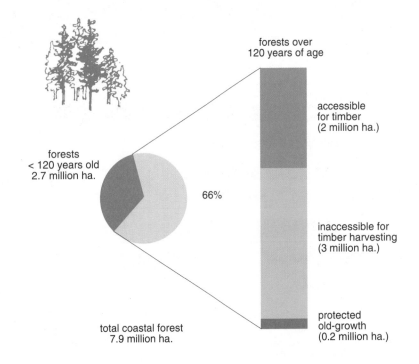

forests over
120 years of age

accessible
for timber
(2 million ha.)

forests
< 120 years old
2.7 million ha.

66%

inaccessible for
timber harvesting
(3 million ha.)

protected
old-growth
(0.2 million ha.)

total coastal forest
7.9 million ha.

can be more readily translated into monetary terms than can spiritual or aesthetic values.

A review of existing protected areas indicates that B.C.'s low elevation, highly productive old-growth ecosystems are under-represented. An Old-growth Strategy project was launched in 1990. Its objectives were to both conserve representative areas of old-growth forests in B.C., and to design a management framework to integrate the broad spectrum of old-growth forest values. A Provincial Protected Areas Strategy team is evaluating nearly 200 study areas for their potential contribution to a provincial protected areas network. These study areas include 14 of the 15 old-growth areas temporarily deferred from timber harvest in 1990.

Box 2.12

The value of old-growth

Sixteen different values of old-growth forests have been identified through B.C.'s Old-growth Strategy:[57,58]

bequest for future generations
biodiversity
community recreation
community stability
gathering of food and medicine
geoclimatic
grazing
heritage
hunting, trapping and fishing
science and education
symbolic
spiritual and aesthetic
timber and manufactured products
tourism
water
wilderness

Striking a balance

Several initiatives throughout the province address the challenge of balancing conflicting timber and non-timber demands in forest management. The Ministry of Forests is currently preparing a Forest Practices Code. The Code will establish the mandatory and uniform application of rules, policies and procedures which guide forest management. The Code will help the Province meet its social and economic needs by recognizing objectives for a broad range of resource values, including the long term ecological sustainability of forest ecosystems. The Commission on Resources and Environment (CORE) is developing a provincial land use strategy that will recognize environmental protection together with economic development in land use decision making. Initiatives are underway to prepare broad Regional Plans. More detailed Land and Resource Management Plans will allocate forests and other resources to various uses.

Wildlife

Wildlife are very important to British Columbians. B.C.'s wildlife support many uses and produce many benefits: recreational, scientific, subsistence, cultural and commercial. On an average day, over 270,000 people in B.C. participate in a wildlife-related activity. Over a whole year, this adds up to over 100 million person-days. A 1983 provincial survey showed that over 87% of B.C. residents are interested in wildlife; 75% are involved in wildlife-associated activities in or near their homes; and 94% feel that wildlife is an important aspect of their trips.

The early 1980s saw a decline in the number of hunters in B.C., followed by a levelling-off in the mid- and late 1980s. Big-game hunting has remained relatively stable. Big-game guiding, geared mainly to nonresident hunters, has long been an important economic activity in rural B.C., especially in the north, and is growing rapidly. Guides are expanding their services to include more residents, and to provide viewing and photographic safaris in the non-hunting season.

The commercial use of wildlife is also growing. Farming of upland game birds and ranching of some furbearers is well developed. Game farming of bison, fallow deer and reindeer is now permitted. Trapping is a traditional activity in the province, especially in rural and northern communities and for aboriginal people. In 1987-88, raw fur sales amounted to $5.2 million. A knowledge of the existence of wildlife is important to many British Columbians, even if only observed through books and magazines, films and television, lectures and wildlife art.

Residents and visitors spend substantial sums of money on wildlife-associated activities — for transportation, food, accommodation, equipment, guide fees, traplines, and preparing and shipping fur pelts. Such spending occurs in all parts of B.C., making a vital contribution to many rural economies. Direct and indirect expenditures by recreational and commercial wildlife users create ripple effects that support the equivalent of over 12,000 person-years of employment for provincial residents.

The status of wildlife

B.C. has more species of wildlife than any other province in Canada. The Ministry of Environment, Lands and Parks currently maintains Wildlife Species Evaluation Lists. Wildlife on the Red List (66 species and subspecies of amphibians, reptiles, birds and mammals) are candidates for legal designation as endangered or threatened under the B.C. Wildlife Act. Wildlife on the Blue List (89 species and subspecies of amphibians, reptiles, birds and mammals) are considered sensitive or vulnerable (Box 2.13). Wildlife on the Yellow List are not considered to be at risk, and are managed to meet particular public uses. Wildlife appreciation, hunting, guiding and trapping are the four major demand categories. In 1991, there were 94 species on the Yellow List (Table 2.5 shows the status of some of these species). The populations of 34 of these species were considered stable, 25 were increasing (or considered "stable to increasing"), and 13 were decreasing. The remaining 22 species

---

Box 2.13

Marbled murrelet

Recently, a small seabird on the Blue List has been receiving a great deal of attention in B.C. Marbled murrelets spend most of their time out on the ocean, can swim underwater, and come ashore only to breed. They normally range as far as 70 kilometres from shore. They are found on both the Asian and the North American sides of the north Pacific ocean. The North American population breeds along the coast from Alaska to northern California. B.C. has an estimated 36,000 birds, accounting for about 20-30% of the North American population. Not enough data have been collected to indicate trends in the size of this population.

Murrelets have a low reproductive rate, producing only one egg per year, and probably do not breed until at least three years of age. Although some have been found nesting on the ground in treeless portions of Alaska, current research indicates that marbled murrelets are dependent on old-growth coastal forests for nesting habitat. Very few nests have been found in B.C., and all have been found on large mossy limbs high in the canopy of coastal old-growth forests. Its low reproductive rate and particular habitat requirements makes the species extremely vulnerable to a number of dangers: oil spills, drowning in fish nets, and habitat destruction through timber harvest. The bird has therefore been added to B.C.'s Blue List, and in 1991 was listed as threatened by the Committee on the Status of Endangered Wildlife in Canada (COSEWIC).

Loss of nesting habitat through logging is considered the greatest threat to marbled murrelets. A number of research and inventory studies have been conducted to learn more about its habitat requirements, behaviour, and vulnerabilities. These studies have involved the federal and provincial governments, universities, industry and many volunteers from environmental groups. This work has provided important data against which future trends can be compared, and its continuation is important to provide the basis for future management decisions.

Table 2.5

Species on the Yellow List

This table presents the status of selected species on the Yellow List. These species were chosen to represent the range of wildlife on the Yellow List. Species on the Yellow List are not at risk, and are managed to meet specific public demands.[62]

Status	Species	Population size (if known)
stable to increasing	beaver	400,000-600,000
	California bighorn sheep	4,500
	cougar	3,000
	moose	175,000
	mountain goat	55,000
	osprey	
	Rocky Mtn. bighorn sheep	3,000
	Rocky Mtn. elk	40,000
stable	Barrow's goldeneye	
	coastal black-tailed deer	200,000
	mule deer	150,000
stable to decreasing	black bear	120,000
decreasing	clouded salamander	
	lynx	20,000-80,000
	painted turtle	
	sharp-tailed grouse	
variable	gray wolf	7,500
	ruffed grouse	3-4 million

Table 2.6

Status of seabird species on the British Columbia Pacific coast [60]

Status	Species	Estimated number	Comments
threatened	marbled murrelet	36,000	loss of nesting habitat
rare (at limit of range)	horned puffin	60	found with tufted puffin
	thick billed murre	20	Triangle Island only
uncommon	Brandt's cormorant	200	irregular breeder
variable	tuffed puffin	78,000	most on Triangle Island
	double-crested cormorant	4,000	restricted to Strait of Georgia
increasing	glaucous-winged gull	58,000	
abundant (trends unknown)	Cassin's auklet	2,700,000	
	Leach's storm-petrel	1,400,000	
	rhinocerous auklet	720,000	
	ancient murrelet	540,000	some impact from rat predation
	fork tailed storm-petrel	400,000	
	pelagic cormorant	9,000	widespread coastal breeder
	pigeon guillemot	9,000	scattered, difficult to census
	common murre	9,000	scarce breeder, most on Triangle Island

either had fluctuating population numbers, some increasing and some decreasing populations, or unknown trends.

Similarly, the Canadian Wildlife Service of the federal government has developed a status report and estimated population numbers of seabird species that breed in colonies along the B.C. Pacific Coast (Table 2.6). Their inventory was completed in 1990 and included all known colonies and newly discovered ones. Population trends for most of these seabirds are largely unknown as there is a lack of reliable historical data. Most seabird species are nocturnal burrow-nesters and are difficult to census. In 1980 only a handful of seabird colonies were protected. Today all but a few are within Ecological Reserves or National Parks.

Factors affecting the status of wildlife

The single most important factor affecting wildlife populations in B.C. is habitat loss. Forestry, agriculture, urbanization, and the construction of reservoirs, highways and roads are among some of the pressures changing or destroying wildlife habitat in B.C. For example, some ungulates require special types of habitat called "winter range" during periods of heavy winter snow. Large clearcut areas may deprive them of this shelter. However, while clearcutting destroys habitat for some species it provides habitat for others.

A complex set of factors affect bird populations. The reproductive biology of Cassin's auklets, rhinoceros auklets and ancient murrelets has been studied in detail and efforts to understand the relationship between these birds and their physical environment have been initiated. Predation by rats and racoons introduced to the Queen Charlotte Islands has been recognized as a threat to some colonies. Some of these seabird species have also been studied for organochlorine contaminants (see Water chapter).

Poaching is a concern for certain species, such as black bear. Improper handling of garbage contributes to another major wildlife concern - problem bears (discussed in Coast and Mountains Ecoprovince). Marine oil pollution can threaten seabirds and other marine animals, and driftnet fishing has resulted in the death of enormous numbers of marine life (Box 2.14).

Actions are being taken to conserve habitat. Eleven Wildlife Management Areas have been designated for the preservation of important wildlife populations. The Habitat Conservation Fund, created in 1981, has supported over 366 wildlife enhancement projects including prescribed burning of vegetation, the placement of nesting structures for waterfowl, small birds and mammals, and the regulation of water levels in marshlands. It has also financed the purchase of large areas of land from private owners for fish and wildlife habitat. The Pacific coast is critical to both migratory birds and resident wildlife. In recognition of this, government agencies and NGOs (non-governmental organizations) in British Columbia, Washington, Oregon and California have formed a partnership known as the Pacific Coast Joint Venture under the North American Waterfowl Management Plan. The goal is to secure, enhance and restore coastal wetlands and associated upland habitat along the Pacific coast from B.C. to northern California.

Marine mammals

B.C.'s coastal waters are inhabited by large numbers of seals, sea lions, whales and dolphins, many of which reside year-round or are regular migrants. Commercial whaling and sealing played a major role in B.C's early history, but today marine mammals in their natural surroundings are valued more for wildlife viewing.

As late as the 1960s, people hunted seals and sea lions in B.C. to reduce their predation on salmon. The pelts of the animals also had commercial value. Harbour seal populations reached historic lows of 10,000 animals before receiving protected status in 1970. Since then, harbour seals have increased in abundance by over 12% per year, and now number about 100,000 (Figure 2.59). Similarly, Steller sea lion populations decreased from about 14,000 to 4,000 animals from 1913 to 1970. Numbers counted at B.C. breeding rookeries indicate that they have slowly increased at a rate of about 2.5% per annum since they were protected in 1970 (Figure 2.60). Biologists suspect that the recovery of the B.C. populations may be slowed by an expanding rookery just north of the

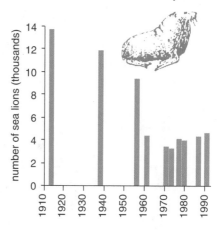

Figure 2.60
Sea lions

The numbers of steller sea lions counted at breeding rookeries in B.C. have increased from record lows in the 1970s, but are still well below numbers earlier in the century. [26]

Queen Charlotte Islands in Alaska, which may have taken over the food resources of the depleted populations.

Harbour seals and sea lions are an important link in the marine food chain. They consume marine fish, and are in turn preyed upon by Orca (killer whales) and sharks. Presently growing populations of seals and sea lions have prompted some commercial fish harvesters to call for animal control measures. The Department of Fisheries and Oceans is now studying the diet of harbour seals and their impact on salmon stocks.

Two distinct types of Orca, differing in appearance and behaviour, occur along the B.C. coast. "Residents" occur in groups of 5 to 50 animals and feed primarily on fish. "Transients" usually travel in groups of 1 to 7 animals and eat seals, sea lions and other marine mammals. Residents appear to be divided into northern and southern communities, with the boundary being somewhere around central Vancouver Island. Since population studies began in the 1970s, the size of the northern group has increased by 2.9% per year, reaching 198 animals in 1991 (Figure 2.61). In contrast, the size of southern group has increased by 1.3% per year to 90 whales. This slower rate of increase is largely due to the fact that juvenile whales were captured from the southern group for exhibits in zoos and aquaria from the mid 1960s to the early

Box 2.14
Driftnets: lifting the "curtains of death"

Asian fleets have historically used thousands of kilometres of fine filament nets to catch large squid in the Pacific Ocean. These nets also ensnare tonnes of North American salmon and hundreds of thousands of marine mammals, seabirds, and other marine life (by-catch).

Over the past four years, the provincial and federal governments have hosted a number of events (including the North Pacific Driftnet Conference in Vancouver) to focus international attention on the issue. Canada also participated in an international observer program to quantify the by-catch problem and help devise solutions. As a result, a global ban on high seas squid driftnet fishery came into effect at the end of 1992.

Figure 2.59
Harbour seals

Harbour seals received protected status in 1970, and have since become increasingly abundant in B.C.[26,59]

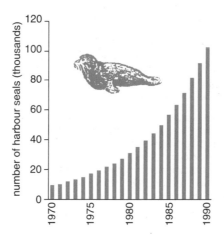

Figure 2.61
Orca (killer whales)

The numbers of southern resident Orcas in B.C. is relatively stable. The number of northern residents was increasing during the past two decades but now also appears stable.[59,26]

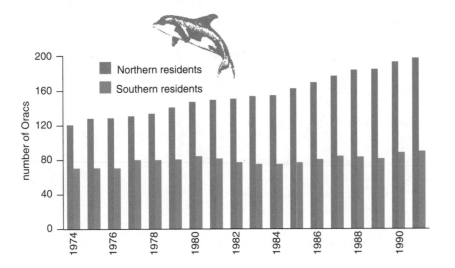

Figure 2.62
Sea otters

The sea otter is one of the four wildlife species legally classified as endangered under the B.C. Wildlife Act.[26]

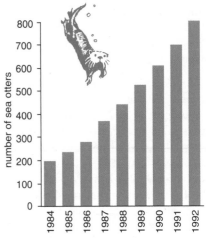

1970s. Efforts are being made to protect important resident Orca habitat such as Robson Bight (Box 2.15). There are about 150 transient individuals, that range from Washington State to southeast Alaska. Relatively little is known about them. A population of at least 150 killer whales has recently been found to inhabit the offshore waters of B.C., but little research has been conducted.

Sea otters were extirpated by hunting along B.C.'s coast by the early 1930s. Between 1969 and 1972, 89 Alaskan

sea otters were transplanted to the Bunsby Islands on the northwest coast of Vancouver Island. By 1977, a second colony had naturally formed at Nootka Island, 70 km south. Overall, the population has steadily increased by about 18% per year, now numbering about 800 animals (Figure 2.62). A colony has also been discovered southwest of Bella Bella, and is now estimated at approximately 200 animals. Sea otters prey heavily on sea urchins, which in turn graze on marine plants such as kelp. When otters

disappeared, a major predator of sea urchins was eliminated. Urchin numbers exploded, decimating many of the kelp "forests" and their associated algae communities along the outer B.C. coast. It is anticipated that as sea otter populations grow, sea urchin populations will again be checked and the kelp habitat will recover. On the other hand, some research scientists are concerned that the expanding sea otter population may threaten the shellfish fishery.

Box 2.15

Robson Bight - beaches for whales

Protection of Orca habitat has lead to some controversies between land use pressures at Robson Bight on the northeast portion of Vancouver Island. A large section of this Bight was renamed the Robson Bight (Michael Bigg) Ecological Reserve. Killer whales gather there annually to "rub" themselves on several unique beaches (called the rubbing beaches) which are comprised of small smooth stones very uniform in size. The bight is located at the mouth of the Tsitika River valley. Those concerned about the whales fear that sediments from upstream logging activities may enter into the Bight and damage the Orca's habitat, and that the logging activities themselves could adversely affect whale behaviour. Increasing numbers of whale-watching boats compound the potential threat.

In 1991, a Killer Whale Committee was appointed by the Federal Minister of Fisheries and Oceans and the Provincial Minister of B.C. Parks to examine the impacts of human activity on the Orca in Johnstone Strait. A number of recommendations were made to the respective governments, one of which was a 5-year moratorium on logging activities in the lower portion of the Tsitika Valley. Timber harvesting activity has since been suspended. An intensive study initiated by the British Columbia Ministry of Forests in 1991 will help to establish the degree of stream siltation within the watershed and the extent to which the cause is natural or the result of human activity.

Conclusions

B.C. has an impressive range of biological diversity, significant on both national and global scales. Loss or change of habitat, introduced species and increasing development activities are several factors threatening significant portions of this diversity. To ensure the conservation of biodiversity, land- and water-use decisions must be based on a sound understanding of ecosystems and the processes that maintain them. Although a great deal of research and cataloguing has been accomplished, the biodiversity picture is not yet complete. There is still much more to learn about B.C.'s biological diversity, and how best to conserve it.

Most information on the state of fish in B.C. focuses on species targeted by the commercial, recreational and aboriginal fisheries. Three quarters of B.C.'s salmon stocks are judged to be stable or increasing. One quarter are decreasing, including coho and chinook in the Strait of Georgia. The stocks of other marine fish species for which we have data are fluctuating, primarily due to fishing pressure. There has been no noticeable change in the populations of most species of freshwater fish in B.C. However, freshwater fish in the southern half of B.C. are experiencing high fishing pressure. Fish harvest is only one of a number of factors that has led to significant reductions in steelhead along the coast. Over the past two decades salmon abundance has been sustained largely by enhancement efforts. The annual stocking of freshwater with 11,000,000 fish has helped reduce angling pressure on wild native Freshwater stocks.

Approximately two-thirds of B.C. is forested, and about half of these forests are mature. Large stands of old-growth trees can still be found in the more inaccessible areas of the province, and some of these are coastal temperate rainforests of global significance. Much of the current inventory information about forests focuses on forestry-related data. This will likely change as forest management adapts to the recent shift in forest values from timber to a broader spectrum of ecological, social and cultural values.

Although there are estimates of population size and/or stability for over 200 wildlife species, there is little trend data illustrating how these populations have changed over time. Marine mammals are the exception, and the species for which we have data appear to be doing well. Of the 636 vertebrate species — excluding fish — in B.C., four are legally designated as endangered, 66 have low abundance and are being considered for legal endangered or threatened status, and 89 are considered to be at risk. The single most important factor affecting wildlife in B.C. is habitat loss (or change). Wildlife will benefit from increased habitat conservation as greater management consideration is given to biodiversity and other non-timber values of our forests.

Land

British Columbia is a province with a dramatic interplay between mountains, ocean and weather. B.C. has two major mountain belts, both running from north to south. The western mountains create a coastal zone of numerous islands and fjords with about 27,000 km of shoreline (if it were straight it would be only 7,000 km long). These mountains are a barrier to weather systems coming in from the Pacific. On the ocean side the climate is mild and moist; on the inland side it is much drier with greater temperature extremes. Some of the inland area is semi-desert. The eastern mountains play a similar role by blocking the flow of cold Arctic air to the central core of the province. The two mountain belts are separated by a diverse and complex area of basins, plateaus, highlands, and hills. North of the mountains, in the northeast part of the province, B.C. extends into the great plains.[1]

The geology of B.C. is the most varied of all the provinces in Canada. The land is composed of lavas, granites, shales, sandstones, and metamorphic rocks. These have been folded, faulted, gouged by glaciers, and eroded by wind, water, and gravity. Within these complex geological structures are significant deposits of coal, copper, gold, silver, molybdenum, lead, zinc, natural gas, and oil.[2] On the surface there is a thin layer of soil. Soil is a mixture of mineral and organic matter. In addition to being essential for the growth of plants, the soil also holds large volumes of groundwater and large amounts of carbon, most of which came from atmospheric carbon dioxide. Thus the soil plays a key role in both the hydrologic cycle and global climate.[2]

Who governs the land?

At the time of Confederation the government viewed the lands and waters of B.C. as a wild and untamed world that was ripe for resource development. In the late 1800s and early 1900s the federal and provincial governments systematically took possession of all the lands and waters of British Columbia and assigned the aboriginal people to some 1,650 widely scattered reserves. The moral and legal issues generated at that time persist today, as the aboriginal people contend that they never willingly relinquished their rights (Box 2.16).[2]

Crown land covers 93% of the province (Figure 2.63). The provincial government issues tenures or licenses that enable private access to resources from public lands. Around the turn of the century about 6 million ha of Crown land were transferred to private ownership. Since then the rate of transfer has been much slower - a total of about 2 million ha in the last 70 years.[8] Long term tenures are intended to promote investment in resource development, generate employment, provide government revenues, and encourage sustainable management practices. In B.C. today, most of the forestry, mining and recreation activities occur on Crown land. Most farm production and urban development occur on private lands.

Figure 2.63
Land ownership

Most of the land in British Columbia is owned by the Crown. The most common human uses of crown land are forestry, grazing, recreation, and mining.[8]

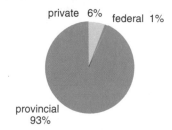

total land area = 1,014,000 km^2

Box 2.16
Aboriginal interests in land and natural resources

"As history shows, the relationship between First Nations and the Crown has been a troubled one. A new relationship which recognizes the unique place of aboriginal people and First Nations in Canada must be developed and nurtured."

"Land, sea and natural resources have always been at the centre of contention between First Nations and the federal and provincial governments. To First Nations, their traditional territories are their homelands. Hereditary title is the source of all of their rights within their traditional territories. The land, sea and natural resources have supported their families, communities and governments for centuries, and form the basis of the aboriginal spiritual, philosophical, and cultural views of the world."

"Treaty negotiations in British Columbia provide an opportunity to recognize First Nation governments on their traditional territories. These treaties will be unique constitutional instruments. First Nations peoples view land, sea and resources as fundamental components of modern treaties. They will identify, define and implement a range of rights and obligations, including existing and future interests in land, sea and resources."

(Excerpts from: The Report of the British Columbia Claims Task Force, June, 1991.)[42]

Much of the federal Crown land in B.C. is held as reserves for the use and benefit of British Columbia's First Nations. There are 1,676 reserves in British Columbia, 350 of them occupied, with a total land area of 344,000 hectares. This land base is divided amongst 196 Bands with an on-reserve population of 46,000 and a total population of 91,000.

First Nations also use substantial areas of Crown lands and waters for traditional activities, including shellfish harvesting, fishing, hunting, gathering, trapping, and the harvesting of medicinal plants. They are increasingly involved in resource and environmental management activities through co-management and joint stewardship agreements, and through the Treaty Negotiation process. Important co-operative examples are the agreement

for a protected area in Haida Gwaii on the Queen Charlotte Islands, and the Fishery Commissions established under the Department of Fisheries and Oceans Aboriginal Fisheries Strategy. Treaty negotiations in British Columbia constitute an opportunity to formulate a new relationship with First Nations on their traditional territories. The British Columbia Treaty Commission, a tripartite organization appointed by First Nations, Canada and the Province, is intended to oversee the treaty negotiations process within British Columbia.

As the population and economy of B.C. have grown, demands on land for human use have increased. We have come to recognize that the land base is indeed limited, and we have become aware of the need for both sustainable use and conservation.

During the last decade the need for improved land allocation, management, and resolution of land use conflicts has sparked several initiatives including the Commission on Resources and Environment (CORE), the Round Table on the Environment and the Economy, the Old Growth Strategy, the Forest Resources Commission, the Protected Areas Strategy, and the Parks and Wilderness Plan for the 90s. The new provincial land use strategy will incorporate three levels of planning: provincial, regional and community. The provincial level will set principles, goals and policies. Negotiation processes will take place at a regional level to determine broad land use allocations. Specific resource and environmental issues will be managed at the community level.[5]

Land suitability

Land use is complicated by divergent values. Some people value land as a commodity, something with economic value that can be used productively, bought and sold. Others value land as part of a life sustaining ecosystem. The dynamics of public opinion and economics in British Columbia influence the distribution of land among competing uses.

A given area of land may be used for a variety of purposes such as agriculture, timber, wildlife, recreation, or conservation (Figure 2.64). However, not all ecosystems have equal capability to satisfy a particular human value, and most are better suited for some uses than others (Box 2.17). Although multiple uses are often possible, we still have to make some difficult choices.

Decisions about land allocation are critical for both the environment and society. These decisions require knowledge of how much land is suitable for each use. The province is

Box 2.17

Capability and suitability

Capability	the maximum potential of an ecosystem to provide a desirable value (e.g.. agriculture, forest, recreation)
Suitability	the ability of an ecosystem to accommodate a specific use

developing several compatible computer information bases (Box 2.18). These will give users access to all land information sources in the provincial government. The data will allow users to consider the many variables involved and make decisions that take into account trade-offs between land capability, environmental impacts, and divergent values. About 40% of the province has been mapped through the Terrain Resource Information Management program.

Figure 2.64

Some lands can support many uses

Most of the land in B.C. is capable of supporting forests. Some of the forested land is also suitable for grazing, but grazing can take place on some non-forested lands as well. The suitability of the land for wildlife depends on the species. Many kinds of land are suitable for recreation, roads and other human developments. Land suitable for crops is limited. (This figure does not indicate actual proportions of land suitable for various uses.)

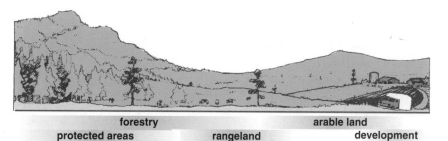

forestry		arable land
protected areas	rangeland	development
	recreation	

Land for forests

British Columbia has approximately 51.8 million hectares of productive forest land (Figure 2.65). Of this, 43.3 million ha is provincial Crown land managed by the Ministry of Forests for timber production, recreation, and wildlife. Of this land, about half is considered suitable for growing commercially harvestable timber. The rest is either inaccessible, non-commercial forest types, environmentally sensitive, or not satisfactorily restocked (NSR).[9] Productive forest land does not include all land with trees; some range land also has forest cover, and many protected areas are forested. About two thirds of B.C. is capable of growing some kind of forest.

Land for range

Rangeland is land that has usable forage for grazing and includes grasslands, open forests, forested range, wet meadows, and pasture land. There are approximately 10 million hectares of rangeland in British Columbia. Most of this area can only support a low density of grazing animals (Figure 2.66). The vast majority of rangeland is Crown range administered by the Ministry of Forests.[8]

In addition to providing forage for cattle, many rangeland areas also support significant wildlife populations such as big horn sheep and elk. The potential for the province's rangeland to support an increased level of grazing is not known. However in some areas, particularly the semi-arid interior, the ability of the ecosystem to support grazing has been approached if not exceeded.

Land for agriculture

Very little of the land in British Columbia (less than 1%) has the combination of soil and climate to support a wide variety of crops. The regions with the largest area of land being used for crops are found in the Boreal Plains and the Central Interior. The Lower Mainland has the best climate and soils, and generates more than half the dollar value of farm sales. Even in the Lower Mainland only 4% of the land is good farm land.[10]

Because of British Columbia's mountainous terrain, farm land is usually limited to the valleys, where farming must compete for space with other uses. In order to protect the limited agricultural land, the Agricultural Land Commission Act has created an Agricultural Land Reserve (ALR). Lands under this classification are not to be used for other purposes - though some golf course use has been

Figure 2.65
Forest land

Forested land includes productive forests, parks and rangeland. Productive forests cover over half of B.C., but less than half of the sites have a good or medium capability for the growth of trees.[8,9]

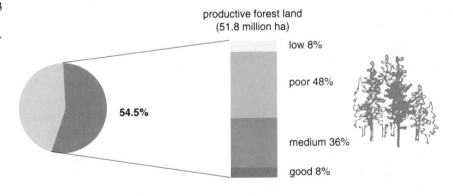

productive forest land
(51.8 million ha)

54.5%

low 8%

poor 48%

medium 36%

good 8%

Figure 2.66
Range land

The better the rangeland, the less area is required for each head of cattle for one month (AUM). In good areas cattle need 2 ha each per month, and in medium areas 5. Most of the rangeland in B.C. is of low productivity, so that more than 10 ha are required per AUM.[8]

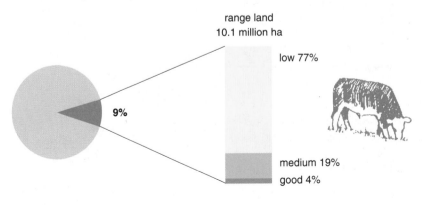

range land
10.1 million ha

9%

low 77%

medium 19%

good 4%

Figure 2.67
Agricultural Land Reserves

Only a small proportion of the land in British Columbia is suitable for agriculture, and only a small proportion of this is capable of producing high crop yields.[8]

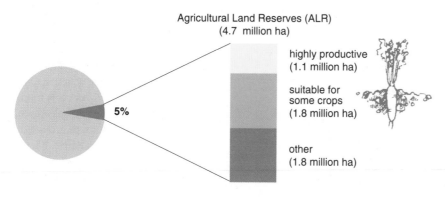

Agricultural Land Reserves (ALR)
(4.7 million ha)

5%

highly productive
(1.1 million ha)

suitable for
some crops
(1.8 million ha)

other
(1.8 million ha)

permitted within the ALR. Almost all of B.C.'s high quality farm land has been placed in the ALR. Of the 4.7 million ha (5% of B.C.) in the ALR, about a quarter is considered prime agricultural land (Figure 2.67).

Mineral and petroleum resources

About 5% of the province's subsurface land has a high potential for mineral and coal production, while another 20% has moderate potential. In addition, extensive areas of the province's northeast and offshore areas have a potential for petroleum production. Some of this potential has already been realized, but many known deposits remain undeveloped.[8]

Only a small area of land is actually used for the extraction of minerals and petroleum resources. Of the 74,000 hectares of land that have been set aside for mining activity, 31,000 hectares have been disturbed. Regulations call for site restoration, but most of the restoration cannot logically take place while the mine is still active. Just over a quarter (27%) of the disturbed area has been restored (Figure 2.68).[11]

Access and utilities

Access corridors and utilities are built for several purposes: roads for public transport, forestry, and mining; reservoirs for hydroelectric energy; and transmission lines and pipelines for conveying energy from where it's produced to where it's needed. These are all important to people, as they provide settlement, employment and development opportunities. They also have social and environmental costs. Both costs and benefits are large relative to the extremely small area of land (less than half a percent)[8] that is actually used. We do not have good quantitative data on how access and utilities affect the state of the environment.

Figure 2.68
Land disturbed by mines and restored

The area disturbed by coal and metal mines has been increasing, but the proportion restored has remained fairly constant over the last decade. Mines generally are not restored until they become inactive.[11]

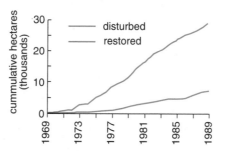

Roads are vital commercial links and provide access and employment for local communities. They are necessary for economic development based on timber harvesting and mining, and the development and maintenance of remote energy sources. Roads also provide access to remote lands for recreation. This access and development leads to a variety of impacts. Direct impacts of construction, such as damage to streams, are largely controlled through a variety of guidelines. It is more difficult to control indirect impacts, such as interruption of habitat continuity and the disturbance or hunting of wildlife. Good road access to an area often leads to further development. This means that both the positive and negative impacts of roads tend to increase over time.

Reservoirs, transmission lines, and pipelines provide for the flow of energy to society. Reservoirs can also have benefits in terms of flood control. The costs of this energy supply include the loss of land, and impacts on fish, wildlife, traditional ways of life, and the visual quality of the landscape. Valuable valley bottom wildlife habitat and agricultural or forest land is lost when flooded by reservoirs. (Examples of the impact of reservoirs are discussed for the Sub Boreal Interior and the Southern Interior Mountains in the Ecoprovinces section). Modified water courses and changed flow patterns affect fish spawning, rearing and migration. Transmission lines and their cleared rights-of-way can affect the aesthetics of wilderness and residential areas.

Linear developments, especially roads, are easier to build in valley bottoms and flat lands. Potential land use conflicts are greatest in these areas because they are valuable for wildlife, urban development, agriculture and other activities.

Recreation

Many different sorts of land can be used for recreation. Some people value wilderness areas; others prefer the amenities available in high use areas. In any case the suitability of the land for recreational use is directly linked to the state of the natural resources. Recreation and tourism are highly dependent on the quality of the environment, including the land, air, water, plants and animals. Tourism is affected by diminishing wilderness and old growth forests, marine and fresh water pollution, degradation of fish and wildlife habitat or populations, and degradation of visual resources. At the same time, tourism can be a major contributor of stress to the environment.

There is the need for better information on the relationship between tourism and environment. In view of this, the World Tourism Organization has undertaken an initiative to develop a set of internationally accepted indicators to improve understanding about tourism's links with, and impacts on the environment.[12]

Human settlements

About 80% of B.C.'s population lives in urban areas. The Georgia Depression has many large urban areas which house 88% of the population in this ecoprovince. Even in the remote areas over half the people are urban based (Figure 2.69).

The major urban centres in British Columbia are growing in area (Figure 2.70). Between 1981 and 1986, Kamloops had the highest rate of growth in area (8.5%). However, its total area only increased by 5 km², compared to 34 km² and 17 km² for the Vancouver and Victoria areas, respectively.[14] In a large urban centre even a small percent growth can lead to a large increase in total area. Nevertheless, smaller urban centres are absorbing rural land at a faster rate than large ones, through the sprawl of shopping areas, transport networks, and low density housing.

Because human settlements tend to centre on the most productive land, the permanent removal of land from agricultural use is a concern. The amount of prime agricultural land converted by the major urban areas in B.C. has declined since the implemen-

Figure 2.69
People in urban areas

In most ecoprovinces over half the population lives in urban areas. The two extremes are the Georgia Depression with almost 90% urban, and the Northern Boreal Plains with no urban areas.[14]

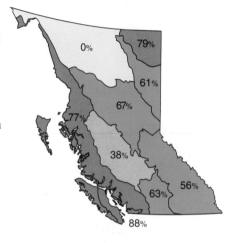

Figure 2.70
Growth of urban areas

Although Kamloops had the highest rate of growth in land area between 1981 and 1986; Vancouver and Victoria (GVRD and CRD) showed the greatest increases in area.[14]

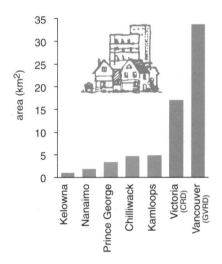

tation of the Agricultural Land Reserve in 1974. Between 1981 and 1986 1,244 hectares of prime agricultural land were converted to urban use (Figure 2.71). Just under half of this land was in the Lower Fraser Valley (see Georgia Depression section).[15]

Human settlements also encroach onto flood plains as the flat land is easy to build on. Not only are these developments prone to flood damage, but they

also limit the biodiversity of river systems. Reduction of wetlands can further impact surface and groundwater quality.

On a local scale urban sprawl can be a major concern. For example, in the Lower Mainland more than 600 hectares of rural lands are converted to urban uses every year.[17] Urban sprawl is an inefficient use of land and diverts capital for roads, parks, schools, and other services from city centres to their margins. Increased areas of pavement can affect the hydrology of ground and surface waters. Water quality, plant species, fish and wildlife are all threatened by pollution from runoff. Urban sprawl also generates long commutes that consume large amounts of fossil fuel and impact air quality.

The impact of settlements goes far beyond the land area actually covered by housing and other amenities. The people in settled areas require resources that are garnered from the surrounding lands, whether these are land-based products such as food, timber, minerals and energy, or whether they are land as a place for recreation and renewal.

We have a growing population that needs to live somewhere. The challenge is to either contain population growth or improve our planning so that the impacts of urban growth are minimized.

Figure 2.71
Urbanization of farm land

Between 1981 and 1986 a total of 6,778 hectares of rural land was converted to urban use in B.C. Of this, 1,244 ha (18%) was prime agricultural land.[15]

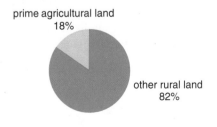

How we change the land

Prior to the arrival of Europeans, native use of the land had little impact on the ecosystems of B.C. European settlers brought in new attitudes and technologies that had more impact on the land. Higher per capita impacts were multiplied by the much higher rate of population growth that came with the new technologies. The industrial age has brought new sets of demands and new impacts. We have become aware that many of these impacts reduce the ability of the land to support human development and natural ecosystems. Sustainable use of renewable resources depends on protecting the productive capacity of the land.

Productivity and productive capacity

Human activities affect the yield of products from the land such as crops, wildlife, and timber— products that we value. They are like the golden eggs in the fable about the goose who laid golden eggs. The rate of laying golden eggs is the *productivity* of the land. A goose that is very well cared for will produce eggs at close to its maximum potential rate.

Humans can also change what the land is capable of producing under ideal conditions. This is the *productive capacity*. Although the difference between productivity and productive capacity is very important in the long term, it is often difficult to discriminate between the two.

In general, we assume that the land produces as much as it is capable of, but this varies with many other factors including weather, losses to insects and disease, and competition by other

Box 2.19
Soil and recovery

The ability of nature to recover from damage depends on the time scale of the processes that have been affected. Vegetation can regrow in a few years if the land has not been degraded. Even old growth forests can regrow in a few hundred years. However, if the soil is lost, recovery is much slower. Lost soil takes a very long time to replace, several hundred years per centimetre. It would take thousands of years to generate enough soil for productive growth.

> "The 'ecological footprint' of urban living extends to other countries, and is a continuing draw on global resources"
>
> Bill Rees, 1992[18]

species (Figure 2.72).

Productive capacity can be reduced in many ways: erosion, compaction, reduction of the organic matter and litter layers, salinization, and changes to the water table. Other changes, such as improved drainage and enhancement of soils can increase the productive capability. The ability of the land to recover from damage is closely related to its productive capacity (Box 2.19).

Loss in productive capacity is sometimes called land degradation. Land degradation is often slow, and therefore difficult to notice. Reduction in productivity due to land degradation is also difficult to recognize because these changes are small compared to the changes caused by other influences, such as climatic variation. Reductions in productivity may also be temporarily masked by increased inputs such as pesticides or fertilizers.[19] The amount of money spent on fertilizer in B.C. has been increasing since 1971, but it is not clear how much of the increase is due to inflation and price increases.[13] Household use of fertilizers and pesticides is on the high side of average compared to the other provinces in Canada (Figure 2.73).

In order to measure soil degradation processes, twenty-two Agricultural Benchmark Sites are being established across Canada, including one in the Fraser Valley. These sites, representing various agro-ecosystems, will serve as environmental indicators for major agricultural practices through long term monitoring. Soil loss rates under different crops are also being measured in both the Peace River region (since 1980) and the lower Fraser Valley (since 1989). Data from these long term studies are not yet available.

Figure 2.72
Factors affecting land productivity

Factors that affect productivity include pest and fire frequencies, water availability and quality, erosion, toxic contaminants, fertilizers, and invasive species. Climate change can influence many of these factors.

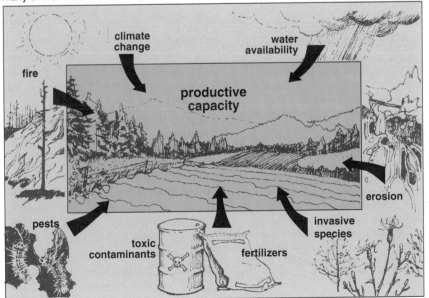

Erosion and degradation impacts are being addressed through a variety of programs. The B.C. Ministry of Forests has issued guidelines that deal with erosion control related to road construction and logging.[21] A National Soil Conservation Program has been established to help farmers adopt crop and animal production systems that are both environmentally sound and economically viable. In British Columbia the program began in 1990 and continues until 1994. Fifteen producer conservation groups have been formed to carry out education and demonstration projects to help farmers implement soil conservation practices. As a further commitment to soil conservation, the Green Plan for Agriculture is currently being developed for British Columbia (see discussion of conservation farming in the Northern ecoprovinces section).

Waste and contaminants

Most (64%) residential, commercial and industrial solid wastes in B.C. are disposed in landfills. There are 236 landfills, of which 60% are expected to reach capacity by the year 2000 if generation rates are not slowed. Only 2% of the land area in B.C. is suitable for landfill siting. Most suitable sites are located in valley bottoms and are in strong competition with other users.[16]

While the majority of landfill materials are relatively innocuous, some have the potential to endanger the environment and human health. Leachates can cause serious local water pollution. Landfill sites can also create wildlife problems. They attract such species as grizzly bear and black bear. This leads to problem encounters with people. Landfills also support large scavenger populations, such as ravens, which reduce other bird populations through predation.

Contaminants can be introduced to the environment through discharges, landfills, storage, and transport of hazardous materials. They can find their way into the soil, groundwater, and adjacent water bodies, sometimes affecting critical habitat or prospective protected areas. The geology and soils

Figure 2.73

Household use of fertilizers and pesticides

Households with lawns, yards, or gardens may use more chemicals on a given area than commercial growers. Although the amounts are not known, about half the households in B.C. (with outdoor space) use fertilizers and about a quarter use pesticides.[13]

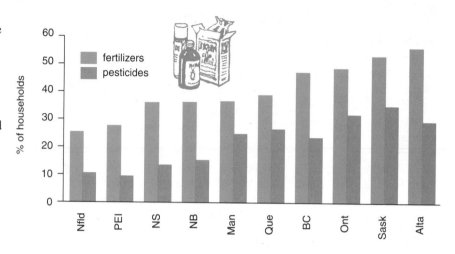

of a region determine the capacity of the land to absorb contaminants of various types. In some areas the soil chemistry can buffer the impacts of contaminants, whereas in other areas porous ground can lead to rapid pollution of soils and groundwater.[22]

Many contaminants, such as inorganic metals, occur naturally and can have negative effects on people (Box 2.20). Distinguishing these from those pollutants released by humans is an intricate and painstaking business.

Contamination of soils and water have

Box 2.20

Radon, a natural contaminant

Radon is a naturally occurring product of the radioactive decay of uranium. It is found as a colourless, odourless gas in soil, rocks and groundwater. The amount of radon in homes is determined by the uranium content of the surrounding ground, how tightly packed the ground is, and the construction of the house. Radon seeps through dirt floors, through cracks in concrete walls or floors, and around drains and joints. If an area is not well ventilated radon concentrations can build up to a level that is a health hazard. Current studies are investigating the link between radon exposures in homes and cancer. Radon has been found in some areas of the Southern Interior Ecoprovince, but is a very localized concern.

been with us since the early days of industrial activity in the province. Historic contamination through dumps, leaks, spills, and discharges has resulted in a backlog of sites requiring cleanup. Site contamination has become a major environmental issue, particularly where former industrial or commercial lands are being redeveloped. Liability for cleanup costs and for possible future claims relating to development is recognized as a prime concern. Purchasers and lending institutions are increasingly aware of problems associated with contaminated sites. This may trigger a site investigation and discovery of a contaminated site (Figure 2.74).[24]

National criteria have been developed for the assessment and remediation of contaminated sites.[25,26] New legislation is being drafted to deal effectively with contaminated sites, and a provincial registry of contaminated sites is planned.

In British Columbia about 3,100 companies and municipalities hold provincial permits which allow them to discharge wastes into the environment. Of these, a small but significant number (about 3%) fail to comply with all the conditions of their permits. Provincial legislation provides for quick action in situations that pose an

Figure 2.74

Awareness of site contamination

In Victoria, the number of files on sites suspected of contamination or undergoing cleanup has been growing. This increase in file numbers is primarily due to increased awareness as well as increased land exchanges and redevelopment. The actual number of contaminated sites in the province is not known.[23]

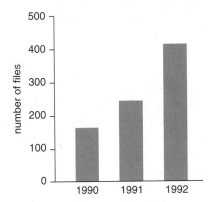

immediate threat. Where there is no acute threat, negotiation is tried first, then prosecution. Since the publication of Non-Compliance Pollution Concern lists in December, 1991, 95 cases (about 50%) have been satisfactorily dealt with and removed from the list.[27]

Special or hazardous wastes are those which need special handling or disposal practices to eliminate or reduce the hazards they pose to people or the environment. They may be poisonous, chemically reactive, corrosive or flammable; or they may increase the incidence of cancer, birth defects or undesirable changes in the cells of living organisms. On escape to the environment they may accumulate throughout the food chain. The danger of improper handling is of particular concern when wastes are being transported. In 1991 almost 200,000 tonnes were moved to, from, or around B.C. [28]

Although most industrial special wastes are appropriately managed, many small firms and households improperly dispose of pesticides, herbicides, paints, varnishes, cleansers, oil, batteries, and disinfectants. These hazardous wastes end up in the same places as regular wastes.[29]

A number of initiatives have been undertaken to develop a waste manage-ment strategy for B.C. The provincial strategy (Box 2.21) for the management of solid waste adopts the "3R" hierarchy to **R**educe, **R**euse and **R**ecycle before materials even enter the waste stream. After these opportunities have been optimized there are two further measures; to **R**ecover energy and materials from the collected wastes and to dispose of the **R**esidue in an environmentally sound manner.

The overall target of the provincial waste management strategy is a 50% reduction in the waste generated per capita by the year 2000. Achieving this goal will require a remoulding of our societal values. Some social change has already been achieved, as shown by participation in various recycling programs (Figure 2.75). Tire collection and battery recycling both surpassed the target capture rates (of 90% and 99.8% respectively) within the first year of the program. Further progress will be monitored through a province wide computerized Municipal Solid Waste Tracking System.[30]

Box 2.21

Provincial targets for waste disposal[30]

Municipal Solid	• reduce by 50% per capita by the year 2000
Waste (garbage)	• special targets for tires, oil, batteries, beverage containers, packaging, litter, etc.
Hazardous wastes	• reduce by 50% by 2000
	• legislation, regulations, and an effective management system for hazardous household wastes by 1993
	• a comprehensive hazardous waste management system by 2000
Contaminated Sites	• an inventory, site assessment criteria, remediation criteria, and legislation
Biomedical Wastes	• a comprehensive system and regulations by 1995
Pesticides	• reduce by 25% by 2000
	• research, information, training, monitoring

Figure 2.75

Use of curbside recycling

Curbside recycling is now available to more than half of the urban households in Canada. Where it is available, most people use it. BC ranks among the top provinces in both availability and use of recycling. This figure shows recycling of metal cans — the numbers are similar for glass and paper, and a little less for plastic.[13]

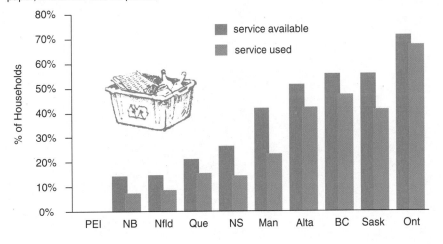

Pesticides

Pesticides are used in many areas of life where there is a need to control undesirable organisms. In British Columbia about 120 different pesticides are used for agriculture, forestry, domestic and industrial purposes (Figure 2.76). Wood preservatives make up the largest amount of pesticide sales by weight (75%) followed by herbicides, fungicides, and insecticides.[31] The area of agricultural land treated with pesticides increased between 1971 and 1986 (Figure 2.77). About $22 million worth of pesticides are applied in British Columbia each year.[29]

The use of pesticides has been an environmental topic for several decades, and concerns remain about both human health and environmental impacts (Box 2.22). Effects on habitats

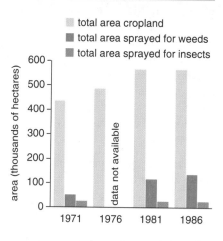

Figure 2.77

Agricultural pesticides in use[14]

- total area cropland
- total area sprayed for weeds
- total area sprayed for insects

area (thousands of hectares)

1971 1976 1981 1986

and biodiversity are growing concerns. The public is also concerned about involuntary exposure to pesticides and the potential consequences to human health. The major source of involuntary exposure is through residues on food or in water, though pesticide application may also lead to direct contact. In the Fraser Valley various Federal and Provincial agencies have monitored drinking water for pesticides. None of the pesticide concentrations exceeded Canadian drinking water guidelines though some exceeded Canadian guidelines for the protection of aquatic life (see Georgia Depression, Ecoprovinces section).[32]

Pesticide residues in both imported and domestically grown foods are tested by

several agencies, although Health and Welfare Canada has the main responsibility for ensuring food safety. These agencies routinely collect samples of food suspected of pesticide residue each year, and test them for up to 130 pesticides. Sampling during 1989 and 1990 showed that no meat or dairy products exceeded acceptable limits, though approximately 2-4% of the suspected samples of produce contained unacceptable pesticide residues (Figure 2.78).

Not all pesticides are of equal concern. Some degrade rapidly, or remain where they are put. Others persist and/or move around to where they are not wanted, and many persistent pesticides accumulate in living organisms. Because of our dependence on pesticides, and the variability in their impacts, regulation has to be specific and complex.

The Province has been developing new directions for pest management. The strategic objectives include promotion of integrated pest management, regulation of sale and use of pesticides, monitoring of effects on humans and the environment, and public information concerning risks, opportunities, and alternatives associated with pesticide use.

Integrated pest management (IPM) is an ecological approach to suppressing pest populations. All available control techniques (including pesticides) are consolidated in a unified program to avoid economic damage and adverse effects on human health and the environment. The government has supported the development of IPM strategies in agriculture for more than 20 years.

Integrated control of orchard mites was initiated in the Okanagan Valley in the mid-1960s. Careful monitoring of harmful plant-feeding mites and beneficial predatory mites resulted in more effective control with fewer pesticide applications. At the present time, IPM programs are available for at least 15 different tree fruit, berry and vegetable crops in B.C. (Box 2.23). Almost half of the cranberries, carrots and onions and more than a third of the

Box 2.22

Gypsy moth spray program

During the spring of 1992 some areas of the Lower Mainland were sprayed with a biological pesticide to combat the risk of an Asian gypsy moth infestation. The Order In Council for the spray program was issued on the condition that a study of the health effects of the spray be undertaken by an impartial agency. The University Hospital at U.B.C. submitted a comprehensive report that indicated no significant health effects.[7]

Figure 2.76

Pesticide use under permit

The use of pesticides on Crown land has stabilized or decreased in the last few years.[31]

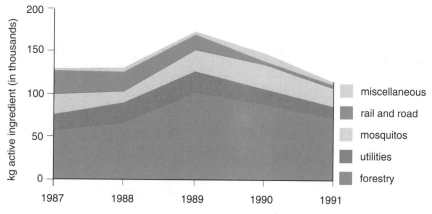

kg active ingredient (in thousands)

1987 1988 1989 1990 1991

- miscellaneous
- rail and road
- mosquitos
- utilities
- forestry

Figure 2.78
Pesticide residues in fruits and vegetables

Fruits and vegetables suspected of exposure to pesticides are tested to determine the level of pesticide residue. Of these a small percent exceeded legally acceptable limits in 1989 and 1990. The limits are designed to ensure that people can eat foods for a lifetime without suffering adverse effects.[33]

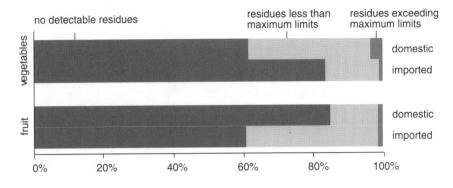

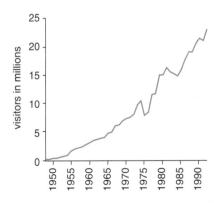

Box 2.23
No coddling for the codling moth

That worm in the middle of an apple is probably a codling moth larva. The codling moth is a major pest of apples and pears, and its control requires multiple applications of pesticide annually. The sterile insect release (SIR) program is raising massive numbers of sterile male codling moths. When these sterile males mate with wild females, no offspring are produced, and the pest population gradually dies out.[34]

the herbicides that they would have used 10 years ago.[39]

potatoes in B.C. are grown under IPM programs. The most successful adoption of IPM has been the B.C. greenhouse vegetable industry, where the use of biological control agents has reduced the use of insecticides by as much as 90%.[36]

Several government agencies have also promoted the biological control of weeds in B.C. To date, four different biological control agents have been established on knapweed in interior grasslands. In total, 42 species of biological control agents have been introduced to control 15 species of weeds in this province.[37]

Use of herbicides to control vegetation under transmission lines is being replaced or supplemented by other methods. For example, grasses and legumes are planted as forage for cattle and wildlife, which help keep the vegetation low through their grazing activity. In some areas sheep are introduced to maintain low growth, and physical controls such as pruning, cutting, and clearing are used. Where chemicals are used, they are often applied selectively - capsules are injected into stems, or a wipe-on herbicide is applied to freshly cut stems to prevent re-sprouting. In the past year B.C. Hydro used only 20% of

The province has developed more stringent regulation of pesticide use. Pesticide permits are now issued by regional offices rather than through Victoria. A new program for training and certifying farmers and commercial users who use federally restricted pesticides has been introduced over the last three years. Since January 1, 1992, all purchasers and users of federally-restricted pesticides have been required to be certified pesticide applicators. The federal and provincial governments are also conducting detailed monitoring surveys, and researching ways of reducing pesticide residues in groundwater in areas of intensive farming.

Protected areas

There are many different types of protected areas in British Columbia. They include networks of parks, wildlife areas, recreation areas, wilderness areas, ecological reserves and more. They range in size from vast wilderness expanses to tiny pockets of nature a few hectares in size.

The purposes of protected areas are diverse. They not only satisfy cultural and recreational needs of the public (Figure 2.79) but also contribute to achieving environmental goals. They allow essential ecological processes to operate, help maintain biological diversity, and promote the sustainable use of the natural environment. Protected areas are an essential component of the province's land use strategy.

Figure 2.79
Visits to protected areas

Protected areas provide a distinctive range of outdoor recreation opportunities. Visits to B.C. park sites have increased rapidly in the last few decades. Visits to the national parks have increased in a similar way.[41]

Figure 2.80

Area protected over time

Before 1920 little attention was paid to protecting ecosystems. Early parks were largely motivated by scenic values. Since the 1970s more and more attention has been focused on ecosystem protection.[14]

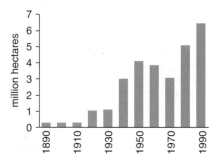

How much should we protect?

Over the last century there has been increasing attention and commitment to the creation of parks and other protected areas (Figure 2.80).

There are currently well over 800 protected areas in British Columbia, encompassing over 6 million hectares, owned or managed by various levels of government or non-government organizations. These areas cover about 6.5% of the total area of land and

freshwater in the province. British Columbia compares well with the other provinces in Canada with respect to protected areas (Figure 2.81).

To promote conservation of natural ecosystems, various national and international organizations (Brundtland Commission, World Conservation Union, World Wildlife Fund Canada and the Canadian federal government) have promoted conservation targets.[37] The Green Plan commits the federal government to the target of setting aside 12% of Canada's total area as protected space. In addition to making direct contributions, the federal government is charged with encouraging and facilitating other institutions and individuals to make such contributions.

What ecosystems are being protected?

British Columbia is composed of a wide variety of ecologically distinct units, each with characteristic species and features. It would be easy to satisfy the 12% goal of area protected by simply taking the least desirable areas and designating them as "pro-

Figure 2.82

Area protected by ecoprovince

All Ecoprovinces except the Taiga Plains and Boreal Plains include protected* areas. Several ecoprovinces are approaching the general guideline of 12% of the area protected.[40]

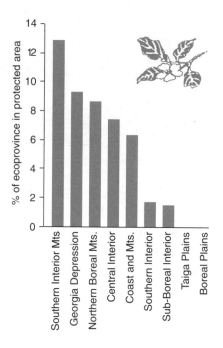

tected". That is not the intent. A great deal of effort is being made to ensure that the protection is evenly distributed among ecoprovinces, and among the smaller ecological units (ecosections) within each ecoprovince (Figure 2.82). The Protected Areas Strategy is designed to protect all major ecosystems and most unique characteristics.

Although some ecological units have a significant proportion of their area in protected area status, significant gaps remain in achieving full representation. Marine ecosystems, wetlands, grasslands and mid- and low-elevation forested ecosystems are, to a large extent, poorly represented in existing protected areas.[6] For example, less than 0.1% of the marine environment is in protected areas, and the level of protection afforded to marine areas that are protected may be insufficient.[35]

The Province is developing a database that contains detailed information on the ecological characteristics of each protected area. When it is complete it will be possible to tell whether the protected areas include all unique or uncommon elements of all ecosystems.

Figure 2.81

Area protected in each province

Only Alberta has a higher percentage protected* area than B.C. The Northwest Territories has a much larger area protected, more than any province.[40]

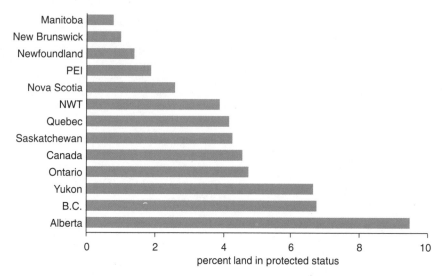

* Protected areas are as defined by IUCN categories I and II (see Table 2.7).

How protected is protected?

The term "protected area" can cover a wide range of use levels ranging from no use by man, even for recreation, to uses that are compatible with conservation and recreation objectives. The International Union for the Conservation of Nature (IUCN) has developed a framework for classifying protected areas according to their objectives and the degree of human intervention permitted (Table 2.7). Protected areas in B.C. have been classified according to this system. Some areas of B.C. have a good representation of what IUCN considers "strictly protected reserves", whereas other areas, such as the north and the interior, have fewer of these (Figure 2.83).

Setting aside an area does not in itself ensure its long-term protection or maintenance of its ecological integrity. The ecological integrity of a natural area determines its capacity to withstand internal and external stresses or threats. Protected areas face many threats, such as: recreation and tourism pressures; oil spills; introduction of exotic species; incompatible land uses within and next to protected areas, and global climate change.

Many protected areas in the province are too small to maintain their ecological integrity and biological diversity.

Figure 2.83
Distribution of strictly protected areas

The percent area that is strictly protected (IUCN Levels I and II, see Table 2.7) has been calculated for various parts of BC. This map shows detail at the ecosection level, that is subunits of the ecoprovinces.[40]

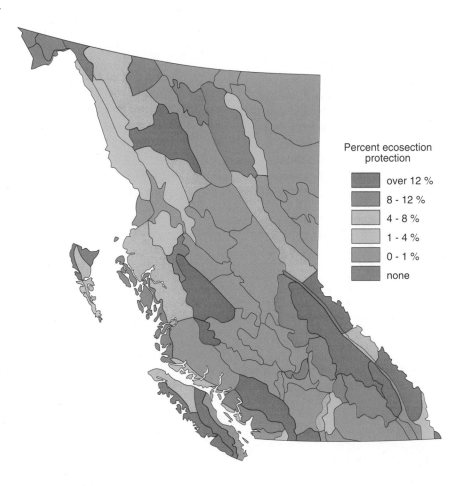

Percent ecosection protection

- over 12 %
- 8 - 12 %
- 4 - 8 %
- 1 - 4 %
- 0 - 1 %
- none

Table 2.7
Classification framework for protected areas.

The International Union for the Conservation of Nature (IUCN) has developed a framework for classifying protected areas according to the degree of human intervention. Categories I and II are considered to be strictly protected.[4]

Category	Example
I	Scientific Reserves Wilderness Areas
II	National and Provincial Parks (and equivalents)
III	Natural Monuments
IV	Habitat and Wildlife Management Areas
V	Protected Landscapes and Seascapes

No protected area in the province is large enough to include all critical habitat requirements of wide ranging mammal species such as grizzly bears, caribou and wolves. Many are becoming "islands in a sea of development", their ecological integrity threatened by fragmentation and encroachment by other land uses such as hydroelectric development, logging, or mining.

Maintaining ecological integrity requires attention to a variety of factors including the size of the protected area, corridors connecting protected areas, management policies and the compatibility of adjacent land uses. A number of specific actions, such as management plans and zoning frameworks, include these factors to enhance the ability of protected areas to maintain natural features and ecological processes.

Many programs, many sponsors

The types of protected area programs in the province vary considerably. A myriad of different programs are in place, with assorted implications in terms of legal securement, function and management objectives (Table 2.8). Federal protected area holdings account for 10% of the total area protected in the province, whereas the array of provincial mechanisms

"A new protected areas strategy will double parks and wilderness areas in B.C. by the year 2000".

Premier Mike Harcourt, May 1992 [38]

account for no less than 89%. Although many programs contribute to the protection of ecosystems, two agencies, B.C. Parks and the Canadian Parks Service, are the stewards for nearly 97% of the total protected area in the province.

Several natural features in British Columbia have been recognized by international conservation programs. Among these are two World Heritage Sites, Ninstints on Anthony Island and part of the Rocky Mountains. One national wildlife area (Alaksen) has been designated as a Wetland of International Importance under the Ramsar Convention. The Canadian Wildlife Service has prepared a list of migratory bird sanctuaries, and is identifying potential Western Hemisphere Shorebird Network sites.

Completing the protected areas system

In 1992 the provincial government committed itself to doubling the existing protected area system by the year 2000. To assist in achieving this goal, the provincial government announced a Protected Areas Strategy for the province, which identified 112 large and 72 small study areas and a time table for their resolution.[20] This is a starting point only and additional study areas will be identified. The overall strategy for protected areas will include federal, provincial and regional initiatives such as parks, wildlife areas, ecological reserves, wilderness areas, and migratory bird sanctuaries.

Also in 1992, the provincial government established the Commission on Resources and Environment (CORE) to oversee land use planning and move the province on a path towards a sustainable society. One of CORE's principal tasks will be to help determine what areas should be designated for protected area status based on their natural, cultural and recreation values. In the same year the B.C. Ministry of Forests released an Old Growth Strategy that recommends the protection of important old growth forest sites within a network of protected areas.

At the federal level, some natural regions remain unrepresented in Canada's National Parks system. The federal government is cooperating with the provincial protected areas strategy to pursue options for establishing three new terrestrial parks plus several National Marine Parks in B.C.

The ecosystem management approach adopted by the protected areas strategy means that protection and sustainability concerns will go beyond the boundaries of the protected areas. The intent is not only to protect areas within the 12% target, but to promote sustainable management in the other 88% of our province. Other processes are in place to deal with the other 88%, including (but not limited to) Land Resource Management Planning (LRMP), Local Resource Use Plans (LRUPs), Forest Practices Code revisions, and regional land use planning under the Commission on Resources and Environment (CORE).

Table 2.8

British Columbia's mosaic of protected areas

There are many types of protected areas in British Columbia. Protected areas vary considerably in their scope, size, objectives, management policies and the level of legislative protection they afford. For example, Provincial Parks and Recreation Areas protect representative landscapes, outstanding natural features and wilderness areas, offer recreation and tourism opportunities and encourage scientific research and education. Ecological Reserves are protected natural areas where human intervention is kept to a minimum and natural change proceeds unimpeded. The goals of Forest Service Wilderness Areas range from preservation of natural landscapes to recreation and limited resource use. Wildlife Management Areas focus on the protection of wildlife species.[40]

Program	Legislation	areas	hectares
National Park / National Marine Park	National Parks Act[1]	6	630,200
Ecological Reserves	Ecological Reserve Act	131	land - 107,321 water - 51,433
Provincial Parks/Recreation	Park Act	393	[2]5,240,294
Regional Parks	Regional Park Act	78	13,384
Wilderness Conservancy	Environment and Land Use Act	1	131,523
Wilderness Areas	Forests Act	4	130,000
Migratory Bird Sanctuaries	Migratory Bird Convention Act[1]	7	3,091
National Wildlife Areas	Canada Wildlife Act[1]	5	2,301
Wildlife Management Areas	Wildlife Act	11	19,299
Creston Valley Wildlife Area	Creston Valley Wildlife Act	1	6,900
NGO Lands[3]	Nature Trust of B.C.	188	12,500
	Nature Conservancy of Canada	17	22,054
	Ducks Unlimited, Canada[4]	748	27,754
	Total	1,592	6,398,054

[1] Federal Act
[2] includes some marine waters
[3] incomplete
[4] land may be secured by government agencies

Conclusions

Although land is a fundamental component of our ecosystems, it is often taken for granted. Our focus has traditionally been on the resources obtained from the land, rather than the land base itself. The land base changes slowly, so it is difficult to notice impacts, except in local dramatic circumstances. Recovery, if possible, is likely to be both slow and expensive.

There are many things we don't know about the state of the land in B.C. Not much is known about changes to the productive capacity, such as soil fertility, or the effect of fertilizer and pesticide use on the land. There aren't even accurate data on the amounts being applied. Contamination of land is also very difficult to sample on a provincial scale. Compared to air or water there is little mixing, so regional scale sampling of contaminants requires more effort.

However, there is significant good news. The Agricultural Land Reserve is keeping virtually all our best agricultural land from other uses. As a society we are developing much better waste management practices that include less waste production and better handling of special wastes. The Province is also well along the way to developing a computer based land information base which will enable resource managers to keep track of land attributes, develop sustainable and coordinated management plans, and monitor land use change. Finally, the evolving protected areas strategy is tackling a difficult problem in a systematic (ecosystematic!) way.

None of this will be easy, nor will it be accomplished without effort and resources. The underlying question is whether our society will continue to promote and support environmental responsibility over the long time frame necessary for sustaining our land base.

Ecoprovinces

The ecoprovince classification for British Columbia has been developed to provide a systematic view of the ecological relationships of the province. The hierarchy of ecosections, ecoregions and ecoprovinces offer a framework for interpreting complex interrelationships between land, air, water and biota including humans.

The hierarchical system allows us to better understand an area in several different contexts: local, regional, provincial and national. Ideally, much of the data to measure and track British Columbia's State of the Environment would be collected and/or compiled within this hierarchy. However, few such data sets exist. Though informa-

tion has been gathered to address particular problems in particular locations, it's generally very difficult to see the overall regional picture. At those sites where data have been collected, monitoring often has not continued for long enough to reveal trends. Nevertheless, some valuable information is available for each

Figure 3.1

Topics discussed in each ecoprovince

Although many issues are relevant in each ecoprovince, a number of topics have been selected. This map indicates the location of the topics discussed on the following pages.

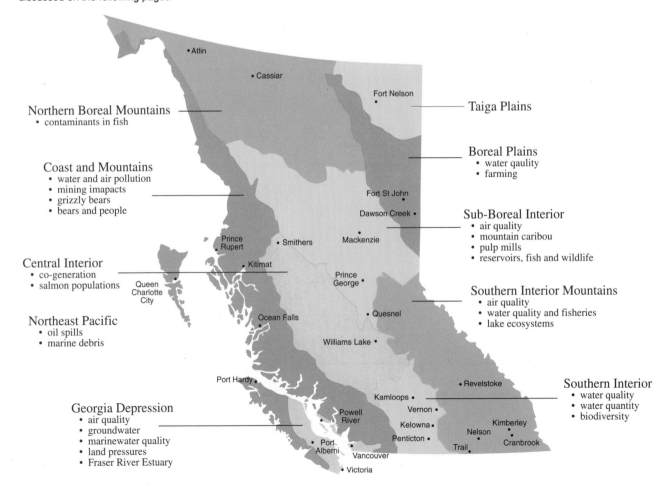

ecoprovince. This information is not always in the form of graphs of indicators, changing over time. Rather, it is often anecdotal information, describing a past, present or future environmental problem.

What follows is a series of short summaries of a range of ecoprovincial topics across British Columbia (Figure 3.1). These examples were chosen to provide an overview of **some** of the more important topics within each ecoprovince. The topics were selected based on feedback from citizens to the B.C. Round Table on the Environment and the Economy during their tour of the province in 1991, and the knowledge of local environmental scientists and planners. Space and information constraints do not permit each ecoprovince to be described comprehensively. Taken together, however, these case examples provide a deeper understanding of how the general environmental topics discussed in the previous sections are manifested locally. They also point to some of the topics requiring more systematic monitoring and management in the future.

The Northern Boreal Mountains, Taiga Plains and Boreal Plains

This section is made up of the three northernmost ecoprovinces: the Northern Boreal Mountains, the Boreal Plains, and the Taiga Plains (Figure 3.2).[1,2] The Northern Boreal Mountains form the western portion of this area, consisting of extensive mountains and plateaus, separated by wide valleys and lowlands. Much of the habitat here consists of high pine, fir or spruce forests, and rolling alpine tundra. The Northern Boreal Mountains are one of the few relatively pristine mountain landscapes left anywhere, almost entirely without

Figure 3.2
The northern ecoprovinces

The three northern ecoprovinces cover more than one quarter of the area of B.C., but house only 1.7% of the total population. [1,2,5]

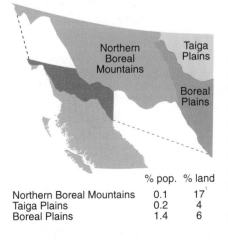

	% pop.	% land
Northern Boreal Mountains	0.1	17
Taiga Plains	0.2	4
Boreal Plains	1.4	6

Figure 3.3
Descriptive statistics

The Northern Boreal Mountains, Taiga Plains and Boreal Plains constitute 27.4% of B.C.'s land area, and are home to 1.7% of B.C.'s population.[4,5]

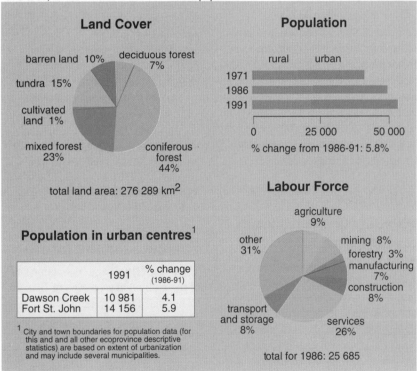

Land Cover

barren land 10%
deciduous forest 7%
tundra 15%
cultivated land 1%
mixed forest 23%
coniferous forest 44%

total land area: 276 289 km^2

Population

rural urban
1971
1986
1991

0   25 000   50 000

% change from 1986-91: 5.8%

Population in urban centres[1]

	1991	% change (1986-91)
Dawson Creek	10 981	4.1
Fort St. John	14 156	5.9

[1] City and town boundaries for population data (for this and and all other ecoprovince descriptive statistics) are based on extent of urbanization and may include several municipalities.

Labour Force

agriculture 9%
other 31%
mining 8%
forestry 3%
manufacturing 7%
construction 8%
transport and storage 8%
services 26%

total for 1986: 25 685

commercial timber value. About 8.7% of the land in the Northern Boreal Mountains is protected area.[3] As one moves east, the landscape becomes dominated by level plateaus and lowlands. The plateaus, plains and prairies of the Boreal Plains contain aspen parkland, spruce forests and some sub-alpine fir. The Taiga Plains is mainly composed of flat lowlands that support muskeg and black-and- white spruce forests. There are no large protected areas in either the Boreal Plains or the Taiga Plains ecoprovinces, though there are some small ecological reserves. Precipitation in these three ecoprovinces is evenly distributed throughout the mild summers and long cold winters. A general description of the ecoprovince is found in Figure 3.3.

Charlie Lake

managing the future by learning about the past

Charlie Lake is located 8 km away from Fort St. John and serves both as a fresh water supply and important recreational site for Fort St. John's 14,000 residents. A study completed in 1985 suggested the overall water quality of Charlie Lake was very poor and in need of improvement. High loadings of phosphorous had created a nutrient enriched (over-fertilized) condition in the lake. The results from preliminary tests also suggested the lake had higher than normal levels of fecal coliforms.[6] The Ministry of Environment, Lands, and Parks is examining sediment cores sampled from the lake bottom in order to understand the historical nutrient changes in Charlie Lake. The Ministry of Health has undertaken fecal coliform studies of the lake to learn more about its current coliform level. In addition, the Province is completing studies to find the major sources of nutrients, herbicides and pesticides within the watershed. The results from these studies will be used to help develop a management strategy for Charlie Lake and its watershed.

Atlin Lake

where are the contaminants coming from?

The liver of burbot is a traditional aboriginal food. In 1991, scientists found high toxaphene levels in the burbot livers collected from Atlin Lake. As a result, the B.C. portion of Atlin Lake was covered by a general advisory, from the local Medical Health Officer, against eating any fish liver. Toxaphene is used as a pesticide, and may bioaccumulate in living organisms, primarily in the fatty tissues. It may be harmful to fish consumers in high doses.

How did toxaphene enter the Atlin Lake ecosystem? Although it is now banned in Canada, other countries continue to use the pesticide. In 1992, considerable effort was undertaken by federal, territorial, provincial, and aboriginal groups to expand fish-testing programs. These programs aimed both to assess potential point sources of contaminants and to evaluate the possibility that winds from distant sources transported the toxaphene. Scientists surveyed other lakes in the area for toxaphene concentrations. Results indicate that at least some of the toxaphene in Atlin Lake must have come from distant sources. However, scientists still do not know if long range atmospheric transport is a major contributing source of toxaphene. PCB's and other pesticides which are chemically similar to toxaphene, and are known to be transported worldwide via the atmosphere, were found in Atlin Lake burbot livers in much lower levels than toxaphene. Another possibility is that there are as yet unidentified sources of toxaphene that have leaked into Atlin and other Yukon River systems lakes.

Farming for the future

The Peace River region contains half of the cultivated crop area of British Columbia. The major crops are grains, oilseeds, and fineseeds. Soil erosion is a serious problem here, partly due to current agricultural practices. The long, gentle slopes of the Peace River region show many visible examples of damage by water erosion from farm runoff. Erosion may partially or completely remove the topsoil as well as the subsoil. This results in low water holding capacity, poor nutrient content, low organic matter and poor cultivation potential. These factors all contribute to poorer farm production and increased sediment loads in rivers. It is difficult to assess the extent and severity of past soil erosion since rates of erosion vary with climate, topography and soil surface features. However, all of the nearly 400,000 ha of grain growing land in the Peace River region is classified as high erosion risk, and 15% already shows evidence of erosion.[7] Soil erosion could ultimately seriously affect the environment and economy of the Peace River region.

The Canada - British Columbia Soil Conservation Program promotes conservation farming to reduce soil erosion in an economical manner for the Peace River grain and oilseed producers. Conservation farming means cultivating the land in a manner that provides long term ecological sustainability, by reducing tillage, increasing winter soil cover with crop residues, and improving the use of green manures. These practices are being encouraged through various incentives and technology and information transfer programs.

It is difficult to estimate to what degree conservation farming will actually be incorporated into future farming practices. However, a recent survey indicated that a majority of Peace River producers plan to purchase conservation tillage equipment in the future; and that they believe their economic status would be maintained or improved by adopting soil conservation management practices.

Sub-Boreal Interior

Located in the north-central portion of the province, this landscape includes broad level plateaus bordered by the Skeena, Omineca and Rocky Mountains.[1,2] Much of this area lies in the rainshadow of the Coastal Mountains, though the mountains receive higher amounts of precipitation. Precipitation is more or less evenly distributed throughout the year. The summers are warm, but in winter cold Arctic air frequently covers the ecoprovince. The Sub-Boreal Interior hosts dense conifer forests, alpine tundra, scattered wetlands, and some deciduous forests. Less than 2% of this ecoprovince is designated as protected area.[3] Prince George is the largest city in the ecoprovince and the fifth largest city in British Columbia. A general description of the ecoprovince is provided in Figure 3.4.

Air quality

reducing total reduced sulphur in Prince George

In general the air quality of this ecoprovince is very good, but in the Prince George area air quality has been a public concern for many years. In 1981, the Ambient Air Monitoring Program, a joint government/industry program, began monitoring the levels of total reduced sulphur (TRS) and sulphur dioxide in the Prince George area. TRS is responsible for an unpleasant odour, to which humans are very sensitive. However, the presence of TRS in the air is not considered to be a health risk. TRS levels now only exceed permissible levels one half to one third as frequently as they did in the early 1980s (Figure 3.5).

The improvement in air quality is largely due to emission reduction programs carried out in 1989 and 1990 at Prince George's pulp mills. As pulp mills install more emission reduction

Figure 3.4
Descriptive statistics

The Sub-Boreal Interior constitutes 14.0 % of B.C.'s land area, and is home to 3.9 % of B.C.'s population.[4,5]

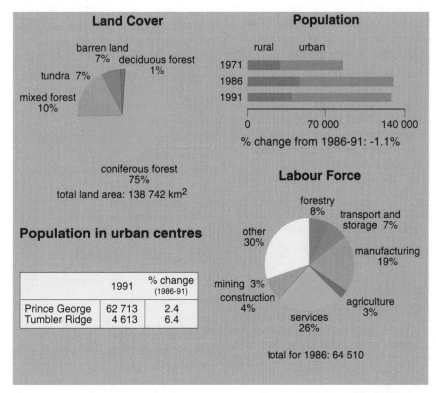

systems, further reductions in TRS levels will occur. Currently, the largest TRS emission source is not the pulp mill stacks but the pulp mill effluent ponds. To reduce TRS levels, many pulp mills are now treating their effluent with a method called steam stripping. This involves injecting steam through concentrated effluents before these effluents are sent to biological treatment ponds. The steam strips out the foul smelling TRS which

Figure 3.5
TRS in Prince George

In the late 1970s, levels of total reduced sulphur (TRS) exceeded objectives 60 - 70% of the time; now they exceed objectives 10 - 30% of the time.[8]

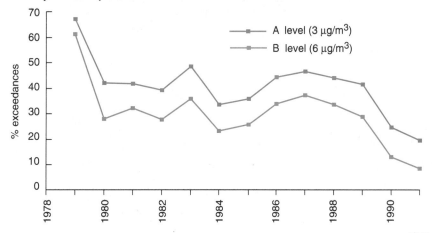

is then directed to an incinerator where it is burned (oxidized) to less odorous SO_2 (sulphur dioxide).

Mountain Caribou
managing with uncertainty

There are two distinct groups of caribou in British Columbia: Northern Caribou and Mountain Caribou (Figure 3.6). Managing caribou and their habitat is difficult. It requires an understanding of how factors such as hunting, poaching, predation, climate, food and habitat availability affect caribou populations today, and how those factors may change in the future. Compared to the Northern Caribou population (12,000), there are relatively few Mountain Caribou (1,700). The Ministry of Environment, Lands, and Parks has "blue listed" the Mountain Caribou, which means it is considered sensitive or vulnerable.

Figure 3.6
Caribou in B.C.

Mountain caribou are found in southeast British Columbia. In the winter months, they live in high elevations and feed mainly on lichens.[9]

Understanding the factors that affect the Mountain Caribou population is essential for their long term survival. Though some factors are consistently important (e.g. the availability of lichen as food), other factors change in importance across different groups. For example, a recent study on the Quesnel Highlands population found that predation by wolves reduced the caribou population during the late 1980s. Fragmentation of habitat, as

well as actual habitat loss, is a major concern.

In 1988, wildlife groups, government agencies, and the local forest industry established a cooperative venture called Mountain Caribou in Managed Forests (MCMF). The goal of the program is to develop integrated solutions that allow both loggers and caribou to share the mountains. After four years of research from this program, there are no definite answers. However, the MCMF has concluded that clearcuts in critical caribou habitat regions are not compatible with the long term survival of caribou populations. They also agreed that maintaining suitable habitat is better than trying to recreate habitat lost to clearcutting. The MCMF is now developing a provincial strategy for caribou habitat management.

Pulp mill effluents
a new monitoring approach

In 1987, the six pulp mills in the mid to upper Fraser River Basin (Figure 3.7) discharged more than 500,000 m³ of effluent per day. These mills are the primary contributors to the 38-fold increase in total wastewater discharges to the upper Fraser between 1965 and 1985. There was a 12-fold increase in the Thompson River during the same period. Although the effluent receives secondary treatment, the treated effluent still represents several possible threats to ecosystems. These include wastewater impacts on overwintering juvenile salmon near dilution zones, effects on fish during low flow periods, effects on bird reproduction, and the cumulative long term impacts of toxic, persistent compounds on various biota including humans.[10,11,12]

To address some of these concerns, the federal and various provincial governments facilitated workshops to promote the development of a consistent approach to pulp and paper mill monitoring in Canada. In 1989, Environment Canada selected the upper Fraser River as the area to carry out a major pilot study called Environmental Effects Monitoring (EEM). EEM provides an objective basis for

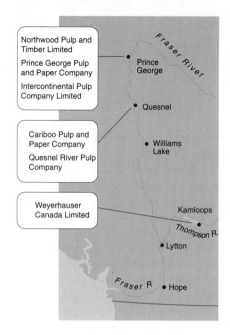

Figure 3.7
Pulp mill effluents

Northwood Pulp and Timber Limited
Prince George Pulp and Paper Company
Intercontinental Pulp Company Limited
Cariboo Pulp and Paper Company
Quesnel River Pulp Company
Weyerhauser Canada Limited

Fraser River
Prince George
Quesnel
Williams Lake
Kamloops
Thompson R.
Lytton
Fraser R
Hope

demonstrating the effectiveness of corrective action and helps to identify areas where improvements are needed.

The 1989 program provided a well integrated assessment of pulp mill effluent characteristics and their environmental impacts on the upper Fraser. The study recommended that further research be carried out to assess the medium to long term responses of aquatic biota in the Fraser River. Major improvements are being made to pulp mill effluent quality (see Water chapter). EEM offers a method to assess the actual environmental response to these improvements. EEM serves as a successful model that can being applied under the Pulp and Paper Effluent Regulations of the Federal Fisheries Act (1992).[13]

The Williston Reservoir
the benefit of electricity but ...

Williston Lake Reservoir is the largest body of fresh water in British Columbia. The reservoir has a surface area of 1736 km², more than two-thirds the size of Greater Vancouver. It was formed in 1968 by the completion of B.C. Hydro's Bennett Dam on the Peace River, about 90 km west of Fort St. John. Discharges from the lake pass from the station downstream to Dinosaur Lake, through the Peace Canyon Dam/Generating Station and then enter the Peace River. The generating station provides more than 6.3 % of B.C.'s annual energy needs.

...loss of fish and wildlife

There was an environmental cost associated with the creation of the reservoir. The flooding of several river valleys eliminated large areas of prime winter wildlife range, important migration corridors and fisheries habitat. Reduced catch rates by anglers indicated declines in some species of sports fish such as rainbow trout and Arctic grayling. Reservoir flooding also forced the relocation of Native villages and ultimately destroyed a traditional way of life for those in the region. The dam also lessened river flow fluctuations at the Peace-Athabasca Delta in Alberta. This reduced the quantity and quality of fish and wildlife habitat, which depended on seasonal flooding.[14]

In 1988, B.C. Hydro and B.C. Environment agreed to cooperate in a fish and wildlife compensation program for the Williston Reservoir watershed. B.C. Hydro agreed to establish two $5 million funds - one for fisheries and one for wildlife, with the annual interest from each fund used to finance activities associated with the management of fish and wildlife in the watershed area. For the short term, the general emphasis of these programs is to determine the present state of the habitat and populations of these resources, and to implement management measures to ensure their sustainability. Over the long-term, some projects will be undertaken to enhance fish and wildlife populations which were reduced due to the establishment of the reservoir.

Central Interior

This ecoprovince is east of the Coast Mountains, between the Fraser Basin and the Thompson Plateau.[1,2] The extensive plateau system includes the flat to rolling Chilcotin, Cariboo, and Nechako plateaus. While the area lies in the Coastal Mountain rainshadow, it is still influenced by the moderating flow of Pacific air. Here the climate consists of cold winters and warm summers. There are seven vegetation zones in the Central Interior ecoprovince, ranging from dry sagebrush/grasslands to dense lodgepole pine forests across most of the plateau's uplands. There are many wetlands and small lakes. About 7.5% of the Central Interior is currently protected area.[3] The Central Interior accounts for about 2% of British Columbia's population. Williams Lake is the largest community. A general description of the ecoprovince is provided in Figure 3.8.

Williams Lake

generating electricity from wood waste

Smoke is a problem in many interior B.C. communities, particularly those with active forest products industries.

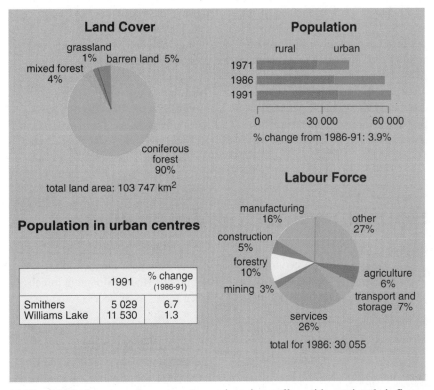

Figure 3.8
Descriptive statistics

The Central Interior constitutes 10.5 % of B.C.'s land area, and is home to 1.9 % of B.C.'s population.[4,5]

Land Cover
grassland 1%
barren land 5%
mixed forest 4%
coniferous forest 90%
total land area: 103 747 km²

Population
rural urban
1971
1986
1991
0   30 000   60 000
% change from 1986-91: 3.9%

Population in urban centres

	1991	% change (1986-91)
Smithers	5 029	6.7
Williams Lake	11 530	1.3

Labour Force
manufacturing 16%
construction 5%
forestry 10%
mining 3%
services 26%
other 27%
agriculture 6%
transport and storage 7%
total for 1986: 30 055

Williams Lake is one such community. Five saw mills and a plywood mill, located near the city, presently burn their waste residues in wood waste burners. The resulting gases and fly ash are released to the atmosphere. The city is in a river valley with restricted air flow. Together, these factors often combine to produce degraded local air quality. And, in the ecoprovince as a whole, smoke is the primary air quality issue.

It is difficult to maintain satisfactory

air quality in Williams Lake with the types of wood waste burners currently in use. Consequently, they are being replaced with a single wood-burning boiler. This new facility, scheduled to begin operation in 1993, will use wood residues to produce electricity. Because wood wastes will be burned in the new facility under a more controlled environment, greater emissions control will be possible for contaminants such as fly ash, and smoke problems should be reduced. However, high temperature combustion in the boiler could result in increased emissions of other air contaminants, such as nitrogen oxides. Atmospheric monitoring has already been initiated to establish background levels of NO_2, ozone, and total suspended particulates as a basis for assessing the overall atmospheric impact of the new plant.

Horsefly River sockeye

a fast rising stock

Historically the Horsefly River was one of the great salmon spawning areas of the Fraser River watershed. In the late 1800s, this river reportedly produced many millions of juvenile salmon. But this came to an abrupt end in the fall of 1898 when a dam, constructed to permit gold mining, dried up the Quesnel River and prevented salmon from returning to spawn in the Horsefly River. Two

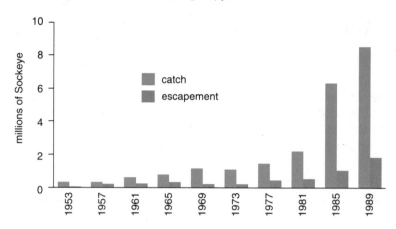

Figure 3.9
Horsefly River sockeye

Catch and escapement data for dominant (peak) years.[15]

years later the mining operation was abandoned, but the dam remained. A fish pass was built in 1903, and by 1909 the salmon run appeared to be restored, with around 4 million sockeye reported on the Horsefly River spawning grounds.

However, disaster soon struck the fish stocks again, this time in 1913-14 during construction of the Fraser Canyon railway line. Waste rock falling into the river, and a massive rock slide at Hells Gate, severely restricted the migration of salmon. In 1941 there were only 1,100 fish recorded on the Horsefly River spawning grounds. Then, in 1945, the Hells Gate fishway was opened, and

3,000 spawning sockeye were observed at the Horsefly River grounds.

Since then, the size of the Horsefly River sockeye stock has grown steadily and especially rapidly in the past decade (Figure 3.9). The Department of Fisheries and Oceans has carefully controlled catches to allow the stock to rebuild. In 1989 nearly 1.9 million sockeye returned to the Horsefly River to spawn and another 8.4 million were caught by fishermen. This indicates that the stock has now been restored to levels recorded in the early 1900s.

Southern Interior Mountains

This ecoprovince spans the vast mountain ranges of southeastern British Columbia, including the Columbia Mountains in the north and the Rocky Mountains to the east.[1,2] Here, the western slopes of the mountains receive considerable amounts of precipitation, and snowfall is heavy

during the winter months. In the winter, the Rocky Mountain trench often serves as an access route for outbreaks of cold, arctic air, but in the summer months this area has warm, clear weather. Dense conifer forests are common in the Southern Interior Mountains ecoprovince, although dry forests do occupy the southern valleys, and alpine tundra and barren rock are found near mountain summits. Of all the B.C. ecoprovinces, this one

contains the highest proportion of protected land (13.6%), with the majority of the protected areas in the high mountains.[3]

About 5% of the population of British Columbia resides in the Southern Interior Mountains ecoprovince. Cranbrook and Nelson are the two largest communities. A general description of the ecoprovince is provided in Figure 3.10.

Figure 3.10
Descriptive statistics

The Southern Interior Mountains ecoprovince constitutes 13.6 % of B.C.'s land area, and is home to 4.9 % of B.C.'s population.[4,5]

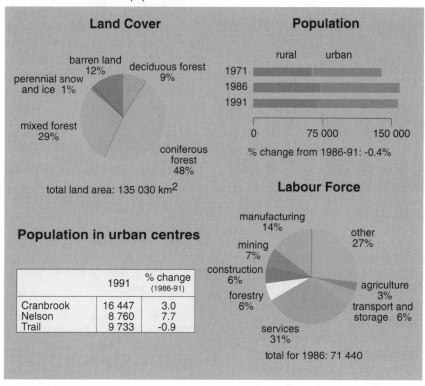

Population in urban centres

	1991	% change (1986-91)
Cranbrook	16 447	3.0
Nelson	8 760	7.7
Trail	9 733	-0.9

Air quality

managing lead and sulphur emissions

Air quality across this ecoprovince is generally very good, but human activities have had major impacts in certain locations. For example, for nearly 100 years, Trail has been a smelting and industrial centre. During this time, atmospheric emissions from the smelters have reduced local and regional air quality, affecting human health, agricultural crops, and nearby ecosystems. Continuous efforts to improve smelter technologies have improved local and regional air quality. However, sulphur emissions remain a concern today, as do emissions of lead, zinc, and particulates.

In the early 1980s atmospheric sulphur dioxide (SO_2) declined as a result of lower emissions from the modernization of the zinc smelter (Figure 3.11). Sulphur dioxide levels in Trail are also controlled by a system, unique in British Columbia, where smelting operations are curtailed during periods

of poor air quality. Further SO_2 emission reductions are expected with replacement of the old smelter, scheduled for completion in 1995.

The lead smelter is currently a major source of metals and particulates to the surrounding atmosphere. Lead levels in Trail's atmosphere are about twice that

measured in Vancouver prior to the removal of lead from gasoline. As shown in Figure 3.12, atmospheric lead levels have declined since the zinc plant was upgraded in the early 1980s. Still, lead concentrations are higher than background levels, as illustrated by measurements for 1974 and 1987 - years in which the smelters were not fully operational due to labour strikes.

In 1969, horses grazing in the vicinity of the smelter were found to have severe lead poisoning. In a subsequent study, children near and downwind of the smelter were found to have high blood lead levels when compared with children living in the control community of Nelson. A more recent study found that average blood lead levels for children living in Trail dropped almost 40% from 1975 to 1992 (Figure 3.13). Blood lead levels in Trail children are still more than double the average for Vancouver children (5.3 µg/dL - micrograms per tenth of a litre)). They are comparable with levels found in children living in Rouyn-Noranda, a Quebec smelter town (11.1 µg/dL).[18,19] Individuals identified as having elevated blood levels receive intervention and appropriate follow-up.

The discovery that some children in Trail have elevated blood lead levels has raised concerns regarding smelter lead emissions. To identify pathways of human exposure to lead, and to recommend corrective actions, the

Figure 3.11
Sulphur dioxide in Trail air

Ambient concentrations at Butler Park. Horizontal line designates limit specified in provincial waste discharge permit.[16,17]

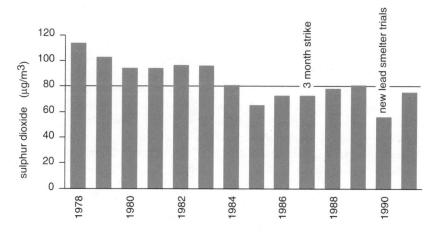

Figure 3.12

Lead in Trail air

Ambient concentrations of lead in suspended particulates at Butler park. Shading indicates B.C. Pollution Control Objectives for lead (1.0 to 2.5 µg/m³).[16,17]

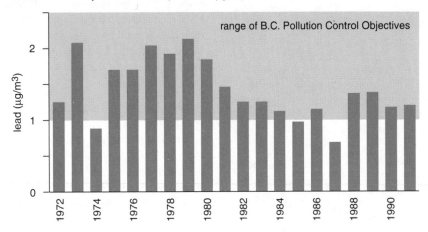

Trail Blood Lead Task Force was established in 1990. The Task Force has discovered a correlation between blood lead levels in children and lead levels in soil and house dust. The Task Force is now investigating remediation measures to complement actions at the smelter to reduce lead emissions.

Figure 3.13

Average blood lead levels

Data are for children living in Trail.[20]

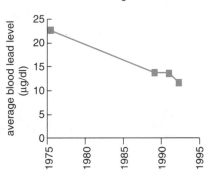

Lower Columbia River

fisheries and water quality

The lower Columbia River is an important water body. It serves as a source of drinking water, and supports a productive fishery. It also receives treated and untreated industrial and municipal wastes. Water quality is generally good, but there are a number of human activities that affect water quality and fish populations.

Water plunging over the Hugh Keenleyside Dam becomes supersaturated with air, and fish downstream can suffer from gas bubbles in their tissues, much like divers who experience the bends. Further downstream is a bleached kraft pulp mill at Castlegar which historically discharged untreated effluent directly to the river. Recent studies there found organochlorine compounds (e.g. dioxins, furans) in fish tissues, prompting officials to issue an advisory restricting human consumption of Mountain and Lake whitefish. Dioxin and furan contamination was significantly lower in the two main sportfish species, rainbow trout and yellow walleye. Under recently approved plans, the pulpmill is to install state-of-the-art pollution control technology by 1993. However, because organochlorine compounds are persistent and reside in river sediments, there may be some delay before these compounds disappear from Columbia River fish.

At Trail, slag and effluents discharged to the river from smelting and industrial activities contain mercury and many other contaminants. In the past, this resulted in mercury contamination of yellow walleye. A health advisory, in effect since 1988, restricted consumption of this fish to one meal a week; this advisory has recently been lifted. Under modernization plans, the lead smelter will no longer be dis-

charging slag or untreated effluents to the river by the end of 1995. But again, mercury and other contaminants already in the ecosystem are expected to persist for a considerable period.

To monitor the environmental state of the river, the Columbia River Integrated Environmental Monitoring Program was established in 1990 to examine water and sediment quality, and aquatic biota.

Kootenay Lake kokanee -

how to restore the food chain?

Kootenay Lake has been renowned for its trophy rainbow trout, known as Gerrard rainbow, which can reach up to 16 kg. Fishing resorts in the vicinity draw visitors from around the world and contribute significantly to the local economy.

Gerrard trout are at the top of a food chain that includes kokanee salmon, microscopic animals (zooplankton), and microscopic plants (phytoplankton) (Figure 3.14). Since the mid 1970s, populations of kokanee salmon, the main food source for the Gerrard rainbow, have been declining (Figure 3.15). The cause lies at the very bottom of the food web, with a dwindling nutrient supply. The very existence of the kokanee population is now at risk, and if the kokanee disappear then the Gerrard rainbow population will be in serious trouble.

Figure 3.14

Impacts on Kootenay Lake

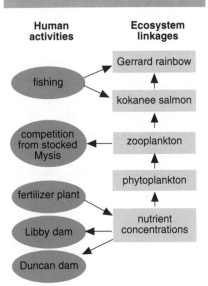

Figure 3.15

Kootenay Lake kokanee

Combined data for Kokanee salmon spawning in the Lardeau River and in Meadow Creek.[21]

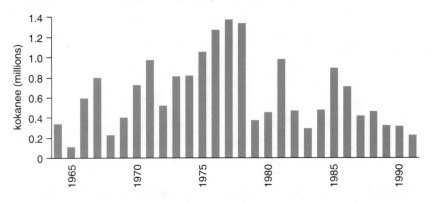

Figure 3.16

Phosphorus in Kootenay Lake [21,22]

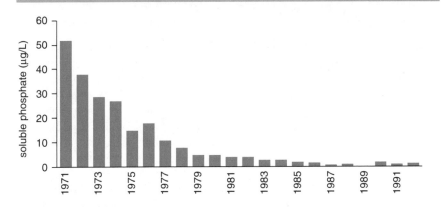

The simple explanation for the kokanee decline is a reduction in availability of phosphorus (Figure 3.16), the nutrient that controls phytoplankton growth in the lake (see Figure 3.14). Construction of the Duncan and Libby Dams reduced *natural* nutrient supplies to the lake, which is downstream. In 1975, pollution control measures at the fertilizer plant in Kimberley greatly reduced inputs of *man-made* phosphorus into Kootenay Lake. Now the annual supply of this critical nutrient is at its lowest level in recent geological history.

The next chapter in this story involves, ironically, an effort to increase fish productivity. Around the middle of this century, fisheries biologists introduced a small shrimp-like organism, *Mysis relicta*, into Kootenay Lake in an attempt to provide another food source for the Gerrard rainbow. Unfortunately, *Mysis* proved to be too large for juvenile trout to consume; more importantly, *Mysis* also feed on the same zooplankton as do the juvenile kokanee. During the period when Kootenay Lake was highly productive due to abundant phosphorus supplies, this competition was of little importance. But now that the lake is limited by this nutrient, *Mysis* competition is a serious additional threat to the lake's kokanee salmon. There is no known way to remove or eradicate *Mysis* from Kootenay Lake.

Faced with very few options, fisheries biologists started an experimental program in 1992 to artificially fertilize Kootenay Lake by the addition of phosphorous. It is hoped that this will increase food production for kokanee, and thereby also enhance the food supply for Gerrard trout.

Southern Interior

This is the southern-most portion of the interior plateau system, and includes the Okanagan and Thompson Basins and their surrounding uplands.[1,2] It lies in the rainshadow of the Coast and Cascade mountains, which, combined with the intrusion of warm air from the western Great Basin to the south, creates some of the warmest and driest areas in the province. Higher elevations receive regular rain and snowfall in the winter, but this is the mildest area in the interior. During the winter and early spring, outbreaks of cold, dense Arctic air occasionally occur because there is not an effective barrier to the north. Habitats include dry grasslands in the major valleys, ponderosa-pine and Douglas-fir forests, large deep lakes, and numerous small wetlands and rivers. About 1.8% of the land in this ecoprovince is protected as a park or wilderness area.[3]

Although this ecoprovince comprises only 4% of the total area of British Columbia, it is home to about 11% of B.C.'s population, and is growing rapidly. The largest cities in this ecoprovince are Kelowna and Kamloops. A general description of the ecoprovince is provided in Figure 3.17. (The section "Land under change" describes this ecoprovince in greater detail).

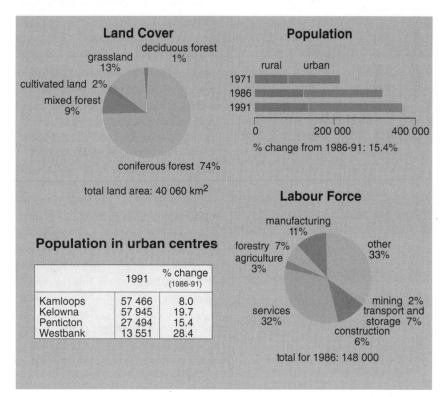

Figure 3.17

Descriptive statistics

The Southern Interior ecoprovince constitutes 4.0 % of B.C.'s land area, and is home to 11.2 % of B.C.'s population.[4,5]

Land Cover

deciduous forest 1%
grassland 13%
cultivated land 2%
mixed forest 9%
coniferous forest 74%

total land area: 40 060 km^2

Population

rural | urban
1971
1986
1991

0   200 000   400 000

% change from 1986-91: 15.4%

Population in urban centres

	1991	% change (1986-91)
Kamloops	57 466	8.0
Kelowna	57 945	19.7
Penticton	27 494	15.4
Westbank	13 551	28.4

Labour Force

manufacturing 11%
forestry 7%
agriculture 3%
other 33%
services 32%
mining 2%
transport and storage 7%
construction 6%

total for 1986: 148 000

Water managment

quantity and quality for both people and fish

Water is in great demand in the Southern Interior. It is used for drinking, irrigation, livestock watering, recreation and various industries. These uses affect both water quantity and water quality. Declines in water quantity and quality, in turn, affect both human uses and wildlife. There is the potential for serious water use conflicts as well as concern for long term fisheries and water management.

The water quality in the main valley lakes of the Okanagan Valley has been affected by human activity for many years. The main problem has been nutrient enrichment - overfertilization which causes algal blooms, oxygen losses and in extreme cases fish kills. Water quality problems came into sharp public focus in 1972 and brought about the Canada/B.C. Okanagan Basin Study.[23] This multi-agency study resulted in many changes, some of which improved water quality and

others of which slowed the rate of deterioration.[24,25] There has been a considerable expenditure of money by the B.C. provincial government and municipal agencies.[26] Where it has been possible to reduce nutrients from municipal sources or agricultural sources, water quality improved.[27,28,29] Where nutrient loadings increased, water quality has deteriorated somewhat.

The fish resource has seriously declined in Okanagan Lake over the past few decades. Stream escapements (numbers of spawning fish) dropped from 450,000 in 1971 to between 50,000 and 200,000 since 1974. The average escapement in seven Okanagan Lake tributaries is between 7% and 56% of their escapement objectives (Mission, Powers, Kelowna, lower Vernon, Peachland, Trepanier and Lambly Creeks). A variety of factors may be contributing to this, including water shortages, overfishing, habitat deterioration, disease, competition, predation, and natural population

fluctuations. An Okanagan Lake Tributaries Plan was completed in March 1992 to identify resource information in the Okanagan Basin, and recommend management strategies for the tributaries known to possess high fisheries values, particularly for kokanee and rainbow trout. The Plan recommends specific water quality and quantity measures for each of the seven streams. These measures include water reservations, the transfer or cancellation of unused water licences, improved management of water usage, and general water conservation to decrease water consumption.[30,31]

Osoyoos

pesticides in groundwater

The area around Osoyoos is intensively cultivated for orchard crops, on which chemicals are used to control pests. The geology in the area supports a plentiful groundwater supply, and there is concern that pesticides used on orchards leach into the groundwater and eventually seep into Osoyoos Lake. As much as 18 million litres of water seep into Osoyoos Lake from groundwater every day.[33] A preliminary survey of groundwater in the Osoyoos area in 1987 found five samples out of 22 to contain detectable levels of pesticides. Although these concentrations were low, their presence indicates that the possibility of groundwater contamination still exists, and monitoring programs have been recommended.[33]

Nitrates in groundwater

Nitrate contamination is evident throughout the Osoyoos area (see the Water chapter and Georgia Depression ecoprovince for more information). Wells located both inland and near the lakeshore have shown high levels of nitrate-nitrogen; 13 of 40 samples had concentrations equal to or greater than 10 ppm, the Canadian drinking water standard. This contamination is likely due to orchard fertilization.[34,35,36] Evidence for this conclusion comes from the Groundwater Quality

Monitoring and Assessment Program, which was initiated in 1983 to identify problem areas and concerns. The program recommended further sampling, and informing residents of the potential hazards of infants drinking water that has nitrate-nitrogen concentrations above 10 ppm.[36] Research is being done on "fertigation" - fertilization with irrigation water - which may reduce fertilizer input or allow fertilizer additions to be timed more closely to plant growth.

Groundwater was also tested north of Armstrong. In February of 1991, three of 26 samples were found to have concentrations above 10 mg/L. Residents using these wells were informed of the possible risks. A 1991 Water Quality Reconnaissance Study recommended increasing the awareness of landowners and water users of how to reduce water quality degradation, and constructing an observation well to monitor local groundwater quality.[40]

Water quality

The Hydraulic Creek watershed near Kelowna provides a source of drinking water for 3,500 people and irrigation water for about 2,000 hectares of agricultural land. The creek is also important for recreational fisheries; rainbow trout spawn in portions of the watercourse, and every year Hydraulic Lake is stocked with 12-15,000 hatchery trout. For years prior to 1984, low intensity selective logging took place in the watershed. In response to a mountain pine beetle outbreak that year, there was a dramatic increase in timber harvest to salvage the wood that was still marketable. This accelerated rate of harvest raised considerable concern about water quality degradation. Subsequent studies concluded that water quality, particularly turbidity (a measure of water clarity) and suspended solids (particles), was being greatly affected by the logging activity.[41,42] The response has been to set water quality objectives for four water quality characteristics, and design weekly monitoring to ensure compliance.

Biodiversity

The northern-most end of the Western Great Basin of North America extends into the southern end of the Okanagan Valley. The south Okanagan basin has low levels of precipitation, hot summers and mild winters. These semi-arid ecosystems are small in size, extremely fragile, and particularly sensitive to disturbance. They also provide habitat for some of the most diverse, unique and rare groupings of plant and animal species in Canada.[43] The south Okanagan basin has more candidate species (mammals, birds, reptiles and amphibians) for vulnerable, threatened and endangered status than any other ecoprovince in B.C. (see Table 2.3).[44]

Many south Okanagan species exist nowhere else in B.C., and some are not found anywhere else in Canada. For example, 15 of the 20 species of bats in Canada are present in the south Okanagan and two of these are found nowhere else in Canada. At least 125 invertebrate species found in the south Okanagan are found nowhere else in B.C., and 37 of these are found nowhere else in Canada.[43] The semi-arid habitats in the Lytton-Lillooet-Kamloops area are also rich in biological diversity.

A number of pressures threaten the biological diversity in the Southern Interior. Urbanization and agricultural development are responsible for much of the loss of natural habitat. Introduced species affect natural systems by competing with native species. There are many introduced species (aside from domesticated plants and animals) in this ecoprovince, including Eurasian watermilfoil (Box 3.1), purple loosestrife, diffuse knapweed, eastern fox squirrel, European starling, English sparrow, chukar, ring-necked pheasant and gulls.[43]

Domestic species can also affect the diversity of native biota. Domestic dogs and cats are of concern in some areas because they prey upon native animals species and are much more abundant than natural predators. Unnatural increases in native species have also occurred. Native raven populations in the Okanagan have increased substantially since 1965, mainly due to increasing quantities of dumped garbage.

A wide variety of stresses affect wildlife, many of them indirectly. Livestock grazing can disturb the soil, and reduce the water supply in

---

Box 3.1
Eurasian watermilfoil

Eurasian watermilfoil, an aquatic plant introduced to B.C. approximately 20 years ago, has had a substantial impact on aquatic systems. It spreads by fragments drifting downstream, and on boating equipment. Its fibrous root system and numerous stems form dense masses, which can hinder or prevent recreational use of lakes, streams and rivers. Native plant growth is displaced and fish spawning areas may be affected. Seven mainstream lakes and one upper elevation lake in the Okanagan Valley are infested with this water weed, affecting approximately 1,000 hectares of shoreline.[37] Once these plants are established, it is almost impossible to eradicate them. Continued action is therefore necessary to prevent further spread, and to allow water-based recreational activities. In 1991 approximately 150 hectares of Eurasian watermilfoil was treated by de-rooting or harvesting throughout the Okanagan Valley.

Eurasian watermilfoil was discovered in Shuswap Lake in 1981, and by 1987 it had spread upstream into south Mara Lake and the lower Shuswap River. The Shuswap infestation totalled 194 hectares in 1991.[38] A Shuswap control program began in 1981 to delay the spread within Shuswap Lake and into downstream waters. The program includes the installation of bottom barriers, diver dredging, derooting and harvesting. In 1992, no spread had been documented into Little Shuswap Lake or the South Thompson River. However, Eurasian watermilfoil has expanded to about 200 hectares of shoreline area, mainly in Salmon Arm of Shuswap Lake.[39] Eurasian watermilfoil has also been found in Nicola Lake.

In addition to helping minimize the further spread of Eurasian watermilfoil, the Ministry of Environment, Lands and Parks has been studying native insects which feed on this plant. The nuisance impact of this plant has been reduced in some situations by one particular insect, milfoil midge, which is now the subject of study to determine its potential as a biological control agent.

temporary water pools on which wildlife depend. Livestock grazing also reduces fuel for natural wildfires. Reduced wildfires (due to both livestock grazing and fire suppression) changes plant species composition in grasslands, thereby altering habitat. Timber harvesting reduces winter range for some species, as well as nesting or roosting habitats such as tree snags for cavity-nesting birds and bats.

Approximately 3000 deer are hit and killed on highways by vehicles each year in the Okanagan sub-region, as are many more smaller animals. High

numbers of road-kills also sustain predator populations at higher-than-usual numbers, by providing carcasses to scavenge. Also, new recreation technologies such as trail bikes, tricycles and quadracycles disturb sensitive wildlife as well as sensitive soils, allowing the invasion of noxious weeds.

As these pressures continue to grow, so does the likelihood that already-threatened species and habitats will disappear and more species and habitats will be placed at risk. In 1991, the region initiated the South

Okanagan Conservation Strategy. The strategy will develop and priorize management activities for the conservation of natural habitat and unique plants and animals in the area.[45]

On a smaller geographic scale, the city of Kelowna identified special natural features remaining within the city. These included rare, threatened or endangered plant communities and wildlife habitat, areas of significant biodiversity, and biological linkages between natural areas. The city also developed a framework for managing these special features.[46]

Coast and Mountains and Northeast Pacific

This section is comprised of two ecoprovinces: The Coast and Mountains and the Northeast Pacific.[1,2] Given the large marine component and the substantial overlap among issues, they are discussed together.

The Northeast Pacific ecoprovince is the ocean portion of B.C. west of the Continental Slope to the 200 mile limit off the west coast of Vancouver Island. It lies almost entirely in the ocean, where fresh water discharge from the coast dilutes the upper layers of the sea. From late autumn to early spring, winds arrive from the southeast or southwest. From late spring to early autumn, coastal winds are generally from the northwest. There are no urban areas, nor protected areas in this ecoprovince.

The Coast and Mountains ecoprovince extends along the length of British Columbia's coastline and encompasses the western edge of the province. It consists of the Coast Mountains, the Continental Shelf, and most of British Columbia's islands. The climate is determined mainly by the arrival of fronts carrying moist air off the Pacific Ocean, causing high rainfall as these fronts are lifted by the mountains. The landscape includes wave-beaten

shorelines, coastal plains and rugged ice-capped mountains cut by wide rivers, fiords and estuaries. Vegetation consists primarily of large temperate rainforests with alpine tundra on the mountain summits. About 6.4% of this ecoprovince is protected area.[3]
Although it covers 27.9% of British

Columbia's land mass, only 9% of British Columbia's population lives here. Prince Rupert and Terrace are the largest communities in this ecoprovince. A general description of the ecoprovince is provided in Figure 3.18.

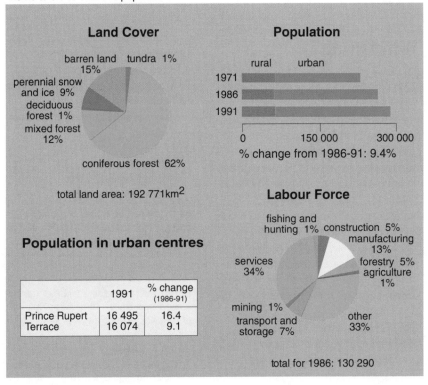

Figure 3.18
Descriptive statistics

The Coast and Mountains ecoprovince constitutes 27.9% % of B.C.'s land area, and is home to 9.0 % of B.C.'s population.[4,5]

Land Cover

barren land 15%
tundra 1%
perennial snow and ice 9%
deciduous forest 1%
mixed forest 12%
coniferous forest 62%

total land area: 192 771km²

Population

rural urban
1971
1986
1991
0   150 000   300 000
% change from 1986-91: 9.4%

Population in urban centres

	1991	% change (1986-91)
Prince Rupert	16 495	16.4
Terrace	16 074	9.1

Labour Force

fishing and hunting 1%
construction 5%
manufacturing 13%
forestry 5%
agriculture 1%
other 33%
mining 1%
transport and storage 7%
services 34%

total for 1986: 130 290

Kitimat

contamination of ecosystems

Kitimat is an important coastal city located near the mouth of the Kitimat River at the head of Douglas Channel. It is also the centre of an area of intensive resource use and concentrated industrial activity. Due to local topography, most of the environmental effects of these activities are concentrated within the long, steep sided inlet of Kitimat Arm and the Kitimat River Valley. Both are ecologically important areas supporting a wide variety of both resident and migratory wildlife. These animals have ecological, commercial and cultural importance. In recent years, concern has been expressed about the potential effects of industrial emissions and resource use on these species, and on the people who depend on them for traditional food, such as the Haisla Indians of Kitamaat Village.

The major sources of industrial effluents and emissions are the Alcan aluminum smelter, the Eurocan pulp and paper mill which produces unbleached Kraft paper, and the Methanex petrochemical plant which produces methanol and liquid ammonia from natural gas.

Contamination and environmental impacts attributable to industries in Kitimat have been measured over a broad area. Contaminants of most concern in the area include fluorides, dissolved aluminum, sulphur dioxide, dioxins, furans, and polycyclic aromatic hydrocarbons (PAHs). Chemical contamination attributable to Kitimat's industries has been measured in sediments as far as 16 km down the inlet. There are also concerns about taste and odour problems in the eulachon (an important native food fish) as a result of pulp mill discharges to the Kitimat River. The pulp mill is currently incorporating a number of modifications to their pulp process (e.g. turpentine recovery, improved brown stock washing) and is pursuing other options (e.g. condensate steam-stripping) to resolve this concern.

About 58 km² of Kitimat Arm are closed to shellfish harvesting due to dioxin and furan contamination. The most likely sources of dioxins and furans in the Arm are from the historical use of chlorophenols (a wood preservative no longer in widespread use) and chlorophenol contaminated wood chips. Elevated levels of PAHs have also been found in upper Kitimat Arm sediments. PAHs are a group of complex organic molecules, derived from combustion processes, that include both benign and carcinogenic compounds. Studies are underway to assess the fate and effects of PAHs in this region. The Province is also developing water quality objectives for PAHs.

Studies conducted by Alcan indicate that fluoride is currently the most significant pollutant of concern affecting the valley. Effects include disappearance of lichens and reduced tree growth (primarily hemlock) in some areas. Reductions in fluoride emission rates have reduced fluoride levels in leaf tissue (Figure 3.19). The effects on more sensitive species such as lichens and mosses are not consistently monitored, but preliminary information is encouraging. Fluoride also can affect animals. It is concentrated in their tissues, potentially interfering with physiological functions and altering bones and teeth. Skeletal fluoride concentrations in voles, shrews and mice are higher close to the mill, possibly due to fluoride deposition from the air. Some of the fluorides emitted are also potent greenhouse gases.

Emissions of fluoride to water are also a concern. In areas immediately adjacent to the smelter, levels of fluoride as high as 246 mg/L have been observed. Out of concern for aquatic organisms, the provincial government has set ambient water quality objectives for fluoride of no more than 1.5 mg/L. Water quality objectives also exist in Kitimat Arm for suspended solids, turbidity, cyanide, fluoride, ammonia, nitrite, pH, cadmium, copper, iron, and lead. In 1990, those objectives checked were met, during the sampling period. Objectives for

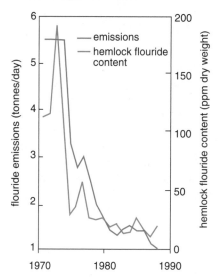

Figure 3.19
Flouride trends

Trends in air emissions of fluoride from the Alcan smelter in Kitimat and concentrations in hemlock foliage, 1971-1988.[47]

some metals and for cyanide have occasionally not been met in previous years.

Industry in Kitimat has recognized the need for reduced emissions. In response to stricter government and industry standards for emissions and public pressure, local industries are decreasing the amount of toxic materials being released into the environment. This is a long term, ongoing process which may take several years.

Buttle Lake

recovery of an ecosystem

Since 1966, a copper-lead-zinc mine operated by Westmin Resources has added heavy metals (cadmium, copper, lead and zinc) to Buttle Lake. Buttle Lake is a water reservoir located in Strathcona Park (B.C.'s oldest provincial park) on central Vancouver Island. The resulting increase in metal concentrations in the lake caused increased metal concentrations in salmon muscle and liver tissues, and declines in both the number of species and abundance of phytoplankton and zooplankton (microscopic floating plants and animals, respectively).[48] Metal levels reached a peak in

1980/81. At that time, the provincial government ordered improved treatment and collection systems at the mine site to address concerns for the health of fish, other aquatic life in the lake, and downstream residents (the town of Campbell River).

Recent studies of Buttle Lake indicate that heavy metal levels in the water have dropped by more than 80% since 1980/81 (Figure 3.20). As metal concentrations have decreased, phytoplankton have become more abundant. In addition, some, although not all, metal-sensitive species of phytoplankton and zooplankton have begun to reappear in the lake. Concentrations of metals in rainbow trout muscle tissue have returned to background levels. Cadmium levels in liver tissue have also decreased significantly, while copper remains elevated. In addition, hepatic metallothionein, an indicator of metal stress in fish, has been restored to normal levels.

Figure 3.20
Zinc in Buttle Lake

Trends in surface concentrations of zinc at Gold River bridge on Buttle Lake from 1970 to 1990. [49]

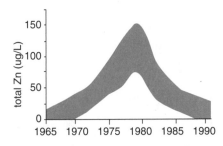

The Nestucca oil spill

In December 1988, 875 tonnes of oil were spilled off Gray's Harbor on the coast of Washington State when the tug Ocean Service collided with its tow, the barge Nestucca. The tug was trying to reattach a broken tow line during rough seas. Ocean currents spread the oil slick hundreds of kilometres northward, eventually reaching the west coast of Vancouver Island (Figure 3.21). About 2 to 3 km of the Island coastline were "heavily

oiled" while an additional 150 km were considered to be "moderately" or "lightly oiled".

Figure 3.21
Nestucca oil spill

About 150 km of the west coast of Vancouver Island were affected. [50]

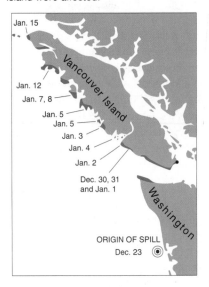

ORIGIN OF SPILL
Dec. 23

The most visible impact of the Nestucca spill was the death of more than 50,000 seabirds offshore from both B.C. and Washington. Other impacts included damage to several thousand bird scavengers and predators who fed on oiled carcasses, and the death of at least one sea otter. Shellfish and crab fisheries in certain areas were also temporarily closed. There was also evidence of widespread low-level contamination of sandy beaches, damaged eel-grass beds, and some significant oiling of saltmarsh habitat. Both the Nestucca oil spill and the much larger Exxon Valdez spill in Alaska a few months later, heightened concern about shipping accidents and our ability to prevent, and respond effectively, to such events (see Water Chapter).

In May of 1992, the federal and provincial governments, along with the Nuu-Cha-Nulth Tribal Council (NTC), successfully negotiated their environmental damage claims from the Nestucca spill. The agreement included payment of $4.4 million towards federal clean-up costs, $1.2 million towards NTC clean-up and environmental costs, and $4.3 million to the

federal and provincial governments to be used jointly for restoration and protection of the environment. [51]

Persistent marine debris
what goes out comes back!

Marine debris includes all man-made objects made of plastic, metal, glass, rubber, and cloth that are lost or discarded into the marine environment, including open ocean, coastal waters, and beaches. About 95% of marine debris collected from B.C. beaches in 1990 was non-biodegradable. [52] Because most marine debris takes years to degrade in the environment, it persists and accumulates.

The density of persistent marine debris at Pacific Rim National Park ranged from 100 to 150 kg/km during surveys between 1987 and 1989. On average, a person would see one piece of debris for every step taken on a walk along the 20 km beach. From 1987 to 1989 in B.C. coastal waters there was a three-fold increase in the number of pieces of marine debris (Figure 3.22). The causes of this increase are not known. They may simply reflect

Figure 3.22
Marine debris

Trends in amount of marine debris observed on beaches and in water along the west coast of Vancouver Island, 1987 to 1989[52,54,55,56]

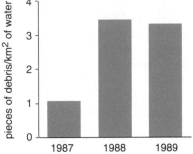

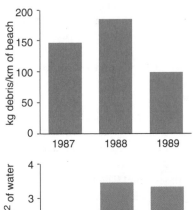

natural year-to-year variability. Most collected debris is styrofoam and plastics (77%), followed by glass and metal (15%), paper and wood (5%), and fishing gear (3%).[52]

Marine debris can originate from many sources, both on land and at sea. In 1987, marine park visitors lost or discarded an estimated 115,000 kg of marine debris. However, recreational boaters, commercial fishermen, cargo ships, and cruise and passenger ships are the heaviest polluters of B.C. beaches, discarding or losing an estimated 850,000 kg of debris annually. Recreational boaters account for almost half of this amount.[52] Winds and oceanic currents also carry marine debris from the central and eastern North Pacific to B.C. beaches. Pieces of squid driftnet from the North Pacific squid driftnet fleet have been found along the coast of B.C. and Alaska.[57]

Marine animals (e.g. birds, seals, and sea lions) can become entangled in debris or can ingest it, threatening their survival. Debris is also a safety hazard since it can get caught in propellers and motors, endangering people who are fishing or boating. Debris which contains sharp objects also poses a health risk. At a minimum, marine debris detracts from the aesthetic enjoyment of beaches and coastal waters.

In 1987, a Working Group on Plastic Debris established by the Department of Fisheries and Oceans recommended to the Federal Government that a clear national policy be implemented, recognizing plastics and other persistent debris in the aquatic environment as an immediate and serious issue. Federal and provincial legislation has tried to deter marine polluters under the Canadian Shipping Act through the Garbage Prevention Pollution Regulations (1978). Other regulations include Section 36 of the Fisheries Act.

The interested public, such as the B.C. Coastal Cleanup Campaign, Pitch-In Canada, schools and club groups, has aided in removing debris from B.C. beaches while at the same time providing valuable data about the amount and types of debris present.

Khutzeymateen Valley
protecting grizzly bears

Since the early 1970s, the Khutzeymateen Valley has been the focus of conflict between timber harvesting interests and grizzly bears. Historically, only small amounts of timber had been harvested from the valley next to the estuary . The timber resource represents 3% of the annual allowable cut for the North Coast timber supply area. In June 1988, the Provincial government decided to study the potential impacts of timber harvest on grizzly bears. The Ministry of Environment, Lands, and Parks and the Forest Service jointly initiated the Khutzeymateen Project, consisting of studies of grizzly bears, fisheries, road engineering, forest inventory, ecological habitats, and terrain and slope stability (Figure 3.23).

The Project found that the Khutzeymateen is important to grizzly bears in north coastal B.C. It con-cluded that timber harvesting could not be carried out without substantial risk to the grizzly bears due to reduced habitat and increased mortality. The Project also found that any unregulated public access into the Khutzeymateen would have tragic results for both people and bears. The study report recommended that, in addition to the large grizzly bear reserve with no hunting (established in 1924) a smaller protected habitat core with no hunting or logging should be established to assure future viability of the grizzly bear population. The Khutzeymateen was recommended as the best candidate for a protected habitat core in north coastal B.C. On June 4, 1992, the provincial government announced the protection of the Khutzeymateen valley as grizzly bear habitat. No timber harvesting will be permitted in this area. This is the first area in Canada to be protected specifically for grizzly bears.[58]

Figure 3.23
The Khutzeymateen valley - a haven for grizzly bears

The Khutzeymateen Project Area, which includes Larch and Cedar Creek, is located 45 km northeast of Prince Rupert and covers 443 square kilometres. The valley is a diverse collection of glaciers, avalanche chutes, bogs, flood plains, a large estuary, and extensive areas of old-growth forests, occupying three biogeoclimatic zones (coastal western hemlock, mountain hemlock, and alpine tundra). Its river system supports runs of chinook, coho, chum, and pink salmon. Seasonally, the area also supports approximately 50 grizzly bears and may play an important role in the population dynamics of grizzly bears over a much larger area. Other wildlife found in the valley include black bear, mountain goat, marten, beaver, seal, wolf, porcupine, wolverine and otter. Common birds include a variety of songbirds, waterfowl, raptors, grouse, shore birds, hummingbirds, swifts, woodpeckers, and kingfishers.[58]

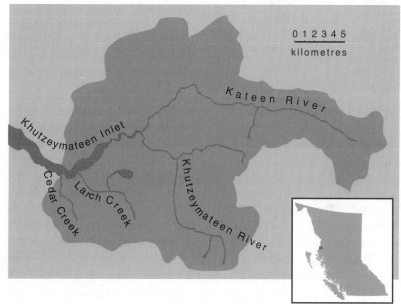

Bears and people

Bears are not always a good news story. There has been a large rise in bear complaints, disposal and relocation in Terrace, Kitimat and Stewart in recent years (Figure 3.24). These bear complaints are a direct result of bear and human interaction and the effects of human activities on bear habitat.

Bear complaints occur when black bears or grizzlies enter human settlements and are seen by people, cause property damage, threaten (or are perceived to threaten) human or animal safety, or actually injure or kill humans or their animals. Most of these incidents are a direct result of the way humans handle their garbage, livestock or fruit crops. In Terrace, Kitimat and Stewart, the landfills are close to residential areas. Residents and businesses in both Kitimat and Stewart have poor garbage storage practices.

Electric fencing has been installed around the landfills in Kitimat and Stewart. Ministry of Environment, Lands and Parks staff are removing habituated bears from these sites and surrounding residential areas. To reduce future bear habituation with garbage, public information campaigns have been launched to change both public attitudes and garbage handling practices.[59]

Figure 3.24
Concerns about bears

Bear complaints, disposal and relocation have risen significantly in recent years in Terrace, Kitimat and Stewart. These figures represent only complaints the Conservation Officer Service handles. R.C.M.P handle many additional complaints. For example, in 1990, Stewart R.C.M.P. handled an additional 100 bear complaints, destroying a significant number of these bears.[59]

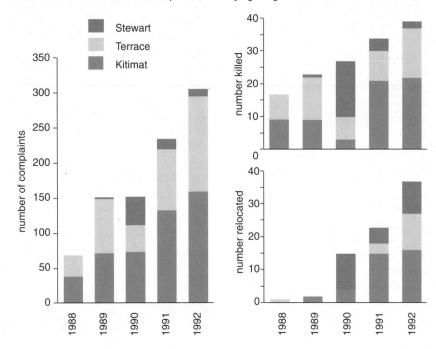

The Georgia Depression

This broad sheltered basin harbours the Strait of Georgia, and includes the Lower Fraser Valley, the Sunshine Coast up as far as Powell River, the Gulf Islands, and the eastern side of Vancouver Island.[1,2] An effective rainshadow appears in the lee of the Vancouver Island Range while more precipitation falls on the Lower Mainland side. The moderate climate and flat lowlands in the Georgia Depression have resulted in a variety of forest habitats. These include Douglas-fir forests, arbutus and Garry oak woodlands, as well as wetlands, agricultural lands, and large estuaries. These habitats support a rich diversity of wildlife species. About 9.4% of this ecoprovince is protected area.[3]

The Georgia Depression makes up only 2.7% of the area of B.C., but contains two-thirds of its people (Figure 3.25). The population density here is about 25 times the provincial average. People are attracted here by the mild climate, a spectacular natural environment, relatively abundant job opportunities, and world class cultural and educational facilities, all within close proximity. During the 1971-1986 period, this ecoprovince absorbed 69% of B.C.'s overall population growth, and grew by almost half a million people (Figure 3.25). Almost two-thirds of this increase occurred in the Lower Mainland, one quarter on southeastern Vancouver Island, and the remainder (11%) on the Gulf Islands. The Gulf Islands population grew particularly rapidly during this period - by 58%. The Islands' many unique qualities are likely to continue to draw more and more people.

The population of the Greater Vancouver Regional District (GVRD) is expected to grow by about 40% over the next 25 years.[60,61] Unless per capita environmental impacts can be reduced by 40% over the same period, we can expect increased stresses on the air, water, land and biota of this ecoprovince. The population of Vancouver Island, for example, is expected to swell from a current level of 559,000 to 777,000 within the next twenty five years. Most of this increase is expected to be absorbed in existing metropolitan areas along the east coast of the Island (Box 3.2).

Less than five percent of the population in this ecoprovince is directly employed in the primary resource sectors of agriculture, forestry, mining, fishing and hunting (Figure 3.25). However, the total *number* of people working in these sectors far exceeds that of all other ecoprovinces. Furthermore, many of the jobs in other labour force categories, such as manufacturing, depend on economically viable resource industries. Other labour force sectors, such as tourism, depend on a high quality natural environment, which can potentially be impaired by

Box 3.2
Growth pressures on Vancouver Island

Vancouver Island offers one of the most attractive environments of any area of Canada. As a result, the population of Vancouver Island is expected to grow from 559,000 to 777,000 by the year 2016 - an increase of nearly 39%.[60] For the east coast of the island itself, growth has been projected to exceed 50% for the same period. It is anticipated that rapid growth will place major demands on the natural resource base of the island. In view of the sheer physical constraints that the island presents, issues of water supplies, liquid and solid waste disposal, and fish and wildlife resources may be more serious than those experienced elsewhere.[100]

resource industries. Much of the economy of the ecoprovince therefore depends on finding a way to use resources so that both economic and environmental sustainability are accommodated.

Ground level ozone
transportation impacts on health and visibility

Air pollution in the Lower Mainland comes from many sources. These include motor vehicles (the major pollution source), natural gas processing and forest industries, municipal incinerators, home heating and outdoor fires. Smog, a brownish haze, is a major air quality problem. One of the primary ingredients of smog is ground-level ozone, which in turn is formed from nitrogen oxides (NO_x) and volatile organic compounds (VOCs) on sunny, warm, calm days. Motor vehicles produce 64% of the NO_x and 54% of the VOC emissions.[64]

Air quality in the region deteriorates during periods of limited air movement. At these times the high coastal mountains restrict movement of regional emissions. Vancouver, Canada's third largest city, is considered the eighth worst city in Canada for ozone problems (Figure 3.26). One advantage Vancouver has over other Canadian cities is that most of the pollution (82%) is generated from within the Greater Vancouver region, and is therefore potentially under local control. The highest concentrations of ozone form in the eastern portions of the region (such as Port Moody and Port Coquitlam) during hot summer days (Figure 3.27). Hourly ozone concentrations of 110-130 ppb can occur as far as 100 km downwind from the major sources of NO_x and VOC emissions. In spite of improvements over the last decade, there are still 100 days per year when one or more stations have only fair air quality for part of the day due to high ozone levels (Figure 3.28).

Computer models of ozone generation indicate that under projected emission levels for the year 2005, high ozone levels will continue to cause fair to poor air quality conditions.[86] These projections assume current climate conditions. If hotter, dryer summers should occur, air quality could further deteriorate.

Figure 3.25
Descriptive statistics

The Georgia Depression ecoprovince constitutes 2.7% % of B.C.'s land area, and is home to 67.4% of B.C.'s population.[4,5]

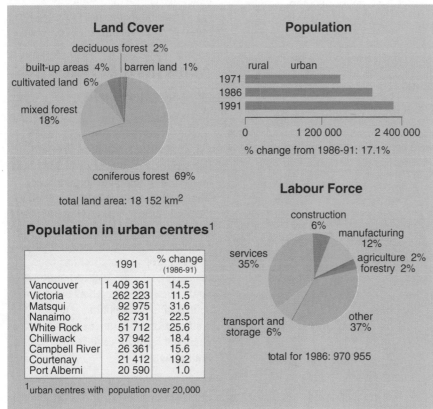

Land Cover
deciduous forest 2%
built-up areas 4% | barren land 1%
cultivated land 6%
mixed forest 18%
coniferous forest 69%
total land area: 18 152 km²

Population
rural urban
1971
1986
1991
0   1 200 000   2 400 000
% change from 1986-91: 17.1%

Labour Force
construction 6%
manufacturing 12%
services 35%
agriculture 2%
forestry 2%
transport and storage 6%
other 37%
total for 1986: 970 955

Population in urban centres[1]

	1991	% change (1986-91)
Vancouver	1 409 361	14.5
Victoria	262 223	11.5
Matsqui	92 975	31.6
Nanaimo	62 731	22.5
White Rock	51 712	25.6
Chilliwack	37 942	18.4
Campbell River	26 361	15.6
Courtenay	21 412	19.2
Port Alberni	20 590	1.0

[1] urban centres with population over 20,000

Figure 3.26
Ground level ozone in Canadian cities

Number of days per year when Canada's 1-hour ozone air quality objective (82 ppb) was exceeded. This air quality objective corresponds to 'poor' air quality line in Figure 3.28. The value for each city is the average of that city's three highest years during 1983-90, and includes several stations.[62,68]

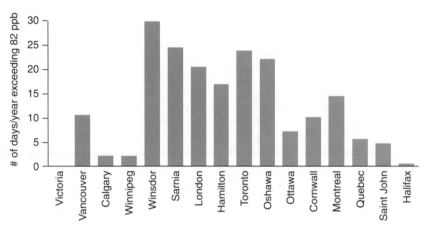

Smog and ozone are not only a concern because they obscure the view. Ozone can affect the health of people, vegetation and animals. It also corrodes materials. As ozone levels approach or exceed 82 ppb (poor conditions in Figure 3.28), short-term exposure may result in irritation, lung inflammation, or mild aggravation of symptoms in sensitive persons. Normally healthy individuals can also experience impaired lung function around this ozone level if they have been vigorously exercising outdoors.[63,66] Long term exposure to ozone may hasten the decline in lung function with age.[67,68] Health effects of ozone on animals, such as livestock in the Fraser Valley, are also a concern. Other impacts on agriculture may be substantial. Preliminary estimates suggest that ozone may be causing up to $9 million annually in crop losses in the Fraser Valley.[69] Ozone has been shown to reduce forest growth in other parts of the world, but detailed local studies have not been completed.

The Greater Vancouver Regional District (GVRD) air quality program has set a goal of reducing total emissions by 50%, by the year 2000. This is only seven years away. Reaching this goal during a period of rapid population growth will require a major reduction in per capita emissions. Actions being considered by the GVRD include: redesigning transportation networks (pedestrians and cyclists first, then transit and movement of goods, and lastly cars); encouraging carpools and high-occupancy vehicle lanes; increasing commuter parking rates; converting government vehicles to cleaner fuels; stronger control of car and industry emissions; and making new residential developments pay for transit costs. The new Air Care vehicle emission program is an important component of the GVRD plan.

The distribution of land for housing makes the GVRD target more difficult to achieve. If automobiles remain the dominant form of transportation of the rapidly growing communities of the Fraser Valley, commuting distances, traffic congestion and ozone formation are all likely to increase. The Capital Regional District of the Victoria area, though currently blessed with much better air quality than Vancouver, faces similar challenges in the future and has initiated an air management program.

Abbotsford aquifer
groundwater quality

The Abbotsford aquifer is an important source of water for domestic, municipal, agricultural, fish hatchery and industrial users in the Lower Mainland and Washington State (Figure 3.29). The aquifer is unconfined (exposed to the land surface) making it particularly vulnerable to contamination from land use practices.[70] Nitrate contamination of the Abbotsford aquifer has been increasing (Figure 3.30). Manure application is suspected as the major source of nitrates but the actual contribution from other sources such as chemical fertilizers and septic fields is not known.

Pesticide contamination has also been observed in some locations.[70] Labora-

Figure 3.27
Ground level ozone in the Lower Mainland

Contours show the maximum 1-hour concentrations, based on an average of the three highest years during 1983-89. These conditions never occurred at the same time at all locations. However, the map shows that many areas occasionally exceed the maximum acceptable objective of 82 ppb. The highest ozone concentrations occur downwind from the major sources of ozone-forming gases.[62,68]

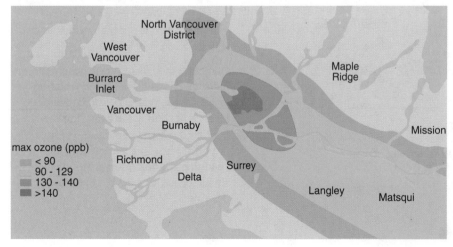

Figure 3.28

GVRD ground-level ozone trends

In spite of improvements over the last decade, there are still 100 days per year when one or more stations have only *fair* air quality for part of the day due to high ozone levels. *Fair* indicates that very sensitive individuals may need to take some precautions. *Poor* conditions occur on average 10 days per year. *Poor* indicates that sensitive individuals of the general population (i.e. with heart or respiratory ailments) may experience irritation and should avoid unnecessary exposure. *Very Poor* indicates concern for sensitive people, while the general population may notice symptoms. These trends are approximate, since the number and location of stations has changed over time.[64]

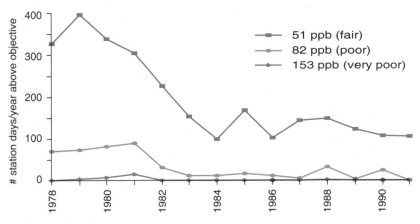

tory analyses were able to detect 12 of the 23 pesticides analysed in groundwater samples, though six of these twelve were only found infrequently (i.e. in 1-3 samples out of 58). None of the pesticides detected exceeded the existing Guidelines for Canadian drinking water quality. However, four pesticides were found at concentrations exceeding the more stringent Canadian

guidelines for protection of freshwater aquatic life.

Nitrate contamination of drinking water is of particular concern for infants, as it can reduce the ability of blood to carry oxygen. Residents relying on well water have been advised to have their water tested, and to not drink water with nitrate-nitrogen concentrations

exceeding the 10 ppm guideline. Pesticides can have a variety of impacts on human health.[72]

How can the aquifer's contamination be reduced and water quality improved? Recommended actions include improved farming practices, enhanced septic field design and maintenance, modified land use activities, additional research, and better regulation of manure applications.[70] The Waste Management Act was amended in 1992 to include control regulations and a code of agricultural practice.[73] This code introduces new standards for agricultural activities to prevent surface and groundwater pollution, specifying appropriate methods of storage, management and application of agricultural wastes. B.C. farmers have formed an Agricultural Environmental Protection Council to support the implementation of the control regulations and code.

The B.C. Ministry of Health, Environment Canada, Agriculture Canada and the University of British Columbia are continuing to study groundwater quality in the Abbotsford aquifer and the general area of the Lower Fraser Valley. In addition to monitoring changes in nitrate and pesticide levels, these studies include evaluations of the impact of septic tanks on groundwater, the quality of water in municipal and communal wells, and the levels of disease organisms in high risk aquifers.

Marine water quality

many sewers discharge into one ecosystem

There are water quality concerns in several areas, including the Fraser River Estuary, Burrard Inlet, the Gulf Islands Victoria Harbour and Esquimalt Harbour (Table 3.1). In general, while "hot spots" exist in sediments and marine organisms near specific pollution sources, these effects are not observable reasonably short distances from the outfalls. Victoria's untreated sewage outfall is an example of such an area. The

Figure 3.29

The Abbotsford aquifer

The aquifer (shaded area) is comprised of extensive sand and gravel deposits in southwestern B.C. and northwestern Washington State, and covers about 200 km² in area.[70]

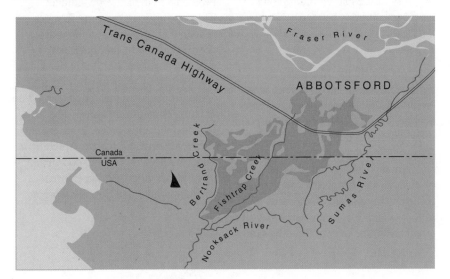

Figure 3.30

Nitrate nitrogen in the Abbotsford aquifer

Average concentrations in sampled wells appear to be increasing. In the South Matsqui part of the aquifer, about 60% of the samples exceed Health and Welfare's drinking water standard of 10 ppm. Two cautionary notes: 1) few samples were taken during the 1982-86 period, so the calculated average is highly uncertain; 2) later sampling has focused on areas with higher nitrate concentrations. (* indicates years with no data) [70,71]

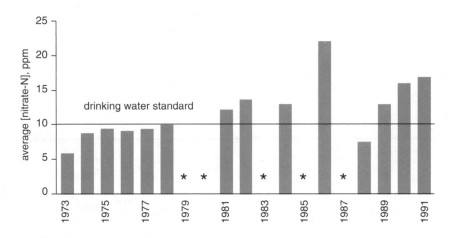

Table 3.1

Marine water quality problems

These are examples of some concerns in the Georgia Depression.[76]

Location	Concerns
Lower Fraser River and Estuary	• organic contaminants from local industries, landfills and sewers • municipal sewage • pulp and paper contaminants • contaminated sediments and biota
Vancouver Harbour	• wood preservative, metal, PAH and PCB contaminatied sediments • combined storm sewer overflows • cancerous lesions in livers of English sole
False Creek	• contaminated sediments • PCBs and organic contaminants
Victoria	• municipal sewage • contaminated sediments
S.E. coast Vancouver Island	• bacterial contamination of shellfish • pulp and paper contaminants
Gulf Islands	• bacterial contamination of shellfish • contamination from Fraser River plume

effluent itself is acutely lethal to fish, though water quality appears to be generally unaffected.[74] Sediment conditions are moderately polluted within 400m of the outfall, and affected up to 2 km away.[74] Another example is the Iona sewage treatment plant, which discharges primary-treated sewage from Greater Vancouver to the ocean. Historic fish kills and highly contaminated sediments led to the installation of a deep water discharge outfall. There is ongoing monitoring of water quality, sediments and biota in the vicinity of the outfall. No major impacts have been identified to date. Coliform levels at Vancouver area beaches have decreased.[75,86] The recovery of the habitat on the Iona Island foreshore is being assessed by the Department of Fisheries and Oceans.

Site specific studies like these do not, however, account for all potential environmental impacts. First, wastes may be transported far from their point of origin due to tidal influences, and deposited in seldom sampled embayments. Municipal sewage discharges are the largest single factor contributing to shellfish closures in B.C. Second, there may be cumulative effects from the over 300 outfalls in this ecoprovince discharging various wastes to the Strait of Georgia and Juan de Fuca Strait. Discharged wastes all end up in the same ecosystem. Although not originating from sewer discharges, the accumulation of dioxins and furans in crabs, shrimp, fish, and seabirds indicate how the effects of individual outfalls can be magnified when the whole ecosystem is considered (see Water chapter).

Sediment core samples taken from the sea bottom of the Strait of Georgia have been contaminated by lead and organochlorines such as dioxins, furans and PCBs. Careful analysis of the cores' layers show that this contamination began in the 1940s, 1960s and 1970s, and increased markedly in concentration in following years (Figure 3.31). Some of these pollutants are gradually being eliminated from sources such as automobile gasoline, incinerated waste and pulp effluents. However, sediment contamination does not simply disappear. The contaminated sediments will slowly be buried over the next several decades by a rain of new sediments from the Fraser and other rivers. This burial will eventually isolate the contaminants from living organisms and lessen their impacts, unless the sediments are again exposed by dredging or other disturbances.[77,78]

The Fraser River Action Plan (see Water Chapter, Box 2.1b), Fraser River Estuary Management Program and the Burrard Inlet Environmental Action Program are addressing water quality, sediment and biological problems in the Lower Mainland. These actions are focusing first on reducing existing contaminant discharges to stop further degradation; next, on ensuring that future discharges are adequately regulated to prevent future impacts; and last, on cleaning up existing contaminated sites. The Province recently entered into a joint Environment Cooperation Agreement with Washington State to coordinate environmental protection efforts, including the Puget Sound-Georgia Basin region.

Figure 3.31
Contaminants in Strait of Georgia sediments

By dating sediments and measuring contaminants from bottom cores, scientists can assess the history of contaminant loads to the Strait of Georgia and Fraser Basin.

a) The appearance of lead coincided with the introduction of lead to automotive gasoline in the 1930s, and today concentrations are about double the natural background levels.[77] The effects of introducing unleaded gasoline in the early 1970s are not yet apparent.

b) The furan TCDF started to enter the sediments in the early 1960s, coincident with chlorine bleaching installations at a number of pulp mills. It steadily increased to 1990. Other data for surface sediments suggest that its concentration is decreasing, in response to pulp mill conversions to chlorine dioxide bleaching.[78]

c) The dioxin OCDD is most likely to have originated from regional and distant waste incinerators, and reached the Strait of Georgia via the atmosphere. Regulation of incineration in the 1970s. is probably responsible for the observed decline.[78]

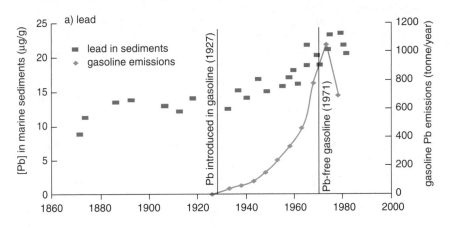

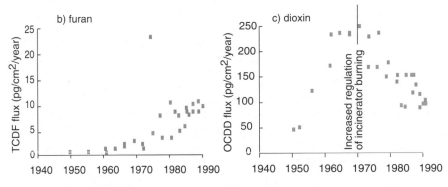

Land use change
and ecosystem change

Rapid population and economic growth is changing the landscape of the Georgia Depression ecoprovince. The main activities causing landscape change are urbanization, forestry, agriculture, recreation development and transportation/utility corridors. These changes are probably affecting the potential of ecosystems to maintain the native plant and animal populations of the region. However, the extent of landscape change is not fully documented for each land use, and the overall ecological consequences are not well understood.

Data are available for rates of urbanization. These data are generated for Urban Centred Regions (or UCRs). UCRs include all of the urbanized area around a major city, including adjacent urban municipalities. In the five years between 1981 and 1986, over 50 km² of rural land in the Vancouver and Victoria UCRs were converted to urban uses (33.8 and 17.2 km² respectively).[79] Though data are not available for the 1986-91 period, it's possible that the Vancouver and Victoria UCRs converted as much as 80 km² of rural land during these five years. (This estimate assumes that between 1981-86 and 1986-91 there was no overall change in the number of people added per square kilometre urbanized.)

Urban centred regions in the Georgia Depression vary widely in the density of development placed on newly urbanized lands. In the 1981-86 period, the Vancouver UCR population increased by 3,329 people for each newly urbanized square kilometre. Victoria added 823/km², Nanaimo 1,364/km² and Chilliwack 253/km².[79] In general, larger centres tend to occupy new land more efficiently, a trend observed throughout Canada.[79] There is a slight trend towards higher densities in the Georgia Depression, in that a greater percentage of people were living in apartments in 1986 (30%) than in 1971 (25%).[80] However, most people occupy single family dwellings (58% in 1986).

Urbanization consumes agricultural land in most areas of the world, and the Georgia Depression is no different. Mountain slopes, the U.S. border and the Strait of Georgia restrict the area in which development can occur, placing extra pressure on agricultural land. The Lower Fraser Basin is one of the most productive agricultural areas in Canada. In 1986, there were 5,600 farms on 890 km² of agricultural land producing 50% of the total gross farm income in the province.[86] Between 1980 and 1987, 750 ha of prime agricultural land in the Lower Fraser Basin was permanently lost to urban uses.[81] The southern third of Vancouver Island ranks behind only the Lower Fraser Basin and the Okanagan in terms of agricultural production, and faces similar pressures. Urbanization is chipping away at the Agricultural Land Reserve (ALR) in the eight regional districts which overlap the Georgia Depression. Between 1973 and 1990, the ALR area in these districts declined by 8.5% (from 2,170 km² to 1,990 km²). Additional lands were permanently converted from farms to golf courses, yet still remain inside the ALR. By contrast, the ALR declined by only 0.4% over the province as a whole.[82]

Cities are sometimes described as forming an "urban shadow", because farm land around cities is seen as a potential site for urban use rather than as an agricultural resource.[83,84] As land pressures grow more intense, it becomes more and more difficult for farmers to survive the economic pressures induced by rising property values, rising costs and land speculation. People living in new subdivisions adjacent to farms may complain about the odour from manure, adding pressure to modify or close agricultural operations. Even if agricultural land uses are maintained, farming practices often intensify to remain profitable. Intensive use of heavy farm machinery on moist soils has led to compaction of soils in the Lower Fraser Basin, with an estimated cost of $6-12 million / year in lost productivity.[85]

In many areas of the Georgia Depression, agricultural land originally displaced waterfowl habitat, yet waterfowl still use these areas as an important supplement to their remaining natural habitat. Removal of agricultural land therefore also affects wildlife. Encroachment onto prime agricultural land and wildlife habitat is not necessarily an inevitable consequence of population growth in this ecoprovince. In the Lower Mainland, for example, much developable land is available elsewhere.[81,99]

Urbanization affects more than agricultural land. As cities expand, they increasingly encroach on streams, rivers and coastal zones. In both the Lower Mainland and southeastern Vancouver Island, urban development and its associated flood protection and drainage projects have eliminated wetlands, stream habitat, and other important fish and wildlife areas. This undermines the basic principle of sustainable development - maintaining the integrity of natural systems to keep options open for future generations.[87] Building in floodplains has serious risks for human populations as well. While natural ecosystems associated with floodplains have adapted to periodic flooding, human populations appear less adaptable.[87] Twice in the

Box 3.3

Flood risks to the Lower Fraser Basin

The greatest Fraser River floods in recorded history occurred in 1894 and 1948. The 1948 flood damaged 2,000 homes, caused the evacuation of 16,000 residents, and cost $20 million (about $109 million in current dollars).[87]

"At the time of the 1894 flood there were few farms along the lower reaches of the Fraser. Damage, reckoned in dollars, (though not in human misery), was relatively small. When, in the spring of 1948, the engineers saw the water rising fast on the Hope gauge, when they looked at the gigantic load of snow in the mountains, and learned of sudden hot weather throughout the interior, they knew they were in for trouble. ...Modern Canada had never seen a flood like this".[88]

last hundred years major flooding has occurred and caused significant damage to people and property in the Fraser River flood plain (Box 3.3) . Future population growth will increase pressures to build in floodplain areas, with potentially devastating consequences.

Maintaining the integrity of the region's ecosystems under the current and future land use changes will be very difficult. It will certainly require a form of integrated environmental management which is proactive, and cuts across traditional political, institutional and community boundaries. It will also require the creative commitment of all residents of the region. The foundation for building

integrated ecosystem management exists in the Fraser River Estuary Management Program (FREMP, see next section) and Fraser River Management Board (formed under the Fraser River Action Plan, Box 2.1b). These programs must be continued, and perhaps extended to other parts of the ecoprovince facing similar stresses (i.e. southeast Vancouver Island, the Gulf Islands).

The Fraser River Estuary

An estuary is the area at the mouth of a river where freshwater and sea water mix, and tides occur. The Fraser River Estuary contains a tremendous diversity and abundance of life. In an average year, about 800 million juvenile salmon and steelhead migrate out of the estuary and 10 million adults pass through on their way upstream to spawn. There are at least 87 species of fish and shellfish in the Lower Fraser.[89] The Estuary is also a vital staging area on the Pacific Flyway, one of the world's major migratory routes extending from the Bering Sea to South America. It supports the highest density of wintering waterfowl, shorebirds, and birds of prey in Canada. In a typical year, about 1.5 million birds (150 species) utilize the estuary, especially during the months from October to December.[90]

Fish and birds in the Fraser River Estuary need a variety of habitats, but marshes are particularly important. Marshes are the foundation of an

Figure 3.32

A Fraser River Estuary food chain

Detritus (e.g. dead marsh plants and microscopic organisms) provide food for invertebrates, which in turn support fish and bird communities.[91] The actual food web is much more complex. Removal of marshes and contamination of water and sediments are major concerns.[86]

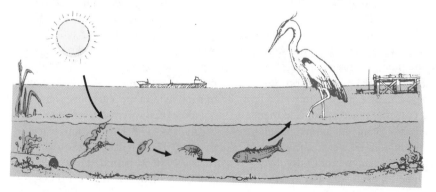

estuary's food chain (Figure 3.32), a place of shelter while fish adjust to salt water before going to sea, a source of shade and cover, and a source of food for juvenile fish. Though the entire Fraser River Estuary is used by birds, the marshes support about a quarter of the total population.[90]

Up to 70% of the original wetlands have been altered due to human settlement.[86] Most of these losses occurred at the turn of the century with dyking and draining of fertile floodplains for agricultural land, and later urban development (e.g. Richmond and Delta). Since then, habitat losses have continued due to dredging and filling in of river marshes and shoreline areas. The total area of wetlands in the southwestern portion of the Fraser lowland declined by 27% between 1967 and 1982.[92] A 1989 inventory estimated that there were 25,200 ha of wetlands in the Fraser Estuary.[93] Of this total, the 4,000 ha of eelgrass beds (an aquatic plant) and 3,200 ha of marshes are particularly important to the Estuary's ecosystem.[93]

In addition to habitat loss, other threats to the estuary ecosystem are from municipal, industrial, and agricultural wastewater (Figure 3.33). Water quality in the Fraser Estuary is generally within the Province's water quality objectives.[94] Ambient water quality is fair to good where large flows flush out most contaminants, except right near the dilution zones of effluent outfalls. There are more serious problems in areas of limited circulation, such as sloughs, side channels and small streams. Here, fish kills have often occurred, due to either low flows or poor water quality.[86]

Over 90% of Greater Vancouver's sewage discharges come from the Iona, Annacis and Lulu sewage treatment plants (53%, 33% and 5% respectively). Together these plants discharge enough wastewater each year to fill B.C. Place Stadium 160 times.[86] Though an impressive volume, this represents only 0.2% of the average annual flow of the Fraser River. As mentioned above, the Iona plant discharges into deeper marine waters.

Figure 3.33
Wastewater sources

The chart shows sources of wastewater flows to the Fraser River Estuary. The pie chart is based on 1987 volumes, and includes estimates of runoff from agricultural lands. The different sources vary greatly in the composition of wastewater.[53,86,95]

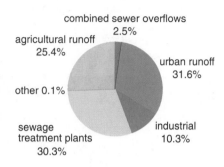

combined sewer overflows 2.5%
agricultural runoff 25.4%
urban runoff 31.6%
other 0.1%
industrial 10.3%
sewage treatment plants 30.3%

annual total: 908 000 000 m³/year

The effects of Fraser River sewage discharges remain a concern. There has been a substantial reduction in the amount of untreated sewage discharged (Figure 3.34). However, the waste only receives primary treatment - removal of large solids and floating substances through settling and screening. Furthermore, discharges are increasing rapidly, with flows from the Annacis plant expected to double by 2036 as the eastern part of the Lower Mainland region grows.[86] In 1985, the discharged effluents were toxic to fish more than half the time at the Annacis and Lulu plants.

Though the sewage is diluted by the Fraser River's flow, there are critical times when dilution is reduced. For example, during winter low flow conditions, the effluent can reside in the estuary for up to 1.7 days, with tides moving the effluent back and forth. Contaminants such as persistent organic compounds and heavy metals may become bound up in sediments or plants, and eventually into food used by fish, birds and other biota. Of the five species of salmon, chinook is the most threatened by contaminated habitat and wastewater discharges, since juvenile fish spend up to one year in the Fraser Estuary before going to sea.[10] Urban runoff (the water released from storm sewers, combined sewer overflows, and direct drainage) adds more nutrients, metals and organic compounds. During the first hour of a rain storm, more contaminants enter the Fraser River from urban runoff than from the three major sewage treatment plants.[11]

Concerted efforts are being made by government agencies, associations and community groups to protect habitats and maintain water quality. The Fraser River Action Plan (Box 2.1b) is working to reverse environmental degradation and restore degraded areas in the Fraser River Basin. The GVRD is implementing secondary treatment at its Lulu and Annacis Island sewage treatment plants by 1995 and 1997. It

Figure 3.34
GVRD untreated sewage discharges

Over the last 25 years, discharges of untreated sewage from the GVRD have decreased by over 90%.[96]

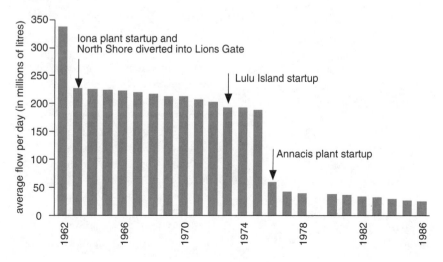

Iona plant startup and North Shore diverted into Lions Gate

Lulu Island startup

Annacis plant startup

average flow per day (in millions of litres)

is also exploring other options for improving the effectiveness of existing treatment plants, reducing the amount of untreated waste and urban runoff, and finding a useful end use for waste by-products such as sewage sludge. This includes experiments to fertilize forests with sewage sludge. The Fraser River Estuary Management Program (FREMP) is a key agency. It coordinates the activities of federal, provincial, and municipal governments to review development proposals, and monitors the health of various parts of the ecosystem (water, sediments, bottom-dwelling organisms, fish). FREMP and the North Fraser Harbour Commission have mapped habitat in the Estuary in terms of its productivity for juvenile salmon.[97,98] These maps are used to locate appropriate development, while protecting remaining habitat. High productivity habitats cannot be altered. A Habitat Compen-sation Bank, consisting of mudflats that have been converted to marshland, is being used to compensate for the loss of medium to low productivity habitats. Over the last three decades conservation efforts have secured large portions of the marshes, such as the South Arm Marshes Wildlife Management area. Other critical areas are not protected from development.[65]

Conclusions on the state of ecoprovinces

There is not sufficient information to provide a comprehensive set of conclusions for each ecoprovince, nor for the overall environmental conditions across all ecoprovinces. However, as the topics discussed are examined from a distance, there are certain overall principles that consistently appear. This is similar to the effect when one steps back from a large tapestry - the individual panels begin to form larger patterns that were not observable when examined separately. Six of these principles are summarized below.

Ecologically sustainable resource management is possible. New practices are being implemented that have not only less environmental impact but in many cases better economic returns (e.g. conservation farming in the Peace River region, cogeneration in Williams Lake, restoration of Horsefly River sockeye stocks).

Environmental problems in B.C. are linked to the rest of the world, in terms of both causes and effects. Some problems appear to be at least partly due to actions taken outside the province: long range transport of incinerator produced dioxins to Strait of Georgia sediments, oil spills and marine debris on the west coast of Vancouver Island, Eurasian watermilfoil in the Southern Interior, and possibly toxaphene in Atlin Lake. Other problems are 'made in B.C.', but have effects which extend beyond provincial boundaries: effects of the Abbotsford aquifer contamination on Washington State, effects of the Bennett Dam on Alberta, pol-lution of the lower Columbia River, and production of greenhouse gases and ozone - depleting chemicals by a Kitimat smelter.

Sustainable development requires firm actions to preserve wildlife habitat, representative ecosystems and agricultural resources. Habitat and land preservation is essential for the mountain caribou of eastern B.C., Khutzeymateen Valley grizzlies, Fraser Estuary fish and birds, Lower Fraser Valley agriculture, and various Southern Interior plants and animals. Major positive actions have already been taken - the Mountain Caribou in Managed Forests program, preservation of the Khutzeymateen Valley, the Fraser River Action Plan, the Fraser River Estuary Management Program, the Agricultural Land Reserve, and the South Okanagan Conservation Strategy. Such actions will probably need to be strengthened if the promise of sustainable development is to be realized in those parts of B.C. experiencing rapid rates of population growth (the Georgia Depression and Southern Interior).

Investments to control pollution may be expensive, but environmental monitoring shows they clearly pay ecological dividends. Environmental monitoring has demonstrated the ecological benefits of a variety of pollution control programs - chlorine dioxide substitution in the Upper Fraser and Thompson pulp mills, improvements to air and water quality from changes to the Trail smelter, reduced fluoride emissions from the Kitimat aluminum smelter, and re-duced metal loading to Buttle Lake from mining operations. Some of these problems require further abatement actions, and other problems lie waiting to be solved. Notable examples include contaminant discharges to the Fraser Estuary, Strait of Georgia and Kitimat Arm; ozone formation from NO_x/VOC emissions in the Georgia Depression, groundwater contamination of the Abbotsford aquifer and Osoyoos area, and local pollution of the Fort St. John water supply.

Living harmoniously requires modified resource demands and management practices. There are many examples of competing demands: water withdrawal conflicts with the needs of fish in the Okanagan Basin, methods of garbage disposal and agriculture conflict with bears in settlements within the Coast and Mountains ecoprovince, and logging conflicts with drinking water and recreational fisheries near Kelowna. Solving such problems requires dialogue, creativity and commitment.

Ecosystems can react in unforeseen ways. The effects of the Bennett Dam on the Peace-Athabasca delta, and of the Duncan and Libby Dam on Kootenay Lake kokanee, were not predicted. Sometimes efforts to improve matters can backfire, as occurred with the introduction of Mysis shrimp into Kootenay Lake. Perhaps the only ways to cope with imperfect environmental knowledge are to maintain a thorough ecosystem perspective in planning and management, and monitor to identify mistakes at an early stage.

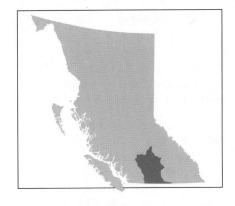

Land under change

The state of sustainability in British Columbia's Southern Interior ecoprovince

Introduction

An ecological perspective to sustainable development requires that society must think, act and plan in terms of ecosystems. This approach to planning strives to understand ecosystems, how their various components interact and how the systems themselves interact. To emphasize these linkages, one ecoprovince, the Southern Interior has been chosen as a case study.

Simply put, all the components of the ecosystem are interdependent. If one component is adversely impacted it can have repercussions for the entire system. To compound the problem we do not really understand the system well enough to know when serious impacts are about to occur. Sometimes we know when such impacts are happening but not why. Also, it is likely that adverse long-term effects are taking place in many ecosystems without us knowing about them. By the time visual manifestations of effects on the ecosystem can be seen in the birds, trees, worms, water, cities and farms, the "invisible" ecosystem interactive functions and processes that sustain all life may have been undergoing degradation for a considerable time. Understanding how ecosystems function through the interplay of environmental, economic and social components is essential if society is to grow and prosper.

The concept of mutually supporting environmental, economic and social systems operating as integral components of ecosystems is relatively easy to understand. The translation from concept to planning and decision-making is not. Existing administrative and single resource focused planning units cannot provide the holistic context for such planning. This case study on the state of sustainability of British Columbia's souther interior ecoprovince illustrates the kinds of information necessary within an ecological framework for planning towards sustainability.

Of British Columbia's ten ecoprovinces, the Southern Interior was chosen for this detailed discussion of sustainability. It is the Province's most densely populated interior region, making up 11% (over 368,000 people) of British Columbia's total population. It also has the most rapid influx of people of all the ecoprovinces. The rapid growth rate has produced a 45% increase in population over the past twenty years. If this trend continues, both Kelowna and Kamloops will soon overtake Prince George as the most populous cities of interior British Columbia (Table 4.1).

Table 4.1

Major population centres of the Southern Interior ecoprovince

The largest city in the interior of British Columbia is Prince George (Sub-Boreal Interior ecoprovince) with a 1991 population near 63,000, an increase of 3% over 1986.[1]

	1971	1986	1991	% change 1986-91
Armstrong	1,648	2,708	3,200	18.2
Ashcroft	1,916	1,914	1,714	-10.4
Cache Creek	1,013	1,147	1,000	-12.2
Chase	1,212	1,933	2,083	7.8
Enderby	1,158	1,842	2,128	15.5
Grand Forks	3,173	3,282	3,610	10.0
Kamloops	26,168	53,218	57,466	8.0
Kelowna	19,412	48,417	57,945	19.7
Lillooet	1,514	1,755	1,782	1.4
Lumby	940	1,181	1,265	7.1
Merrit	5,289	6,180	6,253	1.2
Osoyoos	1,285	2,956	3,403	15.1
Penticton	18,146	23,824	27,494	15.4
Salmon Arm	7,793	5,191	5,746	10.7
Sicamous	N/A	2,428	2,501	3.0
Summerland	5,551	3,643	4,175	14.6
Vernon	13,283	23,298	26,653	14.4
Westbank	N/A	10,553	13,551	28.4

Figure 4.1
Labour force by sector

The diversity of the Southern Interior's labour force (1986) is very similar to that in the rest of B.C.

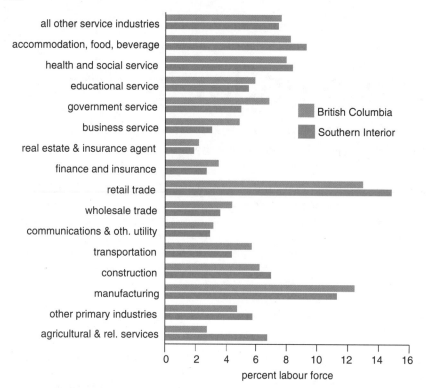

The Southern Interior ecoprovince, with its rapid population increase, and distinct and important environmental, cultural and historical features, serves well as a case study to illustrate ecological linkages between human activities and environmental consequences.

The Southern Interior ecoprovince is comprised of three ecoregions which, in turn, encompass ten ecosections. Three ecosections, those encompassing the Okanagan and Thompson River basins are heavily influenced by urban development; the remaining ecosections are influenced by a variety of resource uses. Within the Southern Interior ecoprovince a complete land use spectrum is represented, ranging from protected ecological reserves to complete urbanization.

The Southern Interior Ecoprovince section of this report provides a general overview of the ecoprovince and some of its major issues. Included is a survey of some of the kinds of environmental, social and economic

information and linkages, that may be needed for assessment of sustainability.

There is full understanding that in many cases, information to determine such linkages is lacking. There are major data gaps, and a lack of sound methodology and assessment procedures to integrate these ecological components. For example, in this case study, data on socio-economic aspects such as employment equity and income are presented to highlight the kinds of information that may be required to be integrated with environmental consideration to provide the ecological context for assessment towards sustainability.

The environmental setting

In the Southern Interior ecoprovince, forestry, agriculture (particularly fruit crop production and cattle ranching), and mining are the predominant primary industries influencing land use, settlement patterns, and income

stability. Adding to the diversity of the commercial base are a wide range of tourist-targeted service enterprises, a strong retail sector, construction, high-tech industry, and considerable manufacturing (Figure 4.1).

The urban centres are concentrated within the three ecosections of the Okanagan and Thompson River Basins. Direct land use conflicts occur with agriculture as these ecosections contain the prime orchard and other farm lands of interior British Columbia. In these areas, total census farmland declined by close to 200,000 hectares or 26% in the 1971-86 period. If declines in census farm land present an accurate picture of farm land alienation, this loss is dramatic. The conversion of agricultural land to largely urban use is an ecosection level impact with provincial significance, because less than 5% of British Columbia's land base is suitable for agricultural purposes (see Box 4.1).

Close to 2% of this ecoprovince is under some sort of protected status. Fifteen provincial parks occur within its boundaries. The Land Chapter of this report discusses further the

Box 4.1

Urbanization of agricultural land - why does it matter?

Responding to Canadian population pressure and urbanization, from 1966 to 1986 about 300,000 hectares (ha) of rural land was converted in urban regions, over half of which was prime agricultural land. For urban regions the size of those in the Okanagan Basin, rural land was converted to urban uses in the period at the rate of about 175 to 200 ha per thousand persons change in population, smaller centres having higher rates of conversion than larger centres. (It should be noted, however, that B.C.'s overall rate of conversion was 51 ha per thousand persons).

These losses are important for at least two reasons. About 75% of Canada's population lived in urban areas in the late 1980s, as did about half the world's population. These populations live by trade with agricultural areas. Furthermore, Canada is one of a small number of reliable international food export supply areas. Consequently, the future of Canada's agricultural land is a matter of global as well as national significance.[3,4]

provincial government's goal to secure 12% of the provincial landbase under protected status. The ecological framework will aid in the application of this objective as the hierarchy provides a context for assessment of ecosystem representation, an integral component of the strategy for protected areas.

Virtually all areas of the ecoprovince are accessible by road. Numerous lake resorts, ski slopes and heliskiing ventures, hiking trails, and wildlife viewing opportunities add to the allure of the area. Fishing, especially sport fishing is important. Game hunting is a seasonal activity that generates significant income to service businesses and their employees. Many of the people who take advantage of these recreational amenities live outside the ecoprovince. With improved communication and transportation links, major population centres in Alberta and the Lower Mainland of British Columbia have increased the recreational pressure on this area. In particular, the Coquihalla Highway connector, which opened in late 1990, has allowed a broader population to take advantage

---

Box 4.2

The sage thrasher: a species at risk

The current plight of the sage thrasher provides a vivid example of the threats posed to wildlife and the challenges facing wildlife managers in the south Okanagan. The sage thrasher is a small bird that in Canada breeds regularly only in the southern Similkameen and Okanagan Valleys in B.C. During the past twenty years, it has been sighted at only four locations in the province, and in the past ten years, at only one. Prior to 1920, populations may have been as high as 30 pairs, but since 1980, numbers have declined to between 5 and 10 pairs. During the breeding season the sage thrasher depends primarily on sagebrush habitat, which has been significantly reduced in quality and quantity by rangeland management practices such as mowing, burning and herbicide applications, and by residential and agricultural development. Just under 50% of the bird's habitat has been lost in the last 70 years. Development pressures are severe on at least three of the four remaining sites with suitable habitat.[6]

---

of the amenities of the area and has provided better access to Vancouver. Specific statistics are not available on this seasonal influx. However, with an increasing population base of over four million to draw from, these pressures are not insignificant.

Since European settlers first came to the Okanagan and Similkameen valleys, four vertebrate wildlife species have disappeared from the area: the sage grouse, the sharp-tailed grouse, the burrowing owl, and the white-tailed jackrabbit. The first two species probably disappeared from over-hunting , whereas, habitat fragmentation may have contributed to the loss of the burrowing owl and the white-tailed jackrabbit. Both of these latter species have been reintroduced to the area. The Short-horned lizard may also have disappeared; it has not been positively identified in British Columbia since 1910.[5]

Presently, about 58% of the threatened and endangered species and 14% of the vulnerable species in British Columbia are found in this ecoprovince.[7] The greatest pressure facing wildlife in this ecoprovince tends to be directed to those species which require valley habitat, the lands which receive the greatest pressure from urbanization (Box 4.2).

In the south Okanagan, for example, wetlands - which are vital for many species - now constitute less than 15% of their original area.[8] Moreover, less than 9% of the area remains in a relatively undisturbed state.[8,9] To emphasize the pressure on valley bottom habitats, most of the wildlife species of management concern are restricted to lower elevations representing less than 1% of the ecoprovince.[10]

Water quantity is currently an issue of concern that may be exacerbated in the future. A decline in the snowpack in recent years has raised worries about widespread water shortages, although the snowpack volumes may be cyclical. If predictions about global warming come to pass, water supply problems could become more exten-

---

sive and more acute.

Water quality is already a matter of much debate. Stream and lake pollution is reported in a number of locations and could have impacts on wildlife, fish and future recreation potential. Degradation of fish habitat and declines in fish populations have been noted in several tributaries to Okanagan Lake including Mission Creek, Kelowna Creek, and Vernon Creek. Approximately 50% of the Lake's rainbow trout and kokanee stream spawning population use Mission Creek, making it the most important tributary to the lake in terms of these two species.[11]

Automobile emissions are a major source of urban smog and the ground level ozone associated with it. Monitoring in Kelowna during the 1983-92 period suggests that ozone is not, at present, a significant problem in the immediate area. The rapid growth of automobile use in the region raises environmental concerns for the future.

Although the present air quality is generally good, there are several localized concerns. In the 1973-89 period, total suspended particulate (TSP) levels in both Lumby and Vernon were generally high and on some days exceeded provincial objectives.[12] Most often, relatively high TSP levels can be traced to woodwaste burners operating in a valley setting. Improvements in air quality in the Lumby area followed the closure of the lumber mill in 1989.

Woodwaste burners are considered to be a major source of dustfall in the Okanagan.[12] During the 1983-89 period, measures of dustfall at 25 sites indicated that over half exceeded desirable levels as outlined by the provincial government. The use of more efficient woodwaste burners to generate electricity is one of several options being considered to reduce emissions from this source.[13]

An odour problem - the familiar "rotten-egg" smell - in Kamloops is associated with hydrogen sulphide, which is emitted by bleached Kraft pulp mills and other industrial processes. 1990 was the worst "smell" year on record, although a substantial improvement was observed in 1991, explainable in part by emission reductions at the mill.[12]

The social and economic setting

The ecoprovince is one of western Canada's prime retirement destinations, and because of the growing economy, relatively mild climate, clean environment and recreation resources, the base population in the urban areas continues to soar. About 60% of the permanent population lives in urban centres, and this proportion is increasing. It is an ecoprovince where close to 90% of the population is located along the Thompson and Okanagan valleys. Seasonal surges of vacationers have to be accommodated, as well.

An aboriginal population of approximately 14,000 people is spread throughout some 30 bands. Of this population, 40% reside outside of Reserve lands. The First Nations

peoples' ties to the land, water, biota and associated resources are closely related to their spiritual, philosophical and cultural views of the world. Such values form an integral component of the social and cultural mosaic of the ecoprovince.

Compared to British Columbia as a whole, the Southern Interior ecoprovince has a greater proportion of people that are 55 years of age or older (Figure 4.2). Many of these are retirees living on pensions from private and public sources. While their earnings are somewhat fixed, incomes are reliable. About 35% of the population is between the ages of 20 and 44 years, and most work in retail stores, service businesses, and manufacturing (Figure 4.1).

While population within the ecoprovince has risen significantly, per capita automobile use has risen even more dramatically. From 1981 to 1991 a population increase of approximately 16% has resulted in a 22% increase in vehicle registrations. The potential certainly exists for increased adverse impacts from related air pollution and increases in the transportation infrastructure.

Labour force participation rates for the ecoprovince suggest that women have not had equal access to some important professions: in 1986, only 29.9% of the managerial and administrative positions; 12.8% of the natural science, engineering and mathematics related jobs; 28.8% of farming and horticultural employment; and 1.9% of construction trades were occupied by women.

This situation is reinforced by the disparity between men and women in professional education. Given the large and growing importance of women in the labour force and the significance of equal opportunity as an ethical issue in defining a sustainable community, the shortfall in the education of women is a serious matter. In 1986, women in the ecoprovince made up: 41.9% of those educated in the social sciences and related fields, 39.9% of those trained in the agricultural and biological sci-

ences, 8.6% of those trained in engineering, applied sciences and related fields, and 31.1% of those schooled in mathematics and the physical sciences.

An inadequate income can severely affect the quality of family life. The situation in the ecoprovince is worrisome. Average family income in 1986 ($32,087) was about 15% lower than B.C. as a whole ($37,675), although in the ecoprovince, lower incomes were offset to some degree by lower expenses for housing and other commodities. Approximately 12% of the families in the ecoprovince were headed by single-parents, who usually have to rely on one income rather than the two incomes enjoyed by many two-

Figure 4.3
Average income

The average female income in 1986 was just over half the average male income.[2]

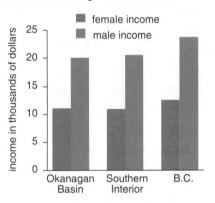

parent families. Moreover, approximately 83% of these single-parent families were headed by women, who tend to have lower incomes than their male counterparts (Figure 4.3).

In terms of formal education, levels of achievement are slightly lower than for British Columbians as a whole. Using 1986 census data, 38% of the adults over 20 years of age had not completed high school (Figure 4.4). Younger adults and children however, are attending school longer and are enrolling in post-secondary training in greater proportions.

The ecoprovince is fortunate to have a diverse economic base. This diversity enhances its ability to adapt to an uncertain economic future. However,

Figure 4.2
Population age distribution

Compared to British Columbia as a whole, the Southern Interior ecoprovince has a greater proportion of people that are 55 years of age or older.[2]

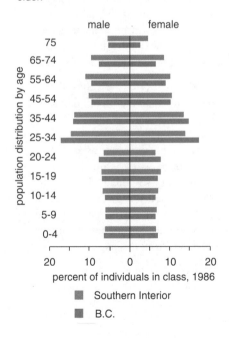

Figure 4.4
Post secondary education

Compared to British Columbia as a whole in 1986, the population of this ecoprovince had a slightly lower formal education level.[2]

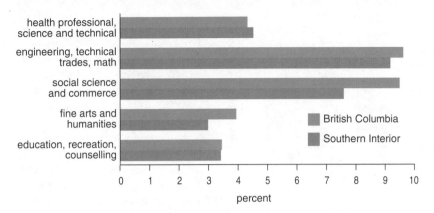

health professional, science and technical

engineering, technical trades, math

social science and commerce

fine arts and humanities

education, recreation, counselling

British Columbia
Southern Interior

percent

the dependence of parts of the ecoprovince on pension and unemployment insurance income is noteworthy. For example, a high proportion of income sources from several Okanagan communities are categorized as "basic" income. For communities such as Kelowna, Oliver-Osoyoos, Penticton, and Vernon, about half the income is based on pension and unemployment income.[14] About 80% of all non-employment income is pension income.

Average annual unemployment rates for the urban area of this ecoprovince have exceeded provincial averages over the past several years. As an example for the 1986-91 period, average unemployment rates were 14.7% in Kelowna and 14.0% in Kamloops, well above Victoria (9.6%), Vancouver (9.1%), and British Columbia as a whole (10.3%). With relatively high unemployment rates, there is a continual pressing need to create jobs: a need which is accentuated by a steady flow of new residents.

The interactions

The most salient and contentious issue affecting the sustainability of the Southern Interior ecoprovince is future land use. It is on this issue where the interplay of social, economic, and environmental forces are most evident and furthest reaching.

For illustrative purposes and to focus the discussion on this interplay, the conflict between urbanization and

agriculture in the Okanagan Basin will be highlighted. This conflict is deeply rooted. Population, pressing on limited land supplies, has increased land values and put cost pressure on agriculture.

The central mechanism governing urbanization pressure on agricultural land is the demand for urban land. Market pressure is indicated by detached bungalow housing prices in selected Okanagan Basin centres. Following the collapse of the real estate boom of 1980/81, these figures show a steady increase. For example, in Kelowna, prices rose from $71,000 in 1982 to $88,500 in 1989. After accounting for inflation, however, the pattern in the Basin is similar to that for B.C. as a whole: following a speculative peak in 1981, real prices collapsed and slowly recovered. However, in the last two years, real estate prices have accelerated to approximately 1981 boom levels.[15,16,17]

An initial analysis of data on demand for urban land supply does not seem to indicate extreme pressure. In the Basin's ecosections, the municipal population density rose from 2.83 persons per hectare in 1981 to a still healthy density of 4.39 in 1991, compared to 28.57 persons per hectare in the City of Victoria, which is certainly not overcrowded by global standards.

However, a significant portion of the land in the Basin's municipalities is

not available for urban development for two reasons: the regulatory constraint imposed by the Agricultural Land Reserve, and the natural restrictions imposed by a sensitive environment. For example, in the city of Kelowna in 1985, about 48% of the land was in the ALR, and over 15% consisted of slopes in excess of 30%, considered unsuitable for building or agriculture.[18] The relative impact of these regulatory and topographic constraints varies from one municipality to another. As a result, it is difficult to generalize about the availability of land for urban development within municipal boundaries in the ecoprovince. Persistent pressure on agricultural land reserves continues. For example, during the period 1974-89, 4,267 requests (involving 10,597 hectares) were made to the B.C. Agricultural Land Commission to exclude land from the ALR in the three regional districts represented in the Okanagan Basin.[19]

Land cost in dollar terms is certainly one input in the determination of land value. However, it is only one factor in the assessment of sustainability. Besides being a source of food for the local populous, orchards and vineyards provide valuable green space and play a significant role in terms of aesthetics. Production of secondary products such as juice, wine and cider increase the value of the role these agricultural uses play in the ecoprovince's economy. Further, the availability of fruit attracts large numbers of tourists who provide major support to the economic base of the ecoprovince. Also, fruit and grape cultivation within the ecoprovince is an important part of Canada's agricultural scene (Box 4.3). These assets should be factored into the assessment of sustainability.

On the negative side, intensive agricultural practices may have adverse environmental effects. The contamination of water draining from irrigated farm fields treated with fertilizers and pesticides affects biota, domestic water supplies, and recreational activities. Widespread use of agricultural chemicals remains an important concern. Between 1971 and

Tree fruits and grapes

The Okanagan is one of three major fruit growing areas in Canada; the other two are the Niagara Peninsula in Ontario and the Annapolis Valley in Nova Scotia. Two agricultural activities of particular importance to the Basin's ecosections are vineyard and tree fruit production. They play a strategic role in the Basin's future for several reasons. First, the Basin's land is unusually suited for these activities, within the spectrum of total Canadian land capability. Second, they are a crucial factor defining the Okanagan Basin in the minds of residents and for the outside world. Third, the overlapping and contiguous nature of agricultural land use with urban land requirements is a source of pressure and conflict. Fourth, they are part of the base for primary, secondary and tourist-related economic activities such as the wine, cider, and agricultural machinery industries.

A major study of fruit land use in the early 1980s showed a serious erosion of tree fruit lands over the 23 year period 1958 to 1981. Fruit land declined from 15,348 ha to 11,883 ha. This loss was partially offset by a rise in vineyard and nurseries. Overall, tree fruit, vineyard and nurseries area declined 13.8%, in the twenty-three year period.

Partly in recognition of this problem, the government of B.C. froze all farmland in 1972 and adopted an agricultural land reserve (ALR) policy in 1974. In 1981, 60% of land in the Okanagan region (including the Similkameen) was in the ALR. The decline in orchard land was reduced for areas within the ALR, from a loss of 615 ha in the six years previous to 1974 to a loss of 94 ha in the following six years — this despite an increase of built-up area within the ALR from 382 ha to 1,234 ha. [22]

1986, the number of hectares treated with fertilizer in the ecoprovince increased significantly, as did the rate of application (ratio of area treated to area cultivated). Pesticide application rates (area treated/area cultivated) and the area of cultivated land treated with pesticides also increased during that period (Figure 4.5). Historically, tree fruit production- the dominant agricultural activity in the Southern Okanagan - has utilized higher amounts of pesticide than any other cropping activity. [20] This heavy use of pesticides raises significant concerns for the health of people, plants and animals. Assessment of such health risks should

Pesticide application

Both the total area and the proportion of cropland treated with pesticides has increased. The area cultivated is the sum of cropland, summer fallow, and improved pasture.[1]

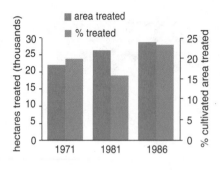

be factored in to the assessment of sustainability.

Urbanization and agricultural practices impact water quality and quantity. Historically, sewage treatment plants have been a principal source of phosphorus contamination in the major lakes. Wide fluctuations of populations in several communities because of tourist influxes, strain the sewage systems of these towns and cities. Recent installation of sophisticated treatment systems in some jurisdictions has reduced phosphorus concentrations substantially. Kelowna, for example, has declined from a discharge 11,000 kg/yr. to 1,000 kg/yr. of total phosphorus from 1980 to 1990.[21]

Nevertheless, phosphorus pollution continues to be a problem in the Okanagan. Some of the gains achieved through improved sewage treatment have been cancelled by increases in phosphorus output from a growing number of septic tank systems.

Water requirements for irrigation and other commercial uses are increasing. Currently, all water in many of the lakes and streams has been formally allocated for defined irrigation, domestic, waterworks and conservation uses.[23] All these kinds of water concerns should also be factored into the assessment of sustainability.

People are attracted to this ecoprovince by its climate and other regional environmental components. The environment is the backbone of the

tourist and general recreational trade. The landscape has cultural and spiritual value to the aboriginal peoples and many others. These considerations should be factored into the assessment.

Sustainability is not a local concept. It should be considered in a regional, national and even global context. In essence, one must understand the whole before the parts make sense. However, many ecological issues may be strongly local. Decisions and actions certainly have local implications. This is where the value of the ecological framework lies. The issues found in Vernon, Kamloops, and the Okanagan Basin can be set in a framework within which local issues and planning options can be linked to broader ones.

How important are the remaining wetlands to the people of Penticton, to the hydrology of the ecoregion or to the wildlife of the ecoprovince? What is considered as old-growth forest in the ecoprovince? What are the timber requirements of the Kamloops mill to maintain the existing work force? And what will the work force look like in the future? The social and economic matrix of the residents of the ecoprovince is changing. The proportion of the total population which is 55 years of age and older approximates 30%. Has this fact any bearing on future direction? These questions serve to suggest possible ecological linkages.

Sustainability is all about trying to come to grips with these ecological linkages. It is about risk assessment, value judgements, and the need to make compromises. Also, it is about keeping as many options open as practical in the decision-making process because there are always ecological surprises.

Regional sustainability: where do we stand?

Although the Southern Interior ecoprovince faces many challenges in the years ahead, when measured by any but the most extravagant standards, its people generally enjoy a high quality of life.

The preservation of the traditions, culture, and natural heritage of the region in the next twenty years does not appear to be seriously threatened by any particular problem. However, the potential cumulative effects of the many environmental concerns that are present may pose a threat to these values. Certainly the region has a responsibility to contribute to the resolution of these problems, but it cannot solve them alone. The region's responsibility is to seek solutions, respond to leadership, and to initiate and participate in programmes to deal with threats to sustainability. Intrinsically, global sustainability is a local issue: it cannot be achieved without commitment and action at the local level where it counts - in the everyday lives of men and women.

The crucial issue for the ecoprovince is the management of growth. Human and vehicle populations and land restructuring have increased the level of stress on the region's ecosystems in the past decade. Every difficulty facing the people of the region will be intensified, and new ones generated, if population growth and associated urban and residential development are not effectively managed. Programs, strategies, and management plans must insure that the necessary public and private institutions are in place to enable the region to seize opportunities, manage growth, and foster sustainability.

We must greatly improve our capacity to live in harmony with the environment. To do this, significant improvements are needed to the information available for environmental monitoring, reporting, and decision making. A first positive step would be to integrate existing economic, social, and environmental information within the ecological framework of ecosections, ecoregions and ecoprovinces. Administrative and institutional boundaries cannot provide this ecological context for analysis and decision-making.

A second step would be to commission long term studies in the ecoprovince that focus on the complex processes linking the environmental, economic, and social components of the ecosystem. A complementary monitoring program is essential. A third step would involve the development of an integrated information system to support the monitoring and management of the full range of sustainability issues at the ecoprovince and higher levels.

A number of efforts designed to create an inventory of databases, identify information needs, establish standards for information collection, and develop information retrieval systems have been undertaken in British Columbia. Many of these efforts are oriented to sustainability issues. These initiatives give hope that planning for sustainability, both in the ecoprovince and British Columbia as a whole, can be placed on a scientifically sound footing. Until then, we lack the necessary information to conclude that the high quality of life enjoyed by the people of the Southern Interior ecoprovince is sustainable over the long term.

Future directions

British Columbians are increasingly concerned about the quality of the environment. This State of the Environment Report addresses this concern and works to provide British Columbians with timely and accurate information on environmental conditions and trends. This report was also prepared to help British Columbians make informed decisions and responsible choices, ultimately for the benefit of the environment, for us and for future generations.

British Columbia offers a rich and spectacular landscape. It still has many environmental options long since foregone in other parts of the world. Decisions that we make now will have an impact on our ability to maintain life support systems, to preserve biological diversity, and to maintain a high standard of human health and quality of life into the future.

Are our actions and choices sustainable over the longer term? What do the environmental signposts and benchmarks reveal? There are three overall conclusions.

Considerable progress

First, considerable progress has been made over the last several decades in protecting and restoring the province's ecosystems. There are many examples in British Columbia that demonstrate that ecologically sustainable management of our natural resources is indeed possible, and that this results in both environmental and economic benefits. For example, levels of dioxins and furans have decreased, lead emission levels have declined, the percentage of protected area has increased and certain species of animals have made a dramatic population recovery.

Room for improvement

Second, there is a lot of room for improvement. Many long standing problems remain unresolved, and new problem areas continue to be discovered. Increasing stresses are evident from rapidly expanding urban centres, and from intensive use of natural resources. Sustainable development presents a real challenge: how to maintain a healthy economy while preserving ecological integrity for future generations. Preserving both nature's 'basic functions' and its biodiversity will require creativity, commitment, dialogue and real changes in how resources are used and how they are managed. Since ecosystems sometimes react in unpredictable ways, there is a need to continue to monitor the effects of our actions.

Linked to the world

Third, human activities and environmental problems in B.C. are closely linked to the rest of the world. Some of our activities have effects which extend far beyond provincial boundaries, and the condition of our local environment is influenced by distant human activities and natural events.

Reporting - now and in the future

This report has provided some, but certainly not all, of the answers and data on the state of the environment and, ultimately, on our achievement of sustainability. It has revealed many gaps in our knowledge base. Much of the environmental information that is collected is dedicated to perceived problem areas or for specific needs. There is a shortage of background information available to provide reliable environmental benchmarks. For many environmental problems, and particularly for those that are emerging, there is no consistent monitoring that will allow a thorough assessment of whether conditions are improving or getting worse (Figure 5.1). And where data are collected, differences in methodologies, definitions, and standards prevent comparative analyses from one area to the next.

Figure 5.1
Measuring the state of the environment

We are still at the early stages of reporting on the environment - there is often no quick and easy way to assess status and trends.

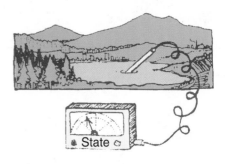

Piecemeal data sets have also limited our knowledge of cumulative and synergistic effects. More importantly, limited information prevents good understanding of the relationship between trends in human use and changes in the environment. While it comes as no surprise that many pieces of the environmental information puzzle are missing, the lack of information does hamper our ability to make sound and informed decisions.

We are at the early stages of reporting on the environment. This report is a first effort at providing a comprehensive assessment of environmental conditions and trends in the Province. To be effective over the longer term, there is the need to establish a firm foundation for state of the environment reporting. A good reporting program is built upon a number of key elements - comprehensive ecological monitoring sites, a solid and easily accessible database, commonly accepted environmental indicators, and the release of information, in a regular and timely manner.

To be effective, state of the environment reporting must contribute to an improved public understanding and awareness of environmental conditions and trends so that informed decisions can be made. In shaping the development of this report and longer term reporting efforts, representatives of the public have indicated that access to objective, timely and relevant information is critical to success. The implications of environmental conditions and trends must be discussed more extensively if improvements in human responses are indeed to be made.

The public has also suggested that future state of the environment reports should comment more extensively on the achievement of targets. Others have recommended that a variety of tools are necessary to communicate effectively with a wide audience that has varying levels of interest and understanding about the environment. It has also been recommended that different interpretations and perspectives surrounding data and information be included in a state of the environment report. Finally, members of the public have requested that reports address the notion of sustainability directly. In the words of one member of the public, "what do reported trends reveal about our ability to support ourselves in a sustainable manner?"

These comments go some distance to describing a more elaborate reporting framework for British Columbia. There's no question that there are many other aspects that could, and should, be reported upon over time. It is important, though, that the process of environmental reporting has begun.

It's up to all of us

British Columbia faces major environmental and economic challenges. Solutions to these challenges will require a shared responsibility on the part of all British Columbians (Figure 5.2). All citizens can benefit from increased awareness of the state of British Columbia's environment. With this knowledge, we can all make certain that our actions help to secure the environmental, economic and social sustainability of the province for both present and future generations.

Figure 5.2
Components of State of the Environment Reporting

State of the environment reporting requires that appropriate indicators be defined, that these be measured through a monitoring program, then analyzed and stored in an accessible data base. Periodic reports would be produced, and information would be available on an 'as needed' basis. In order for these components to function, people (government, scientists and the public) must participate in the process.

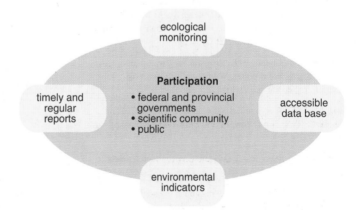

Comments on this report should be directed to:

Ministry of Environment, Lands and Parks
State of Environment Reporting
Corporate Policy, Planning and Legislation
810 Blanshard Street
Victoria, B.C.   V8V 1X4

Environment Canada
State of Environment Reporting
Conservation and Protection
224 West Esplanade
North Vancouver, B.C.   V7M 3H7

References

Perspectives

References cited

1. British Columbia Round Table on the Environment and the Economy. 1991b. Sustainable Communities. British Columbia Round Table on the Environment and the Economy, Victoria, B.C. 24 pp.

2. British Columbia Round Table on the Environment and the Economy. 1991a. Sustainable Land and Water Use. British Columbia Round Table on the Environment and the Economy, Victoria, B.C. 60 pp.

3. British Columbia Round Table on the Environment and the Economy. 1992. Sustainability Strategy for Energy. British Columbia Round Table on the Environment and the Economy, Victoria, B.C. 61 pp.

4. British Columbia Round Table on the Environment and the Economy. 1990. Sustainable Development and Energy. British Columbia Round Table on the Environment and the Economy, Victoria, B.C. 24 pp.

5. British Columbia Ministry of Environment, Lands and Parks. 1992. Municipal Solid Waste Tracking System: 1990 Data Analysis Summary Report. British Columbia Ministry of Environment, Lands and Parks, Environmental Protection Division, Municipal Waste Branch, Victoria, B.C.

6. British Columbia Ministry of Finance and Corporate Relations. 1990. British Columbia Population Forecast 1990-2016. British Columbia Ministry of Finance and Corporate Relations, Planning and Statistics Division, Victoria, B.C. 37 pp.

7. Ministry of Environment. 1991. Program for Participation. How B.C. is Managing Solid Waste. Ministry of Environment, Municipal Waste Branch, Victoria, B.C. booklet. 18 pp.

8. Wilson, M. 1990. Wings of the eagle. In: J. Plant and C. Plant (eds.). Turtle Talk. New Society Publishers, Philadelphia, pp. 76,79.

9. Data provided by Statistics Canada and Environment Canada, 1993.

10. Rowe, J.S. 1990. Home place: essays on ecology. Canadian Parks and Wilderness Society, Henderson Book Series No. 12. Edmonton: NeWest Publishers Ltd.

11. Data provided by B.C. Hydro, 1992.

12. Data provided by J. Mathers. Federal Environmental Assessment Review Office, Vancouver. 1993.

13. Environment Canada. Indicators Task Force. 1991. A report on Canada's progress towards a national set of environmental indicators. SOE Report No. 90-1, Environment Canada, State of the Environment Reporting, Ottawa. Ont.

14. Statistics Canada. 1992. National Income and Expenditure Accounts, Annual Estimates, 1980-1991. Ministry of Industry, Science and Technology, Ottawa, Ont. Cat. 13-201.

15. Data provided by British Columbia Ministry of Environment, Lands and Parks, Victoria. 1993.

Additional reading

British Columbia Round Table on the Environment and the Economy. 1992. Towards a Strategy for Sustainability. British Columbia Round Table on the Environment and the Economy, Victoria, B.C. 141 pp.

Ministry of Finance and Corporate Relations 1991. The Structure of the British Columbia Economy: A Land Use Perspective. Prepared for the British Columbia Round Table on the Environment and the Economy. Planning and Statistics Division, Ministry of Finance and Corporate Relations, Victoria, B.C. 51 pp.

Government of Canada. 1991. The State of Canada's Environment - 1991.

Air

References cited

1. Environment Canada. 1989. Ecoclimatic Regions of Canada. Ecological Land Classification Series. Ottawa: Supply and Services Canada, Ottawa, Ont. No. 23 118 pp.

2. Gullett, D.W. and W.R. Skinner. 1992. The State of Canada's Climate: Temperature Change in Canada 1895-1991. Environment Canada, Atmospheric Environment Service, Ottawa, Ont. SOE Report 92-2. En1-11/92-2E. 36 pp.

3. McBean, G.A., O. Slaymaker, T. Northcote, P. LeBlond, and T.S. Parsons. 1992. Review of models for climate change and impacts on hydrology, coastal currents, and fisheries in B.C. Environment Canada, Ottawa, Ont., Climate Change Digest CCD 92-02. 15 pp.

4. Oak Ridge National Laboratory. 1991. Trends '91: A Compendium of Data on Global Change. Carbon Dioxide Information Analysis Center, Oak Ridge National Laboratory, Oak Ridge, Tennessee.

5. British Columbia Ministry of Environment, Lands and Parks. 1992. Greenhouse gas inventory and management options. British Columbia Ministry of Environment, Lands and Parks, Victoria. ENV 200234/2-692. 58 pp.

6. Burrows, W.R., M. Vallée, and I.J. Wilson. 1992. Climatology of Daily Total Ozone and Ultraviolet-B Radiation Levels. Atmospheric Environment Service, Environment Canada. MSRB Research Report No. 92-005.

7. Archibald, D., J. Towns, and D. Smith. 1992. Ozone depleting greenhouse gases: Part 1 - British Columbia inventory and emissions. Prepared by Peat Marwick Stevenson & Kellogg Management Consultants for Ministry of Environment, Environment Canada, Greater Vancouver Regional District. 43 pp.

8. British Columbia Ministry of Environment, Lands and Parks. 1988. Acid rain in British Columbia. Ministry of Environment, Lands and Parks, Victoria, B.C. 13 pp.

9. Whitfield, P.H. and N. Dalley. 1987. Rainfall driven pH depressions in a British Columbia coastal stream. In: Proc. Symp. on Monitor., Modelling, and Mediating Water Quality. Amer. Water Resour. Assoc. pp. 285-294.

10. Whitfield, P.H., N. Rousseau, and E. Michnowsky. 1992. Rainfall induced changes in chemistry of a British Columbia coastal stream. Northwest Sci. 67(1): 1-6.

11. Data provided by Conservation and Protection Service, Environment Canada, Ottawa, Ont., 1992.

12. Ministry of Environment. 1993. Atmospheric Report for British Columbia. British Columbia Ministry of Environment, Lands and Parks, Victoria, B.C.

13. van Barneveld, J.W., P.D. Marsh, J.H. Wiens, and K.J. Wipond. 1989. Port Alice SO_2 impacts: air quality, soil vegetation, and health. Ministry of Environment, Waste Management Branch, Victoria, B.C.

14. Interim Acid Deposition Critical Loadings Task Group. 1990. Interim Acid Deposition Critical Loadings for Western and Northern Canada. Prepared for Technical Committee Western and Northern Canada Long Range Transport of Atmospheric Pollutants. 31 pp.

Additional reading

ARA Consulting Group et al. 1992. Evaluation of CO_2 management measures. Prepared for British Columbia Ministry of Environment, Lands and Parks, Victoria.

Association of B.C. Professional Foresters. 1991. Discussion Paper on Are We Overcutting Our Forests?

B.C. Clean Air Policy Steering Committee. 1992. Smoke management for the '90s. British Columbia Ministry of Environment, Lands and Parks, Victoria. ENV 112091.292. 61 pp.

B.H. Levelton & Associates Ltd. et al. 1991. An inventory and analysis of control measures for methane in British Columbia. Prepared for British Columbia Ministry of Environment, Lands and Parks, Victoria. 139 pp. and 10 Appendices.

Canada. 1991. Chapter 2: Atmosphere. In: The State of Canada's Environment. Government of Canada, Ottawa. pp. 2-1 to 2-25.

CCME. 1990. Management plan for nitrogen oxides (NO_x) and volatile organic compounds (VOCs). Phase I. Canadian Council of Ministers of the Environment, Winnipeg. CCME-EPC/TRE-31E. 176 pp. and 4 Appendices.

Concord Environmental Corporation. 1992. British Columbia emission inventory of nitrogen oxides, volatile organic compounds and ozone (NO_x/VOC/O_3) as greenhouse gases. Prepared for British Columbia Ministry of Environment, Lands and Parks, Victoria. 124 pp. and 9 Appendices.

Long-range Transport of Air Pollutants Program. 1990. Report of the Federal-Provincial acid rain agreement. AES, Environment Canada, Downsview, Ontario.

Ministry of Environment. 1992. Ensuring clean air: Developing a clean air strategy for British Columbia. Ministry of Environment, Lands and Parks, Victoria, B.C. ENV112100.392. 45 pp.

Task Group on Atmospheric Change. 1992. CRD Healthy Atmosphere 2000: Final Report of Recommendations of the CRD Task Group on Atmospheric Change. Task Group on Atmospheric Change, Capital Regional District, Victoria, B.C.

Water

References cited

1. British Columbia Round Table on the Environment and the Economy. 1991. Sustainable Land and Water Use. British Columbia Round Table on the Environment and the Economy, Victoria, B.C. 60 pp.

2. Environment Canada. 1990. Water - Here, There and Everywhere. Environment Canada, Conservation and Protection, Ottawa, Ont. Fact Sheet: No. 2: Water, 8 pp.

3. Data provided by Hydrology Branch, British Columbia Ministry of Environment, Lands and Parks, 1992

4. Crippen Consultants. 1990. Municipal Water Supply Issues in British Columbia. Prepared for the British Columbia Round Table on the Environment and the Economy.

5. Leith, R.M. 1991. Patterns in snowcourse and annual mean flow data in British Columbia and the Yukon. In: Using Hydrometric Data to Detect and Monitor Climatic Change: Proceedings of NHRI Symposium No. 8, April, 1991. NHRI, Saskatoon, Saskatchewan, pp. 225-231.

6. Northcote, T.G. and P.A. Larkin 1989. The Fraser River: a major salmonine production system. In: D.P. Dodge (ed.). Proceedings of the International Large River Symposium. Can. Spec. Publ. Fish. Aquat. Sci. 106: 272-104.

7. Hall, K.J., H. Schreier and S.J. Brown. 1991. Water quality in the Fraser River basin. In: A.H.J. Dorcey and J.R. Griggs (eds.). Water in Sustainable Development: Exploring our Common Future in the Fraser River Basin. Westwater Research Centre, Vancouver, British Columbia, Part II: Chap. 3, pp. 41-75.

8. Servizi, J.A. 1989. Protecting Fraser River salmon (*Oncorhynchus* spp.) from wastewaters: an assessment. In: C.D. Levings, L.B. Holtby, and M.A. Henderson (eds.). Proceedings of the National Workshop on Effects of Habitat Alteration on Salmonid Stocks. Can. Spec. Publ. Fish. Aquat. Sci. 150. pp. 135-153.

9. Environment Canada. 1990. Water Works!. Environment Canada, Conservation and Protection, Ottawa, Ontario, Fact Sheet: No. 4: Water. 12 pp.

10. McNeill, R. and D. Tate. 1991. Guidelines for Municipal Water Pricing. Environment Canada, Conservation and Protection, Inland Waters Directorate, Water Planning and Management Branch, Ottawa, Ontario, Social Science Series No. 25. 66 pp.

11. Tate, D.M. and D.M. Lacelle. 1992. Municipal Water Rates in Canada, 1989: Current Practices and Prices. Environment Canada, Conservation and Protection, Ottawa, Ontario, Social Science Series No. 27. 22 pp.

12. British Columbia Ministry of Environment, Lands and Parks. 1991/1992. News Releases (4).

13. CEPA. 1991. Canadian Environmental Protection Act. Priority Substances List Assessment, Report No. 2. Effluents from Pulp Mills Using Bleaching.

14. CEPA. 1990. Canadian Environmental Protection Act. Priority Substances List Assessment, Report No. 1. Polychlorinated Dibenzodioxins and Polychlorinated Dibenzofurans.

15. Data provided by Conservation and Protection, Environment Canada, Pacific and Yukon Region, 1992.

16. CEPA. 1992. Pulp and Paper Mill Effluent Chlorinated Dioxins and Furans Regulations. Extract: Canada Gazette, Part II, May 20, 1992. Department of the Environment.

17. Bothwell, M.L. 1992. Eutrophication of rivers by nutrients in treated kraft pulp mill effluent. Environment Canada, Conservation and Protection, National Hydrology Research Institute, Inland Waters and Lands Directorate, Saskatoon, Saskatchewan, Contribution No. 92026. 30 pp. and figures.

18. Ministry of Environment. 1991. Background Paper: Regulatory Restrictions on Sanitary and Stormwater discharges in British Columbia. Environmental Protection Division, Ministry of Environment. Victoria, B.C. 7 pp.

19. British Columbia Ministry of Environment, Lands and Parks. 1992. Environmental Action Plan for British Columbia. British Columbia Ministry of Environment, Lands and Parks. Victoria, B.C.

20. Ministry of Environment. 1992. Urban Runoff Quality Control Guidelines for The Province of British Columbia. Municipal Waste Branch, Environmental Protection Divisionn Ministry of Environment, Victoria, B.C. Prepared by Waste Management Group, British Columbia Research Corporation, Vancouver, B.C.

21. Data provided by Mine Development Assessment Branch, Ministry of Energy, Mines and Petroleum Resources, 1992.

22. Filion, F.L., E. DuWors, A. Jacquemot, F. Bouchard, P. Boxall, P.A. Gray and R. Reid. 1989. Importance of wildlife to Canadians in 1987: Highlights of a national survey. Environment Canada, Canadian Wildlife Service, Ottawa, 45 pp.

23. Errington, J.C. and K.D. Ferguson. 1987. Acid mine drainage in British Columbia: today and tomorrow. In: Acid Mine Drainage: Proceedings of the Eleventh Annual British Columbia Mine Reclamation Symposium. Convened at the Discovery Inn, Campbell River, British Columbia, April 8-10, 1987. Organized by the Technical and Research Committee on Reclamation. Sponsored by the Mining Association of B.C., British Columbia Ministry of Energy Mines and Petroleum Resources, British Columbia Ministry of Environment, Lands and Parks. pp. 7-29.

24. Errington, J.C. 1992. History and future of mine reclamation in British Columbia. In: Mine Reclamation "From Exploration to Decommissioning": Proceedings of the Sixteenth Annual British Columbia Mine Reclamation Symposium. Convened at the Hudson Bay Lodge, Smithers, British Columbia, June 15-18, 1992. Organized by the Technical and Research Committee on Reclamation. Sponsored by the Mining Association of B.C., British Columbia Ministry of Energy, Mines and Petroleum Resources, British Columbia Ministry of Environment, Lands and Parks with support from The University of British Columbia, and The Coal Association of British Columbia.

25. Ministry of Energy, Mines and Petroleum Resources. 1991. Annual Report, Resource Management Branch. Ministry of Energy, Mines and Petroleum Resources, Mineral Resources Division, Victoria, B.C. 23 pp.

26. Data provided by Dangerous Goods Incident Database, Ministry of Environment, 1992.

27. Data provided by Environmental Emergency Services Branch, British Columbia Ministry of Environment, Lands and Parks, 1992.

28. Chatwin, S.C., D.E. Howes, J.W. Schwab, and D.N. Swanston. 1991. A Guide for Management of Landslide-Prone Terrain in the Pacific Northwest. B.C. Ministry of Forests, Victoria, B.C., Land Management Handbook No. 18. 212 pp.

29. Data provided by Water Quality Branch, British Columbia Ministry of Environment, Lands and Parks, 1992.

30. Ministry of Health and Ministry Responsible for Seniors. 1990. Giardiasis and other water-borne disease. British Columbia Ministry of Health and Ministry Responsible for Seniors, Burnaby, B.C., No. 10, Sept. 1990. 1 pp.

31. Canadian Council of Resource and Environmental Ministers. 1991. Canadian Water Quality Guidelines. Prepared by the Task Force on Water Quality Guidelines of the Canadian Council of Resources and Environment Ministers, Environmental Quality Guidelines Division, Water Quality Branch, Inland Waters Directorate, Environment Canada, Ottawa, Ont.

32. Data provided by Bureau of Communicable Disease Epidemiology, Heath and Welfare Canada, 1992.

33. Dwernychuk, L.W., G.S. Bruce, G. Gordon, and G.P. Thomas. 1992. Fraser and Thompson Rivers: a comprehensive organochlorine study 1990/91 (drinking water/mill effluent/sediment/fish). Prepared for Northwood Pulp and Timber Limited, Prince George, B.C.; CANFOR Corporation, Prince George, B.C.; Cariboo Pulp and Paper Company, Quesnel, B.C.; and Weyerhaeuser Canada Ltd., Kamloops, B.C., 6 pp. and tables and figures.

34. Data provided by Environmental Health Protection Service, Ministry of Health, 1992.

35. British Columbia Ministry of Agriculture, British Columbia Ministry of Energy, Mines and Petroleum Resources, Ministry of Environment, Ministry of Forests, Ministry of Health, British Columbia Ministry of Environment, Lands, and Parks Ministry of Housing, and Ministry of Municipal Affairs. 1980. Guidelines for Watershed Management of Crown lands used as Community Water Supplies. Ministry of Environment, Victoria, B.C. 48 pp and appendices.

37. Hess, P.J. 1986. Ground-Water Use in Canada, 1981. National Hydrology Research Institute, Inland Water Directorate, Environment Canada, Ottawa, Ontario, NHRI Paper No. 28, IWD Tech. Bull. No. 140. 43 pp. and 6 maps.

38. Data provided by Groundwater Section, Water Management Branch, British Columbia Ministry of Environment, Lands and Parks, 1992.

39. Data provided by the Groundwater Section, British Columbia Ministry of Environment, Lands and Parks, 1992.

40. British Columbia Ministry of Agriculture, Fisheries and Food, in cooperation with B.C. Federation of Agriculture, and the Poultry Industry of B.C. 1992. Environmental Guidelines for Poultry Producers in British Columbia. British Columbia Ministry of Agriculture, Fisheries and Food, Soils and Engineering Branch, Abbotsford, B.C., B.C.F.A. British Columbia Federation of Agriculture 1992 issue. 70 pp.

41. Data provided by Petrochemical, Mining and Special Waste Unit, Technical Services and Special Wastes Section, Industrial Waste and Hazardous Contaminants Branch, British Columbia Ministry of Environment, Lands and Parks, 1992.

42. Kohut, A.P., W.S. Hodge, and F. Chwojka. 1986. Groundwater quality variations in fractured bedrock aquifers of the Gulf Islands, British Columbia. In: Proceedings: Third Canadian Hydrogeological Conference. International Assoc. of Hydrogeologists, Canadian National Chapter, pp. 185-192.

43. Kay B.H. 1989. Pollutants in British Columbia's Marine Environment - A Status Report. Supply and Services Canada, 59 pp.

44. Wells, P.G. and S.J. Rolston (eds.) 1991. Health of Our Oceans: A Status Report on Canadian Marine Environmental Quality. Conservation and Protection, Environment Canada, Ottawa and Dartmouth.

45. Colodey, A.G. and P.G. Wells. 1992. Effects of pulp and paper mill effluents on estuarine and marine ecosystems in Canada: a review. J. Aquat. Ecosystem Health 1: 15-40.

46. Sullivan, D.L. 1987. Compilation and Assessment of Research Monitoring and Dumping Information in Active Dump Sites in British Columbia and Yukon Coasts from 1979 to 1987. Environment Canada, Conservation and Protection, Environmental Protection, Pacific and Yukon Region, Vancouver, B.C., Regional Manuscript Report 87-02.

47. Data provided by National Analysis of Trends in Emergency Systems (NATES) database (1972-83 data) and Emergencies Division, Environment Canada, Pacific & Yukon Region (1984-92 data)

48. Cross, S.F. 1990. Benthic impacts of salmon farming in British Columbia. Volume 1: Summary report. Manuscript prepared for the British Columbia Ministry of Environment, Water Management Branch, Victoria, B.C. 78 pp. and appendices.

49. Anderson, E. 1992. Benthic recovery following salmon farming study site selection and initial surveys. Prepared for the British Columbia Ministry of Environment, Lands and Parks, Water Quality Branch.

50. Caine, G., J. Truscott, S. Reid, and K. Ricker. 1987. Biophysical Criteria for Siting Salmon Farms in British Columbia. Ministry of Agriculture and Fisheries, Victoria, B.C. and The Aquaculture Association of B.C., Nanaimo, B.C. 50 pp.

51. B.C. Government. 1988. Environmental Monitoring Program for Marine Fish Farms. Waste Management Branch and Water Management Branch, Victoria, B.C. 77 pp.

52. GESAMP. 1990. Long-Term Consequences of Low-Level Marine Contamination: An Analytical Approach. IMO/FAO/Unesco/ WMO/WHO/IAEA/UN/UNEP, Joint Group of Experts on the Scientific Aspects of Marine Pollution, Reports and Studies No. 40.

53. Noble, D. 1990. A State of the Environment Report - Contaminants in Canadian Seabirds. Supply and Services, Ottawa, Ontario, SOE Report No. 90-2. 75 pp.

54. Brothers, D.E. 1990a. Benthic sediment chemistry: West Coast survey - Phase I. Regional Data Report 90-04.

55. Brothers, D.E. 1990b. Benthic sediment chemistry: West Coast survey - Phase II. Regional Data Report 90-05.

56. Brothers, D.E. 1990c. Benthic sediment chemistry: B.C. ocean dump sites, October, 1987. Regional Data Report 90-06.

57. Brothers, D.E. 1990d. Benthic sediment chemistry: B.C. ocean dump sites, October, 1988. Regional Data Report 90-07.

58. D.B. Regan and Associates Ltd. 1992. CanadianOxy industrial chemicals limited partnership: 1991 crab survey. A report prepared for CanadianOxy Industrial Chemicals Limited Partnership, Squamish Chlor-Alkali Plant, Squamish, B.C., File No. 2691.

59. Harding, L. 1990. Dioxin and furan levels in sediments, fish and invertebrates from fishery closure areas of coastal British Columbia. Environment Canada, Environmental Protection Regional Data Report 90-09.

60. Elliott, J.E., D.G. Noble, R.J. Norstrom, and P.E. Whitehead. 1989. Organochlorine contaminants in Seabird eggs from the Pacific Coast of Canada, 1971-1986. Environ. Monit. Assess. 12: 67-82.

61. Whitehead, P.E. 1991. Update: monitoring dioxin and furan contamination of heron and cormorant eggs collected from the Strait of Georgia indicates a downward trend - 1991. Canadian Wildlife Service, Pacific and Yukon Region, 4 pp. and figures.

62. Bellward, G.D., R.J. Norstom, P.E. Whitehead, J.E. Elliot, S.M. Bandiera, C. Dworschak, T. Chang, S. Forbes, B. Cadario, L.E. Hart, and K.M. Cheng. 1990. Comparison of Polychlorinated Dibenzodioxin level with Hepatic mixed-function oxidase induction in Great Blue Herons. J. Toxicol. Environ. Health 30: 33-52.

63. Hart, L.E., K.M. Cheng, P.E. Whitehead, R.M. Shah, R.J. Lewis, S.R. Ruschkowski, R.W. Blair, D.C. Bennett, S.M. Bandiera, R.J. Norstrom, and G.D. Bellward. 1991. Dioxin contamination and growth and development in Great Blue Heron embryos. J. Toxicol. Environ. Health 32: 331-344.

64. Whitehead, P.E., R.J. Norstrom, and J.E. Elliott. 1992. Dioxin levels in Eggs of Great Blue Heron (*Ardea herodias*) Decline Rapidly in Response to Process Changes in a Nearby Kraft Pulp Mill. 12th International Symposium on Dioxin and Related Compounds, August 1992. University of Tampere, Tampere, Finland.

65. Data provided by Department of Fisheries and Oceans, 1992.

66. Burlinson, N.E. 1991. Organochlorine Compounds in Marine Mammals from the Strait of Georgia. British Columbia Environment, Ministry of Environment, Lands and Parks, Victoria, B.C. 9 pp.

67. Dwernychuk, L.W., G. Bruce, and B. Gordon. 1991. Organochlorine Contamination in Various Environmental Compartments Related to Chemical/Combustion Sources: Lower Mainland/Vancouver Island Skeena/Interior Regions. B.C. Environment, British Columbia Ministry of Environment, Lands and Parks, Victoria, B.C. 68 pp. and appendices.

68. Teschke, K., S. Kelly, M. Wiens, C. Hertzman, H.D. Ward, J.E.H. Ward, and J.C. Van Oostdam. 1992. Chlorinated Dibenzo-p-dioxins and Dibenzofurans in the Adipose Tissue of British Columbia Residents. British Columbia Ministry of Environment, Lands and Parks, Victoria, B.C. 28 pp. and appendices.

69. Garrett, C.L. 1985. Chemicals in the Environment, Pacific and Yukon Region: II. Cadmium. Environment Canada, Environmental Protection Service, Pacific & Yukon Region, Summary Report. 47 pp.

70. Indicators Task Force. 1991. A report on Canada's progress towards a national set of environmental indicators. Environment Canada, State of the Environment Reporting, Ottawa, Ont., SOE Report No. 91-1.

71. Whitehead, P.E. 1989. Toxic chemicals in Great Blue Heron (*Ardea herodias*) eggs in the Strait of Georgia. In: K. Vermeer and R.W. Butler (eds.). The Ecology and Status of Marine and Shoreline Birds in the Strait of Georgia, British Columbia. Special Publication. Canadian Wildlife Service, Environment Canada, Ottawa, Ont. pp. 177-183.

72. Noble, D.G. and J.E. Elliott. 1986. Environmental contaminants in Canadian Seabirds, 1968-1984: trends and effects. Canadian Wildlife Service, Ottawa, Ont. Technical Report Series No. 13.

73. Muir, D.C.G. and R.J. Nortstrom. 1990. Marine mammals as indicators of environmental contamination by PCBs and dioxins/furans. In: L.E. Harding (ed.). Monitoring Status and Trends in Marine Environmental Quality: Proceedings of a symposium in conjunction with the 17th Annual Aquatic Toxicity Workshop, Vancouver, British Columbia, November 5-8 1990. Prepared for Environment Canada by Richard Banner, Polestar Communications, pp. 134-139.

74. Muir, D.C.G., C.A. Ford, B. Rosenberg, M. Simon, R.J. Norstrom, and K. Langelier, 1991. PCBs and Other Organochlorine Contaminants in Marine Mammals from the Strait of Georgia. Fisheries and Oceans, Winnipeg, Manitoba; Canadian Wildlife Service, Hull, Quebec; and Island Veterinary Hospital, Nanaimo, B.C. Abstract No. 135 as found in Society of Environmental Toxicology and Chemistry. 12th Annual Meeting, November 3-7, 1991, Seattle Convention Center, Seattle, Washington.

75. Energy, Mines and Resources. 1974. The National Atlas of Canada. Macmillan Publishers Ltd. in association with Energy, Mines and Resources of Canada. Ottawa, Ont. 4th ed. revised. 254 pp.

76. Martel, P.H., T.G. Kovacs, B.I. O'Connor, and R.H. Voss. 1993. A survey of pulp and paper mill effluents for their potential to induce mixed function oxidase enzyme activity in fish. Proceedings of 79th Annual Meeting of the CPPA in Montreal.

77. Carey, J.H., P.V. Hodson, K.R. Munkittrick, and M.R. Servos. 1991. Recent Canadian studies on the physiological effects of pulp mill effluent on fish. Proceedings of a SEPA Conference held in Stockholm, Sweden, 19-21 November 1991.

78. Data provided by Canadian Wildlife Service, Environment Canada, Vancouver. 1993.

Additional reading

British Columbia Ministry of Environment, Lands and Parks. 1992. Municipal Solid Waste Tracking System: 1990 Data Analysis Summary Report. British Columbia Ministry of Environment, Lands and Parks, Environmental Protection Division, Municipal Waste Branch, Victoria, B.C.

Day, J.C. and J.A. Affum. 1990. Toward Sustainable Water Planning and Management in British Columbia. Prepared for the British Columbia Round Table on the Environment and the Economy. 46 pp.

Dorcey, A.H.J. and J.R. Griggs (eds). 1991. Water in Sustainable Development: Exploring our Common Future in the Fraser River Basin. Westwater Research Centre, Vancouver, B.C. 288pp.

Environment Canada. 1985. Cadmium in the Aquatic Environment. Environment Canada, Environmental Protection Service, Pacific & Yukon Region, Chemicals in the Environment: Fact Sheet. 2 pp.

Environment Canada. 1985. Lead in the Aquatic Environment. Environment Canada, Environmental Protection Service, Pacific & Yukon Region, Chemicals in the Environment: Fact Sheet. 2 pp.

Environment Canada. 1985. Mercury in the Aquatic Environment. Environment Canada, Environmental Protection Service, Pacific & Yukon Region, Chemicals in the Environment: Fact Sheet. 2 pp.

Environment Canada. 1985. Polychlorinated Biphenyls (PCBs) in the Aquatic Environment. Environment Canada, Environmental Protection Service, Pacific & Yukon Region, Chemicals in the Environment: Fact Sheet. 2 pp.

Environment Canada. 1989. Municipal Water Rates in Canada: Current Practices and Prices. Environment Canada, Ottawa, Ont. 4 pp.

Environment Canada. 1990. Arsenic in the Aquatic Environment. Environment Canada, Environmental Protection Service, Pacific & Yukon Region, Chemicals in the Environment: Fact Sheet. 2 pp.

Environment Canada. 1990. Chlorophenols in the Aquatic Environment. Environment Canada, Environmental Protection Service, Pacific & Yukon Region, Chemicals in the Environment: Fact Sheet. 2 pp.

Environment Canada. 1990. Clean Water — Life Depends on It!. Environment Canada, Conservation and Protection, Ottawa, Ont. Fact Sheet: No. 3: Water. 12 pp.

Environment Canada. 1990. Groundwater - Nature's Hidden Treasure. Environment Canada, Conservation and Protection, Ottawa, Ont. Fact Sheet: No. 5: Water. 12 pp.

Environment Canada. 1991. Review and Recommendations for Canadian Interim Environmental Quality Criteria for Contaminated Sites. Environment Canada, Conservation and Protection, Inland Waters Directorate, Water Quality Branch, Ottawa, Ont. Scientific Series No. 197.

Deparament of Fisheries and Oceans. 1992. Backgrounder: dioxins and furans. Fisheries and Oceans, News Release dated May 1, 1992. 2 pp.

Hartman, G.F. and J.C. Scrivener. 1990. Impacts of Forestry Practices on a Coastal Stream Ecosystem, Carnation Creek, British Columbia. Department of Fisheries and Oceans, Ottawa, Ont., Can. Bull. Fish. Aquat. Sci. 223. Contribution No. 150 to the Carnation Creek Watershed Project. 148 pp.

Kay, B.H. 1986. West Coast Marine Environmental Quality: Technical Reviews. Environment Canada, Conservation and Protection, Environmental Protection, Regional Program Report 86-01. 154 pp.

Kohut, A.P. 1987. Groundwater Supply Capability: Abbotsford Upland. British Columbia Ministry of Environment and Parks, Water Management Branch, Victoria, B.C. 38 pp.

Kruus, P., M. Demmer, and K. McCaw. 1991. Chemicals in the Environment.

Liebscher, H., B. Hii, and D. McNaughton. 1992. Nitrates and pesticides in the Abbotsford Aquifer, Southwestern British Columbia. Environment Canada. 83 pp.

Mah, F.T.S., D.D. MacDonald, S.W. Sheehan, T.M. Tuominen, and D. Valiela. 1989. Dioxins and Furans in Sediment and Fish from the Vicinity of Ten Inland Pulp Mills in British Columbia. Environment Canada, Conservation and Protection, Inland Waters, Pacific and Yukon Region, Vancouver, B.C. 77 pp. and errata sheets.

Ministry of Environment. 1991. Sustaining the Water Resource. British Columbia's Environment: Planning for the Future. B.C. Environment, Water Management Division, Victoria, B.C., ENV111983.791. 18 pp.

Ministry of Environment. 1991. The Attainment of Ambient Water Quality Objectives in 1990. Ministry of Environment, Water Management Branch, Victoria, B.C. 204 pp.

Ministry of Health. 1990. Nitrate contamination in well water. Ministry of Health, Burnaby, B.C., From the Health Files No. 5, June 1990. 1 pp.

Rieberger, K. 1992. Metal Concentrations in Bottom Sediments from Uncontaminated B.C. Lakes. British Columbia Ministry of Environment, Lands and Parks, Water Quality Branch, Water Management Division, Victoria, B.C. 332 pp.

States/British Columbia Oil Spill Task Force. 1990. Final report of the States/British Columbia Oil Spill Task Force. Province of British Columbia, State of Washington, State of Oregon, State of Alaska, and State of California, 127 pp.

Plants and Animals

References cited

1. Harper, B., T. Lea, and B. Maxwell. 1991. Habitat Inventory in the South Okanagan. Bioline 10(2): 12-16.

2. Ministry of Environment. 1991. Managing Wildlife to 2001, A Discussion Paper. Wildlife Branch, Victoria, B.C. 150 pp.

3. British Columbia Ministry of Environment and Parks. 1987. Wildlife in British Columbia. Wildlife Branch, Victoria, B.C. 15 pp.

4. McKelvey, R. 1981. Winter distribution, mortality factors, and habitat conditions of the Trumpeter Swan in British Columbia. Proceedings and Papers f the 6th Trumpeter Swan Society Conference. Anchorage, Alaska. 101 pp.

5. Ehrlich, P.A and A.H. Ehrlich. 1992. The Value of Biodiversity. Ambio 21(3): 219-226.

6. Data provided by Conservation Data Centre, British Columbia Ministry of Environment, Lands and Parks, Victoria, B.C., 1992.

7. Data provided by Fisheries Branch, British Columbia Ministry of Environment, Lands and Parks, Victoria, B.C., 1992.

8. Cannings, R.A. and A.P. Harcombe. 1990. The vertebrates of British Columbia: scientific and English names. Heritage Record No. 20, Royal British Columbia Museum and Wildlife report N. R-24, Wildlife Branch, Victoria, B.C.

9. Harding, L., P. Newroth, R. Smith, B. Smiley, M. Waldichuk, R. Cranston and A. Sturko. 1993. New Introductions: Alien Species in British Columbia. In: L.E. Harding and E.A. McCullum (eds.). Biodiversity in British Columbia: Our Changing Environment. Chapter 16. (in press)

10. McAllister, D. 1990. List of the Fishes of Canada. Syllabus #64. National Museum of Canada.

11. Data provided by Wildlife Branch, British Columbia Ministry of Environment, Lands and Parks, Victoria, B.C., 1992.

12. Campbell, R.W., N.K. Dawe, I. McTaggart-Cowan, J.M. Cooper, G.W. Kaiser, and M.C.E. McNail. 1990. The Birds of British Columbia. Volume 2. Mitchell Press, Vancouver, B.C. 636 pp.

13. McMinn, R.G., S. Eis, H.E. Hirvonen, E.T. Oswals, and J.P. Senyk. 1976. Native vegetation in British Columbia's Capital Region. Environment Canada, Forestry Service Rep. B.C.-X-140, Victoria, B.C.

14. Thilenius, J.F. 1968. The Quercus garryana forest of the Willamette Valley, Oregon. Ecology 49(6): 1124-1133.

15. Douglas, D. 1914. Journal kept by David Douglas during his travels in North America 1823-1827. Wesley and Son, London, 364 pp.

16. Riegel, G.M., B.G. Smith, and J.F. Franklin. 1992. Foothill Oak Woodlands of the Interior Valleys of Southwestern Oregon. Northwest Sci. 66(2): 66-76.

17. Goward, T. 1991. Lichens and the vanished grasslands. B.C. Naturalist 29(4): 8-9.

18. Harper, W.L., E.C. Lea, and R.E. Maxwell. 1992. Biodiversity inventory in the South Okanagan. In: M.A. Fenger, E.H. Miller, J.A. Johnson and E.J.R. Williams (eds.). Our Living Legacy. Proceedings of a Symposium on Biological Diversity. British Columbia Ministry of Environment, Land and Parks, Ministry of Forests and Royal B.C. Museum, Victoria, B.C. (in press).

19. Dorey, R.J. 1975. A fire history investigation and the effects of fire exclusion on a ponderosa pine forest in southeastern British Columbia. Thesis, Faculty of Forestry, University of British Columbia, Vancouver, B.C.

20. Roberts, A. 1992. A report on ecology of the Junction Wildlife Management Area. Prepared for Wildlife Section, Ministry of Environment, Williams Lake. Unpublished report.

21. Data provided by Ecodistricts Database, Environment Canada, 1992

22. Pilon, P. and M.A. Kerr. 1984. Land Use Change on Wetlands in the Southwestern Fraser Lowland, B.C. Environment Canada.

23. Kellogg, E. (ed.). 1992. Coastal Temperate Rain Forests: Ecological Characteristics, Status and Distribution Worldwide. Ecotrust and Conservation International Occasional Paper Series No. 1, 64 pp.

24. Moore, M.K. 1991. Coastal Watersheds: An Inventory of Watersheds in the Coastal Temperate Forests of British Columbia. Earthlife Canada Foundation and Ecotrust/Conservation International, 54 pp.

25. United Nations Environment Program. 1992. Convention on Biological Diversity, 5 June 1992.

26. Data provided by Pacific Biological Station, Department of Fisheries and Oceans, Nanaimo, B.C., 1993.

27. Haist, V. and J.F. Schweigert. 1992. Stock assessment for British Columbia herring in 1991 and forecasts of the potential catch in 1992. Can. Manu. Rep. Fish. Aquat. Sci. No. 2146, 82 pp.

28. Data provided by 1992 Fact Sheets, Institute of Ocean Sciences, Department of Fisheries and Oceans, Sidney, B.C., 1992.

29. Tripp, A., Nixon, and R. Dunlop. 1992. The application and effectiveness of the Coastal Fisheries and Forestry Guidelines in Selected Cut Blocks on Vancouver Island. Prepared for the British Columbia Ministry of Environment, Lands and Parks, Fish and Wildlife Division, 24 pp.

30. Tunnicliffe, V. 1991. Biodiversity: the marine biota of British Columbia. In: Our Living Legacy. A Conference on the Biodiversity of British Columbia. Proceedings of a Biodiversity Conference in Victoria, October 1991. (in press).

31. Pacific Stock Assessment Review Committee (PSARC). 1991. Annual Report.

32. Data provided by Annual Summaries of Catch Statistics, Institute of Ocean Sciences, Department of Fisheries and Oceans, Sidney, B.C., 1992.

33. Data provided by International Pacific Halibut Commission, Seattle, Washington, U.S.A., 1992.

34. Data provided by Fisheries Branch, British Columbia Ministry of Environment, Lands and Parks, Nanaimo, B.C., 1992.

35. Rieberger, K. 1992. Metal Concentration in Fish Tissue from Uncontaminated B.C. Lakes. British Columbia Ministry of Environment, Lands and Parks, Water Quality Branch.

36. Forestry Canada. 1990. Forestry Facts.

37. Hosie, R.C. 1975. Native Trees of Canada. Canadian Forestry Service, Department of the Environment, Ottawa, Ont., Seventh Edition. 380 pp.

38. British Columbia Ministry of Environment, Lands and Parks. 1992. British Columbia Freshwater Results of the 1990 National Survey of Sport Fishing.

39. Ministry of Environment. 1991. Conserving Our Resource: Fisheries Program Strategic Plan 1991-1995. Ministry of Environment, Fisheries Program, Victoria, B.C. 22 pp.

40. Data provided by Inventory Branch, Ministry of Forests, Victoria, B.C., 1992.

41. Data provided by Protection Branch, Ministry of Forests, Victoria, B.C., 1992.

42. Van Sickle, A.G. 1992. Forest Insect and Disease Conditions, British Columbia and Yukon, 1973-1991. Forest Insect and Disease Survey, Forestry Canada, Pacific Forestry Centre, Victoria, B.C.

43. Ministry of Forests. 1992. Annual Report 1991-92 (in press).

44. Ministry of Forests. 1991. Annual Report 1990-91.

45. Ministry of Forests. 1990. Summary of Backlog Not Satisfactorily Restocked Forest Land. 35 pp.

46. British Columbia Ministry of Crown Lands. 1989. British Columbia Land Statistics. Victoria, B.C. pp. 23-29.

47. Canadian Council of Forest Ministers. 1992. Compendium of Canadian Forestry Statistics - 1991: National Forestry Database. Forestry Canada, Ottawa, 86 pp.

48. Data provided by Ministry of Forests, Annual Reports.

49. Data provided by Timber Harvesting Branch, Ministry of Forests, Victoria, B.C., 1992.

50. Data provided by Timber Harvesting Branch, Ministry of Forests, Victoria, B.C., 1992.

51. Data provided from Statistics Canada, 1992.

52. Ministry of Finance and Corporate Relations. 1992. British Columbia Origin Exports, July 1992. Statistics Branch, Victoria, B.C. Issue 92-07.

53. Ernst and Young. 1992. The tertiary component of the forest sector in British Columbia. In: Rising to the Challenge. Discussion Paper, Forest Summit Conference, September 22-24, 1992, Vancouver, B.C.

54. Data provided by Ministry of Forests, Victoria, B.C., 1993.

55. Hall, T. 1992. Recreation Program Annual Report, 1990/91. Ministry of Forests, Recreation Branch, 23 pp.

56. Government of Canada. 1991. The State of Canada's Environment. Supply and Services Canada, Ottawa.

57. Ministry of Forests. 1992. Towards an Old Growth Strategy. Public Review Draft. Old Growth Strategy Project, 72 pp.

58. Ministry of Forests. 1992. Old Growth Values Team Report. 38 pp. plus appendix.

59. Olesiuk, P.F., M.A. Bigg, and G.M. Ellis. 1990. Recent trends in the abundance of harbour seals, *Phoca vitulina*, in British Columbia. Can. J. Fish. Aquat. Sci. 47(5): 992-1003.

60. Data provided by Canadian Wildlife Service, Environment Canada, 1993.

61. Margalef. R. 1969. Perspectives in Ecological Theory. University of Chicago Press, 111 pp.

62. Data provided by Wildlife Branch, British Columbia Ministry of Environment, Lands and Parks, Victoria, B.C., 1993.

Additional reading

Anderson, K. and L. Harmon. 1985. The Prentice-Hall dictionary of nutrition and health. Prentice Hall, New Jersey.

Archer, S.G. and C.E. Bunch. 1953. The American grass book. A manual of pasture and range practices. University of Oklahoma Press, Norman.

Association of B.C. Professional Foresters. 1991. Discussion Paper on Are We Overcutting Our Forests?

Burlinson, N.E. 1991. Organochlorine Compounds in Marine Mammals from the Strait of Georgia. Ministry of Environment, British Columbia Ministry of Environment, Lands and Parks. 9 pp.

Filion, F.L., E. DuWors, A. Jacquemot, F. Bouchard, P. Boxall, P.A. Gray and R. Reid. 1989. Importance of wildlife to Canadians in 1987: Highlights of a national survey. Environment Canada, Canadian Wildlife Service, Ottawa, 45 pp.

Forestry Canada. 1992. The State of Canada's Forests 1991. Forestry Canada, Ottawa, 85 pp.

Health and Welfare Canada. 1992. A Vital Link. Supply and Services Canada, Ottawa, 160 pp.

Hertzman, C., N. Ames, H. Ward, S. Kelly, and C. Yates. 1991. Childhood Lead Exposures in Trail Revisited. Can. J. Public Health 82: 385-391.

Lynch-Stewart, P. 1983. Land Use Change on Wetlands in Southern Canada: Review and Bibliography. Environment Canada, Lands Directorate, Canada Land Use Monitoring Program. Working Paper No. 26. 115 pp.

Manitoba Centre for Remote Sensing. 1991. Unpublished land cover data derived from AVHRR satellite measurements, at 1km^2 resolution.

Maser, C. 1988. The Redesigned Forest. R.E. Miles, San Pedro, California, 234 pp.

Ministry of Environment. 1991. Environment 2001: Strategic Directions for British Columbia's Environment: Planning for the Future. B.C. Environment, Water Management Division, 25 pp.

Ministry of Forests. 1992. British Columbia's Forests: Monocultures or Mixed Forests. Ministry of Forests, Silviculture Branch, Victoria, B.C.

Muir, D.C.G. and R.J. Nortstrom. 1990. Marine mammals as indicators of environmental contamination by PCBs and dioxins/furans. In: L.E. Harding (ed.). Monitoring Status and Trends in Marine Environmental Quality: Proceedings of a symposium in conjunction with the 17th Annual Aquatic Toxicity Workshop, Vancouver, British Columbia, November 5-8 1990. Prepared for Environment Canada by Richard Banner, Polestar Communications, pp. 134-139.

Muir, D.C.G., C.A. Ford, B. Rosenberg, M. Simon, R.J. Norstrom, and K. Langelier, 1991. PCBs and Other Organochlorine Contaminants in Marine Mammals from the Strait of Georgia. Fisheries and Oceans, Winnipeg, Manitoba; Canadian Wildlife Service, Hull, Quebec; and Island Veterinary Hospital, Nanaimo, B.C. Abstract No. 135 as found in Society of Environmental Toxicology and Chemistry. 12th Annual Meeting, November 3-7, 1991, Seattle Convention Center, Seattle, Washington.

Noble, D. 1990. Contaminants in Canadian Seabirds; A State of The Environment Report. Environment Canada SOE Report Vol. 90-2, 75 pp.

Northcote, T.G. and M.D. Burwash. 1991. Fish and fish habitats of the Fraser River Basin. In: A.H.J. Dorcey (ed.). Perspectives on Sustainable Development in Water Management: Towards Agreement in the Fraser River Basin. Westwater Research Centre, pp. 117-141.

Olesiuk, P.F. and M.A. Bigg. 1990. Life history and population dynamics of resident killer whales (*Orcinus orca*) in the coastal waters of British Columbia and Washington State. In: P.S. Hammond, S.A. Mizroch and J.P Donovan (eds.). Individual Recognition of Cetations: Use of Photo-Identification and Other Techniques to Estimate Population Parameters. Report to the International Whaling Commission, Special Issue 12, pp. 209-243.

Sims, P.L. 1988. Grasslands. In: N.G. Barbour and W.D. Billings (eds.). North American Terrestrial Vegetation. Cambridge University Press, New York, N.Y. pp. 265-286.

Smiley, B. and A. Eade. 1992. Department of Fisheries and Oceans Topic Sheets About Some Indicators for State of Environment Reporting. Draft. Department of Fisheries and Oceans and Department of Environment.

Teschke, K., S. Kelly, M. Wiens, C. Hertzman, H.D. Ward, J.E.H. Ward, and J.C. Van Oostdam. 1992. Chlorinated Dibenzo-p-dioxins and Dibenzofurans in the Adipose Tissue of British Columbia Residents. British Columbia Ministry of Environment, Lands and Parks, Victoria, 28 pp. and appendices.

Wells, P.G. and S.J. Rolston (eds.). 1991. Health of Our Oceans: A Status Report on Canadian Marine Environmental Quality. Conservation and Protection, Environment Canada.

Whitehead, P.E. 1991. Update: monitoring dioxin and furan contamination of heron and cormorant eggs collected from the Strait of Georgia indicates a downward trend - 1991. Canadian Wildlife Service, Pacific and Yukon Region, 4 pp. and figures.

Land

References cited

1. Munn, B. 1992. Personal communication.

2. British Columbia Round Table on the Environment and the Economy. 1991a. Sustainable Land and Water Use. British Columbia Round Table on the Environment and the Economy, Victoria, B.C. 60 pp.

3. British Columbia Claims Task Force. 1991. The Report of the British Columbia Claims Task Force, June, 1992. First Nations of British Columbia, Government of British Columbia and Government of Canada.

4. The World Conservation Union (IUCN). 1990. A Framework for the Classification of Terrestrial and Marine Protected Areas. 1990. The World Conservation Union, 29 pp.

5. B.C. Commission on Resources and Environment. 1992. Report on a Land Use Strategy for British Columbia. Commission on Resources and Environment. 47 pp.

6. K. Lewis and A. MacKinnon (eds.). 1992. Gap Analysis of B.C.'s Protected Areas by Biogeoclimatic and Ecoregion Units: Draft. British Columbia Ministry of Environment, Lands and Parks and British Columbia Ministry of Forests, Victoria, B.C. 89 pp. and appendices.

7. Noble, M.A., P.D. Riben, and G.J. Cook. 1992. Microbiological and Epidemiological Surveillance Programme to Monitor the Health Effects of Foray 48B BTK Spray. Submitted to The Ministry of Forests, Province of British Columbia, Sept. 30/92.

8. British Columbia Ministry of Crown Lands. 1989. British Columbia Land Statistics. British Columbia Ministry of Crown Lands, Land Policy Branch. 58 pp.

9. Data provided by Inventory Branch, Ministry of Forests, Victoria, B.C., 1992.

10. Agriculture Canada. 1988. Agriculture and Food in British Columbia: A Look at the Industry and its Prospects for Development. Agriculture Canada, New Westminster, B.C. 82 pp.

11. Errington, J.C. 1992. Mine reclamation in British Columbia. Int. Mine Waste Manage. News 2(1): 5-12.

12. Data provided by B.C. Lands, British Columbia Ministry of Environment, Lands and Parks, 1992.

13. Statistics Canada. 1992. Households and the Environment 1991. Statistics Canada, Household Surveys Division, Ministry of Industry, Science and Technology, Ottawa, Cat. 11-526 Occasional. 39 pp.

14. Data provided by Statistics Canada and Environment Canada, 1993.

15. Warren, C.L., A. Kerr, and A.M. Turner. 1989. Urbanization of Rural Land in Canada, 1981-1986: A State of the Environment Fact Sheet. Environment Canada, Conservation and Protection, Ottawa, Ontario, SOE Fact Sheet No. 89-1. 12 pp. and supplementary tables.

16. Ministry of Environment. 1991. Program for Participation. How B.C. is Managing Solid Waste. Ministry of Environment, Municipal Waste Branch, Victoria, B.C. booklet. 18 pp.

17. Moore, K.E. 1990. Urbanization in the Lower Fraser Valley, 1980-1987. Canadian Wildlife Service, Pacific and Yukon Region. Tech. Rept. Ser. No. 120. 12 pp.

18. Rees, B. 1992. Ecological footprint and appropriated carrying capacity: what urban economics leaves out. Environment and Urbanization.

19. Anderson, M. and L. Knapik. 1984. Agricultural land degradation in western Canada: a physical and economic overview. Prepared for Regional Development Branch, Agriculture Canada, 138 pp.

20. Government of British Columbia. 1992. Towards a Protected Areas Strategy.

21. Chatwin, S.C., D.E. Howes, J.W. Schwab, and D.N. Swanston. 1991. A Guide for Management of Landslide-Prone Terrain in the Pacific Northwest. Ministry of Forests, Victoria, B.C., Land Management Handbook No. 18. 212 pp.

22. Templeman-Kluit, D.J. 1992. Letter from Templeman-Kluit re: soil and contaminants. 2 pp.

23. Data provided by Industrial Waste and Hazardous Contaminants Branch, British Columbia Ministry of Environment, Lands and Parks, 1993.

24. Jungen, J. 1992. Contaminated sites - state of the environment information - additional notes. 4 pp.

25. Canadian Council of Ministers of the Environment (CCME). 1991. Interim Canadian environmental quality criteria for contaminated sites. Subcommittee on Environmental Quality Criteria for Contaminated Sites. 20 pp.

26. Environment Canada. 1991. Review and Recommendations for Canadian Interim Environmental Quality Criteria for Contaminated Sites. Environment Canada, Conservation and Protection, Inland Waters Directorate, Water Quality Branch, Ottawa, Ontario, Scientific Series No. 197.

27. British Columbia Ministry of Environment, Lands and Parks. 1991/1992. News Releases (4).

28. Bindra, K.S. 1992. Data for the State of the Environment Report - Environmental Indicators. 2 pp.

29. Ministry of Environment. 1989. Environmental Priorities 1989.

30. Data provided by Municipal Waste Branch, British Columbia Ministry of Environment, Lands and Parks, 1992.

31. Data provided by Pesticide Management Branch, British Columbia Ministry of Environment, Lands and Parks, 1987.

32. Gartner Lee Limited. 1992. Fraser Valley ground water/drinking water study: final report. Prepared for Ministry of Health, Publich Health Protection Branch, GLL 91-744. 37 pp. and appendices.

33. Health & Welfare Canada, Agriculture Canada, Ministry of Agriculture, Fisheries and Food, and British Columbia Ministry of Environment, Lands and Parks. 1992. Monitoring of Pesticide Residues in Foods in British Columbia. Health Protection Branch, Health and Welfare Canada, Burnaby, B.C., pamphlet ENV126960.1192.

34. Dyck, V.A. and M.G.T. Gardiner. 1992. Sterile-insect release program to control codling moth *Cydia pomonella* (L.) (Lepidopteria: Olethreutidae) in British Columbia, Canada. Acta Phytopathol. Hung. 27(1-4): 219-222.

35. Westwater Research Centre. 1992. Marine Protected Areas (MPA) in British Columbia. Final report to the Law Foundation of British Columbia.

36. Gilkeson, L.A. 1992. Agricultural crops grown under integrated pest management programs in British Columbia: 1991. Results of a survey of pest management consultants conducted by the Pesticide Management Program, British Columbia Ministry of Environment, Lands and Parks.

37. Turner, A.M., C.D.A. Rubec, and E.B. Wiken. 1992. Canadian ecosystems: a systems approach to conservation. In: J.H.M. Williston et al. (eds.). Science and the Management of Protected Areas. Elsevier Science Publishers, Amsterdam, Netherlands, pp. 117-127.

38. British Columbia Ministry of Environment, Lands and Parks, and B.C. Ministry of Forest. 1992. Government unveils protected areas strategy: parks and wilderness action plan detailed. British Columbia Ministry of Environment, Lands and Parks, Victoria, B.C., News Release dated May 6, 1992.

39. B.C. Hydro. 1992. B.C. Hydro Annual Report. B.C. Hydro.

40. Morrison, K. and T. Turner. 1992. Protected areas in British Columbia. A submission to the State of the Environment Report for British Columbia Project, Final Draft, Nov. 16/92. 24 pp.

41. Data provided by British Columbia Ministry of Environment, Lands and Parks, 1993.

42. The Report of The British Columbia Claims Task Force, June 1991. The British Columbia Claims Task Force 1991.

Additional reading

Agriculture Canada. 1990. Exploring Sustainability in the Agriculture and Food Industries. Agriculture Canada, New Westminster, B.C. 106 pp.

British Columbia Ministry of Environment, Lands and Parks. 1991. Striking the Balance: B.C. Parks Policy. British Columbia Ministry of Environment, Lands and Parks, Victoria, B.C. 28 pp.

British Columbia Ministry of Energy, Mines and Petroleum Resources. 1991. Mine Reclamation in British Columbia: Policy Overview. British Columbia Ministry of Energy, Mines and Petroleum Resources, Resource Management Branch, Reclamation and Permitting, Victoria, B.C. September 1991. 9 pp.

Boydell, A.N. 1990. Waste Management Issues in British Columbia. Prepared for the British Columbia Round Table on the Environment and the Economy, Victoria, B.C. 20 pp. and appendix.

Cain, L. 1991. Environmental sustainability in B.C. agriculture: an overview of the provincial issues and (preliminary) priorities for the federal Green Plan program. Agriculture Canada. 29 pp.

Eng, M. 1992. Vancouver Island gap analysis. Ministry of Forests, Research Branch, Victoria, B.C., Unpubl. document.

Environment Canada. 1991. State of the Parks: 1990 Report. Environment Canada.

Ministry of Environment. 1991. Environment 2001: Strategic Directions for British Columbia. Ministry of Environment, Victoria, B.C. 71 pp.

Ministry of Environment. 1991. New Directions in Pesticide Management. British Columbia's Environment: Planning for the Future. Ministry of Environment, Pesticide Management Program - Five-Year Strategic Plan, Victoria, B.C. ENV007320.791. 12 pp.

Ministry of Parks. 1990. Parks Plan 90: Preserving Our Living Legacy: Landscapes for BC Parks. Ministry of Parks, Victoria, B.C. 48 pp. and map.

Ministry of Parks. 1990. Parks Plan 90: Preserving Our Living Legacy: Recreation Goals for BC Parks. Ministry of Parks, Victoria, B.C. 68 pp.

Trant, D.F. 1989. Estimating agricultural soil erosion losses from census of agriculture crop coverage data. Paper prepared for Environment and Natural Resources Group, Analytical Studies Branch, Statistics Canada. No. 27.

Ecoprovinces

References cited

1. Wareham, B., G. Whyte, and S. Kennedy. n.d. British Columbia Wildlife Viewing Guide. British Columbia Wildlife Watch, Habitat Conservation Fund, and Lone Pine.

2. Demarchi, D.A. and K.T. Lewis. 1992. Appendix 3: Synopsis of the ecoregion classification system of British Columbia. In: K. Lewis and A. MacKinnon (eds.). Gap Analysis of B.C.'s Protected Areas by Biogeoclimatic and Ecoregion Units: Draft. British Columbia Ministry of Environment, Lands and Parks and British Columbia Ministry of Forests, Victoria, B.C. 89 pp. and appendices.

3. Vold, T. 1992. The Status of Wilderness in British Columbia: A Gap Analysis. Appendix A. Ecosystem Representation (Ecoregion and Biogeoclimatic Classification). Wilderness Management, Recreation Branch, British Columbia Ministry of Forests, Victoria, B.C.

4. Manitoba Centre for Remote Sensing. 1991. Unpublished land cover data derived from AVHRR satellite measurements, at 1km^2 resolution.

5. Data provided by Statistics Canada and Environment Canada, 1992.

6. Nordin, R.N. and L.W. Pommen. 1985. Peace River area Charlie Lake sub-basin water quality assessment and objectives: Technical appendix. British Columbia Ministry of Environment, Lands and Parks, Water Management Branch, Victoria, B.C. 34 pp.

7. Anderson, M. and L. Knapik. 1984. Agricultural land degradation in western Canada: a physical and economic overview. Prepared for Regional Development Branch, Agriculture Canada. 138 pp.

8. Data provided by Ministry of Environment, 1992.

9. Ministry of Environment, Canada-British Columbia Partnership Agreement on Forest Resource Development (FRDA II), British Columbia Ministry of Environment Lands and Parks, and Ministry of Forests. n.d. Mountain Caribou in Managed Forests. Published by Ministry of Environment, Prince George, B.C. MCMF brochure.

10. Servizi, J.A. 1989. Protecting Fraser River salmon (*Oncorhynchus* spp.) from wastewaters: an assessment. In: C.D. Levings, L.B. Holtby, and M.A. Henderson (eds.). Proceedings of the National Workshop on Effects of Habitat Alteration on Salmonid Stocks. Can. Spec. Publ. Fish. Aquat. Sci. 105.

11. Schreier, H., S.J. Brown, and K.J. Hall. 1991. The land-water interface in the Fraser River basin. In: A.H.J. Dorcey, and J.R. Griggs (eds.). Water in Sustainable Development: Exploring our Common Future in the Fraser River Basin. Research Program on Water in Sustainable Development: Volume II. Westwater Research Centre, Faculty of Graduate Studies, The University of British Columbia, Vancouver, B.C. pp. 77-116.

12. Marmorek, D.R., J. Korman, and D.P. Bernard. 1992. Fate and Effects of Pulp Mill Effluents in the Fraser River Ecosystem. Inland Waters, Environment Canada.

13. Fisheries Act. 1992. Pulp and Paper Effluent Regulations. Extract: Canada Gazette, Part II, Vol. 126, No. 11, May 7, 1992.

14. Townsend, G.H. 1975. Impact of the Bennett Dam on the Peace-Athabasca Delta. J. Fish. Res. Bd. Can. 32: 171-176.

15. Data provided by Department of Fisheries and Oceans, Vancouver, B.C., 1992.

16. White, E.R., C.A. Johnson, and R.J. Crozier. Trail air quality: compilation and synopsis of ambient air quality and industrial emissions data 1975-1985. Ministry of Environment, Nelson, B.C.

17. Data provided by Environmental Protection, British Columbia Ministry of Environment, Lands and Parks, Cranbrook, B.C., 1992.

18. Hertzman, C., N. Ames, H. Ward, S. Kelly, and C. Yates. 1990. Trail Lead Study Report. Prepared for the Ministries of Health and Environment. Department of Health Care and Epidemiology, University of British Columbia, Vancouver, 26 pp. plus tables, figures and appendices.

19. Hertzman, C., N. Ames, H. Ward, S. Kelly, and C. Yates. 1991. Childhood Lead Exposures in Trail Revisited. Can. J. Public Health 82: 385-391.

20. Data provided by Trail Community Lead Task Force, 1992.

21. Data provided by Environmental Protection, British Columbia Ministry of Environment, Lands and Parks, Nelson, B.C., 1992.

22. Crozier, R.J. and W.F.A. Duncan, 1984. Kootenay Lake: Compilation and synopsis of physical, chemical, and biological data from 1968 to 1984. Ministry of Environment, Nelson, B.C.

23. Anonymous. 1974. Limnology of the Major Okanagan Basin Lakes. Canada/B.C. Okanagan Basin Agreement. Technical Supplement 5. B.C. Water Reserces Service. 261 pp.

24. Anonymous. 1982. Report on the Okanagan Basin Implementation Agreement. Okanagan Basin Implementation Board. ISBN 0-7719-9054-5. 126 pp.

25. Anonymous. 1985. Phosphorous in the Okanagan Valley Lakes: Sources Water Quality Objectives and Control Possibilities. Ministry of Environment. 163 pp.

26. Nickel, R.A. 1990. Project Overview Globe '90 presentation. Ministry of Environment. 7 pp.

27. Bryan, J.E. 1987. Effects of Wastewater Releases by City of Vernon on Vernon Creek and Vernon Arm of Okanagan Lake in 1984 and 1985. Ministry of Environment. BC Environment Technical Report ISBN 0-7726-07206. 35 pp.

28. Bryan, J.E. 1991. Some Effects of Wastewater from Brenda Mines and Water Quality Aquatic Organisms of Forage Crops. Ministry of Environment. BC Environment Technical Report ISBN 0-7726-1379-6, 40 pp. and BC Environment Technical Report ISBN 0-7726-1182-3, 69pp.

29. Nordin, R.N., J.E. Bryan, and E.V. Jensen. 1990. Nutrient controls and water quality in the Okanagan Lakes 1969-1989. Proceedings of the 43rd Conference. Canadian Water Resources Association. pp. 335-346.

30. Wild Stone Resources. 1992a. Okanagan Lake Tributaries Plan, Volume 1: Mission Creek Management Plan. Ministry of Environment, Pentiction, B.C. 36 pp.

31. Wild Stone Resources. 1992b. Okanagan Lake Tributaries Plan, Volume 1: Powers Creek Management Plan. Ministry of Environment, Penticton, B.C.. 32 pp.

33. McNaughton, D.C. n.d. Pesticides in ground water, Osoyoos, British Columbia. National Hydrology Research Institute, Saskatoon, Saskatchewan, Internal Report "Unedited Draft". 27 pp. unpubl. report.

34. Hodge, W.S. 1985. Groundwater Quality Monitoring and Assessment Program - Assessment of Water Quality and Identification of Water Quality Concerns and Problem areas, Osoyoos. Ministry of Environment, Water Management Branch, Victoria, B.C. 28 pp. and appendices.

35. Hodge, W.S. 1986. Groundwater Quality Monitory and Assessment Program. Assessment of Water Quality and Identification of Water Quality Concerns and Problem Areas, Osoyoos. Memorandum. Ministry of Environment, Water Management Branch, Victoria, B.C. 4 pp. and appendices.

36. Hodge, W.S. 1989. Groundwater Quality Monitoring and Assessment Program - Assessment of Water Quality and Identification of Water Quality Concerns and Problem Areas, Osoyoos, 1987. Ministry of Environment, Water Management Branch, Victoria, B.C. 12 pp. and figures and tables.

37. Ference Weicker & Company. 1991. Evaluation of the Socio-economic Benefits of the Okanagan Valley Eurasian Water Milfoil Control Program. British Columbia Ministry of Environment, Lands and Parks, Victoria, B.C. 88 pp.

38. Einarson, E.D. 1991. The 1991 Eurasian Watermilfoil Surveillance and Control Program in Shuswap and Mara Lakes. Ministry of Environment, Water Management Division, Victoria, B.C. 40 pp.

39. Dale, A.R. and D.H. Haberstock. 1992. The 1991 Christina Lake Eurasian Watermilfoil Control Program. Ministry of Environment, Water Management Division, Victoria, B.C. 36 pp.

40. Hodge, W.S. 1991. Water Quality (Nitrate) Reconnaissance Study - Armstrong, B.C. British Columbia Ministry of Environment, Lands and Parks, Water Management Division. 12 pp. and appendices.

41. Singleton, H.J. 1990a. Okanagan Area Hydraulic Creek and its Tributaries Water Quality Assessment and Objectives. Ministry of Environment. 10 pp.

42. Singleton, H.J. 1990b. Okanagan Area Hydraulic Creek and its Tributaries Water Quality Assessment and Objectives. Technical Appendix. British Columbia Ministry of Environment, 44 pp.

43. Harper, B., T. Lea, and B. Maxwell. 1991. Habitat Inventory in the South Okanagan. Bioline 10(2): 12-16.

44. Page, R., D. Meidinger, and E. Hamilton. 1991. Biodiversity Research Strategy, Summary of Conclusions and Research Recommendations. First Draft. Ministry of Forests, Forest Science Research Branch, Victoria, B.C. 28 pp.

45. Hlady, D.A. 1990. South Okanagan Conservation Strategy 1990-1995. Ministry of Environment, Victoria, B.C. 31 pp. and appendices.

46. Christie, B., R. Collins, D. Clarke, C. Thompson, J. French and C. Siddle. 1991. Kelowna Natural Features Inventory Summary Report. Reid, Collins and Associates, Vancouver, B.C. 69 pp. plus appendices.

47. Bunce, H.W.F. 1992. Fluoride emissions and forest growth measurements of second growth - 1982-1988. Prepared by Reid, Collins and Associates, A Division of H.A. Simons Ltd., Vancouver, B.C. for Alcan Smelters and Chemicals Ltd.

48. Austin, A. and N. Munteanu. 1984. Evaluation of changes in a large oligotrophic wilderness park lake exposed to mine tailing effluent for 14 years: the phytoplankton. Environ. Pollut. (Series A) 33: 39-62.

49. Deniseger, J. and L. Erickson. 1991. Trends in Water Quality of Buttle Lake and the Campbell River - Continuing Decreases in Metal Concentrations from 1987 through 1990. British Columbia Ministry of Environment, Lands and Parks, Environmental Protection Branch, Victoria, B.C. 39 pp.

50. Harding, L.E. and J.R. Englar. 1989. The Nestucca oil spill: fate and effects to May 31, 1989. Environment Canada, Environmental Protection, West Vancouver, B.C., Regional Program Report 89-01.

51. Government of Canada and British Columbia Ministry of Environment, Lands and Parks. 1992. Settlement reached on environmental damage from Westucca oil spill. News Release. 2 pp.

52. Eade, A. 1992. Persistent marine debris in B.C. Department of Fisheries and Oceans. unpubl. data.

53. GVRD. 1988. Greater Vancouver Liquid Waste Management Plan. Stage 1. Combined Sewer Overflow and Urban Runoff Committee Report.

54. Mio, Shin-ichi and Shu-ichi Takehama. 1987. Estimation of distribution of marine debris on the 1986 sighting survey. (Document submitted to the 34th Annual Meeting of the International North Pacific Fisheries Commission).

55. Nasu, Keiji and Kazuhiko Hiramatsu. 1989. Distribution and density of marine debris in the North Pacific based on sighting surveys in 1988. (Document submitted to the Annual Meeting of the International North Pacific Fisheries Commission, 1989 October).

56. Nasu, Keiji and Kazuhiko Hiramatsu. 1990. Distribution and density of marine debris in the North Pacific based on sighting surveys in 1989. (Document submitted to the Annual Meeting of the International North Pacific Fisheries Commission, 1990 October).

57. Shaw, W. 1990. 1990 Summary of marine debris sightings during Canadian high seas research surveys, 1989 -1990. (Document submitted to the Annual Meeting of the International North Pacific Fisheries Commission, November, 1990).

58. Ministry of Forests and British Columbia Ministry of Environment, Lands and Parks.1992. Khutzeymateen Study Report, May 1992.

59. Data and background information provided by Ministry of Environment, Skeena Region, 1992.

60. B.C. Ministry of Finance and Corporate Relations. 1990. British Columbia Population Forecst 1990-2016. B.C. Ministry of Finance and Corporate Relations, Planning and Statistics Division, Victoria, B.C. 37 pp.

61. GVRD. 1988. Vancouver Metropolitan Population Forecast 1986-2001. Regional Population, Burnaby, Greater Vancouver Regional District.

62. CCME. 1990. Management plan for nitrogen oxides (NO_x) and volatile organic compounds (VOCs). Phase I. Canadian Council of Ministers of the Environment, Winnipeg. CCME-EPC/TRE-31E. 176 pp. and 4 Appendices.

63. Lippmann, M., P.J. Lioy, G. Leikanf, K.B. Green, D. Baxter, M. Morandi, B.S. Pasternak, D. Fife, and F.E. Speizer. 1983. Effects of ozone on the pulmonary function of children. Advan. Modern Environ. Toxicol. 5: 423-446.

64. GVRD. 1992. Air Quality Management Plan Discussion Paper.

65. Butler, R.W. and R.W. Campbell. 1987. The birds of the Fraser River delta: populations, ecology and international significance. Can. Wildl. Serv. Occas. Paper No. 65, Ottawa.

66. Horstman, D.H., L.J. Folinsbee, P.J. Ives, S. Abdul-Salaam, and W.F. McDonnell. 1990. Ozone concentration and pulmonary response relationships for 6.6-hour exposures with five hours of moderate exercise to 0.08, 0.10 and 0.12 ppm. Amer. Rev. Respir. Dis. 142: 1158-1163.

67. Lippmann, M. 1989. Health effects of ozone: a critical review. J. Amer. Pollut. Contr. Assoc. 39(5): 672-695.

68. Thomson, J. 1992. A State of the Environment Fact Sheet: Ground-level ozone in Canada. Environment Canada, Ottawa, Ont., SOE Fact Sheet No. 92-1. 12 pp.

69. Rafiq, M. 1986. Ozone impact on Fraser Valley crops: a preliminary assessment. 26 pp. Published by B.C. Ministry of Environment, Lands and Parks.

70. Liebscher, H., B. Hii, and D. McNaughton. 1992. Nitrates and pesticides in the Abbotsford Aquifer, Southwestern British Columbia. 83 pp.

71. Gartner Lee Limited. 1992. Fraser Valley ground water/drinking water study: final report. Prepared for Ministry of Health, Public Health Protection Branch, Victoria, B.C. GLL 91-744. 37 pp. and appendices.

72. EPA. 1991. Drinking water regulations and health advisories. U.S. Environmental Protection Agency.

73. Agricultural Waste Management Control Regulation, and Code of Agricultural Practice for Waste Management Act. Adopted April 1992.

74. Colodey, A.G., R.A. Salmon, P.G. Lim. 1992. Environmental monitoring near the Macaulay Point and Clover Point Marine Sewage Outfalls at Victoria, British Columbia in 1989 and 1990. Environment and Protection Regional Data Report: DR 92-14. Environment Canada.

75. GVRD. 1992. Iona Deep Sea Outfall 1991. Environmental Monitoring Program. Summary Report. Quality control Division, Greater Vancouver Regional District. June 1992. 35 pp.

76. Wells, P.G. and S.J. Rolston (eds). 1991. Health of Our Oceans: A Status Report on Canadian Marine Environmental Quality. Conservation and Protection, Environment Canada.

77. Macdonald, R.W., D.M. Macdonald, M.C. O'Brien, and C. Gobell. 1991. The accumulation of heavy metals (Pb, Zn, Cu, Cd), carbon and nitrogen in sediments from Strait of Georgia, B.C. Mar. Chem. 34: 109-135.

78. Macdonald, R.W., W.J. Cretney, N. Crewe, and D. Paton. 1992. A history of OCDD,2,3,7,8, TCDF and PCB 77 contamination in Howe Sound, British Columbia, 1992. Environ. Sci. Technol. 26: 1544-1550.

79. Warren, C.L., A. Kerr, and A.M. Turner. 1989. Urbanization of Rural Land in Canada, 1981-1986: A State of the Environment Fact Sheet. Environment Canada, Conservation and Protection, Ottawa, Ontario, SOE Fact Sheet No. 89-1. 12 pp. and Supplement.

80. Data provided by Statistics Canada, 1992.

81. Moore, K.E. 1990. Urbanization in the Lower Fraser Valley, 1980-1987. Canadian Wildlife Service, Pacific and Yukon Region. Tech. Rept. Ser. No. 120. 12 pp.

82. Provincial Agricultural Land Commission. 1990. Agricultural Land Reserve Statistics, January 1, 1990. Provincial Agricultural Land Commission. 85 pp.

83. Gertler, L.O., R.W. Crowley, and W.K. Bond. 1977. Changing Canadian Cities: The Next 25 Years. McClelland and Stewart.

84. Government of Canada. 1991. The State of Canada's Environment. Supply and Services Canada, Ottawa.

85. Dumanski, J., D.R. Coote, G. Luciuk, and C. Lok. 1986. Soil conservation in Canada. J. Soil Water Conserv. 41: 204-210.

86. Environment Canada and British Columbia Ministry of Environment, Lands and Parks. 1992. State of the Environment for the Lower Fraser River Basin. SOE Report No. 92-1.

87. Smith, S. 1991. Floodplain management in the Fraser Basin. In: A.H.J. Dorcey (ed). Perspectives on Sustainable Development in Water Management: Toward Agreement in the Fraser River Basin. Westwater Research Centre, pp. 115-132.

88. Hutchison, B. 1950. The Fraser. Toronto: Clarke Irwin.

89. Birtwell, I.K., C.D. Levings, J.S. Macdonald and I.H. Rogers. 1988. A review of fish habitat issues in the Fraser River system. Water Pollut. Res. J. Can. 23(1): 1-30.

90. Butler R.W. and R.J. Cannings. 1989. Distribution of birds in the intertidal portion of the Fraser River Delta, B.C. Technical Report Series. No. 93. Canadian Wildlife Service, Pacific and Yukon Region, British Columbia.

91. Kistritz, R.U. 1992. Discover your estuary: Understanding and exploring the aquatic environment of the Fraser River Estuary. 120 pp.

92. Pilon, P. and M.A. Kerr. 1984. Land Use Change on Wetlands in the Southwestern Fraser Lowland, B.C. Environment Canada.

93. Ward, P. 1992. Wetlands of the Fraser Lowland, 1989: Summary Report. Canadian Wildlife Service, Pacific and Yukon Region, Tech. Rept. Ser. 156. 36 pp.

94. Fraser River Estuary Management Program (FREMP). 1990. Status Report on Water Quality in the Fraser River Estuary - 1990. Standing Committee on the Fraser River Estuary Water Quality Plan.

95. Fraser River Estuary Management Program (FREMP). 1990. A Recommended Waste Management Activity Plan. New Westminster: Waste Management Activity Program Working Group.

96. McConnell, H.D. 1991. Planning for metropolitan liquid waste management in the GVRD: An innovative approach towards sustainable development. In: A.H.J. Dorcey (ed). Perspectives on Sustainable Development in Water Management: Toward Agreement in the Fraser River Basin. Westwater Research Centre, pp. 271-287

97. Fraser River Estuary Management Program (FREMP). 1990. Habitat Inventory and Classification of Fraser River Main Arm, Pitt River, Sturgeon Bank, Roberts Bank and Boundary Bay. Maps at 1:2,500 and 1:10,000 and User's Guide for the Map Sheets. Prepared by R.U. Kistritz Consultants Ltd., Richmond, B.C.

98. Fraser River Estuary Management Program (FREMP). 1990. Habitat Inventory and Classification of Fraser River North and Middle Arms (North Fraser Harbour). Maps at 1:2,500 and User's Guide for the Map Sheets. Prepared by G.L. Williams and Associates Ltd., Coquitlam, B.C.

99. B.C. Agricultural Land Commission. 1990. Non-farmland with Long Term Urban Potential in the Lower Mainland, Burnaby. British Columbia Ministry of Agriculture and Food.

100. British Columbia Ministry of Environment, Lands and Parks. 1991. Environmetal impact of intensive east coast Vancouver Island development. British Columbia Ministry of Environment, Lands and Parks, Victoria, B.C.

Additional reading

Alcan Smelters and Chemicals Ltd. 1990. Alcan Vegetation Study Report.

Anonymous. n.d. Williston/Peace Fisheries Compensation Program. Peace/Williston Fish and Wildlife Compensation Program, Prince George, B.C. 17 pp.

Anonymous. n.d. Williston Reservoir Compensation: Wildlife Management Activities: Appendix 1. Peace/Williston Fish and Wildlife Compensation Program, Prince George, B.C.

B.C. Hydro and Ministry of Environment. 1992. The Peace/Williston Nature Line. Peace/Williston Fish and Wildlife Compensation Program, Prince George, B.C., February 1992, No. 2.

British Columbia Ministry of Crown Lands. 1989. British Columbia Land Statistics. B.C. Ministry of Crown Lands, Land Policy Branch. 58 pp.

Child, K.N., S.K. Stevenson, and G.S. Watts. 1992. Mountain caribou in managed forests: cooperative ventures for new solutions. A progress report for the year ending March 31, 1992.

Derksen, G. 1981. Environmental review of the Northwood, International, and Prince George pulp mills at Prince George, B.C. Regional Progress Report No. 82-4. Environmental Protection Service, West Vancouver, B.C.

Dwernychuk, L.W., G.S. Bruce, G. Gordon, and G.P. Thomas. 1992. Fraser and Thompson Rivers: a comprehensive organochlorine study 1990/91 (drinking water/mill effluent/sediment/fish). Prepared for Northwood Pulp and Timber Limited, Prince George, B.C.; CANFOR Corporation, Prince George, B.C.; Cariboo Pulp and Paper Company, Quesnel, B.C.; and Weyerhaeuser Canada Ltd., Kamloops, B.C.

Esposito, N.P., T.O. Teirnan, and F.E. Drydan. 1980. Dioxins. Industrial Environmental Research Laboratory, Office of Research and Development, U.S. Environmental Protection Agency.

Hall, K.J., H. Schreier and S.J. Brown. 1991. Water quality in the Fraser River basin. In: A.H.J. Dorcey and J.R. Griggs (eds.). Water in Sustainable Development: Exploring our Common Future in the Fraser River Basin. Westwater Research Centre, Vancouver, British Columbia, Part II: Chap. 3, pp. 41-75.

Kohut, A.P., W.S. Hodge, and F. Chwojka. 1986. Groundwater quality variations in fractured bedrock aquifers of the Gulf Islands, British Columbia. In: Proceedings: Third Canadian Hydrogeological Conference. International Assoc. of Hydrogeologists, Canadian National Chapter, pp. 185-192.

McLeay, D. and Associates. 1987. Aquatic toxicity of pulp and paper mill effluent: a review. EPS Report 4/PF/1.

McNeill, R. and D. Tate. 1991. Guidelines for Municipal Water Pricing. Environment Canada, Conservation and Protection, Inland Waters Directorate, Water Planning and Management Branch, Ottawa, Ontario, Social Science Series No. 25. 66 pp.

Ministry of Environment. 1992. 1991 Air Quality Data Summary for Prince George. B.C. Environment, Environmental Protection, Northern Interior Region, Prince George, B.C. Prepared for the Prince George Ambient Air Technical Committee.

Ministry of Environment, Environment Canada, Northwood Pulp and Timber Ltd. (Canfor Prince George Pulp and Paper Mills, Cariboo Pulp and Paper Company, Quesnel River Pulp, and Hatfield Consultants Ltd.). 1990. Summary of the Upper Fraser River environmental effects monitoring program: 1989. 23 pp.

Ngan, P. 1990. British Columbia Population Forecasts and Issues. Prepared for the British Columbia Round Table on the Environment and the Economy, 18 pp.

Rogers, I.H., J.A. Servizi, and C.D. Levings. 1988. Bioconcentration of chlorophenols by juvenile chinook salmon (Oncorhynchus tshawytscha) overwintering in the Upper Fraser River: field and laboratory tests. Water Poll. Res. J. Can. 23: 100-113.

Seip, D.R. 1992. Habitat Use and Population Status of Woodland Caribou in the Quesnel Highlands, British Columbia. Faculty of Forestry, University of British Columbia Report for British Columbia Ministry of Environment, Lands and Parks. Wildlife Program, Williams Lake, B.C. Wildlife Bulletin No. B-71, April 1992.

Wood, M. 1992. Williston Wildlife Compensation Program. Project highlights: 1992 Public Workshops. Hudson's Hope - March 28, 1992; Mackenzie - April 25, 1992. Peace/Williston Fish and Wildlife Compensation Program, 10 pp. and maps.

Land Under Change

References cited

1.   Data provided by Statistics Canada, 1992.

2.   Data provided by PCENSUS, Statistics Canada Census, 1986.

3.   Warren, C.L., A. Kerr, and A.M. Turner. 1989. Urbanization of Rural Land in Canada, 1981-1986: A State of the Environment Fact Sheet. Environment Canada, Conservation and Protection, Ottawa, Ontario, SOE Fact Sheet No. 89-1. 12 pp. and Supplement.

4.   World Bank. 1989. Social Indicators of Development 1989. Published by The World Bank, the Johns Hopkins University Press, Baltimore and London.

5.   Harper, B., T. Lea, and B. Maxwell. 1991. Habitat Inventory in the South Okanagan. Bioline 10(2): 12-16.

6.   Cannings, R.J. 1991. Status Report on the Sage Thrasher *Oreoscoptes mantanus* in British Columbia. University of British Columbia, Vancouver, B.C.

7.   Hlady, D.A. 1990. South Okanagan Conservation Strategy 1990-1995. Ministry of Environment, Victoria, B.C. 31 pp. and appendices.

8.   Harper, W.L., E.C. Lea, and R.E. Maxwell. 1992. Biodiversity inventory in the South Okanagan. In: M.A. Fenger, E.H. Miller, J.A. Johnson and E.J.R. Williams (eds.). Our Living Legacy. Proceedings of a Symposium on Biological Diversity. B.C. Ministry of Environment, Land and Parks, Ministry of Forests and Royal B.C. Museum, Victoria (in press).

9.   Redpath, K. 1990. Identification of relatively undisturbed areas in the South Okanagan and Similkameen valleys, British Columbia. Canadian Wildlife Service, Pacific and Yukon Region, B.C., Tech. Rept. Ser. No. 108. 9 pp.

10.   Data provided by the Wildlife Section Head. Ministry of Environment, Penticton, B.C., 1992.

11.   Shephard. 1990. Okanagan Lake Management Plan. Recreational Fisheries, Ministry of Environment.

12.   Richardson, H., E.V. Jensen, and J.E. Bryan. 1991. Air Quality in Several Okanagan Communities, Princeton, and Grand Forks 1973 - 1989. Ministry of Environment.

13.   Data provided by the Senior Science Advisor, Air Resources Branch, Ministry of Environment, Victoria, B.C., 1992.

14.   Horne, G. and C. Penner. 1992. British Columbia Community Employment Dependencies. Ministry of Finance & Corporate Relations, Planning and Statistics Division.

15.   Royal LePage Real Estate Services Ltd. 1986. Survey of Canadian House Prices.

16.   Royal LePage Real Estate Services Ltd. 1988. Survey of Canadian House Prices.

17.   Royal LePage Real Estate Services Ltd. 1992. Survey of Canadian House Prices.

18.   City of Kelowna Planning Department. 1986. Kelowna Community Plan 1985 - 2004. City of Kelowna, Planning Department.

19.   British Columbia Agriculture Land Commission (B.C. ALC). 1990. Agricultural Land Reserve Statistics January 1, 1990. Provincial Agricultural Land Commission.

20.   Clutton, E.H. (ed). 1989. Pest Contral in Canada: a reference manual. PACS.

21.   Richardson, H., S.R. Adams, and J.E. Bryan. 1991. Lumby-Lavington Air Quality 1975 - 1990. Ministry of Environment.

22.   Kerr, M.A., EW. Manning, J. Séguin, and L.J. Pelton. 1985. Okanagan Fruitlands: Land-use Change Dynamics and the Impact of Federal Programs. Lands Directorate, Environment Canada, Ottawa, Ont.

23.   Data provided by Regional Manager, Water Management, Southern Interior Regional Headquarters. British Columbia Ministry of Environment, Lands and Parks, 1993.

Glossary

acid mine drainage (AMD): The seepage of sulphuric acid solutions from mines and their removed wastes (rock and tailings) dumped at the surface. Sulphuric acid is produced through natural reactions between exposed sulphide minerals, air and water (groundwater and/or percolating precipitation). This is a special case of the more wide-spread phenomenon of acid rock drainage (ARD) which occurs wherever sulphide-bearing rocks are exposed to water and air (e.g. highway and railroad rock cuts or naturally exposed rock surfaces).

acid deposition (*acid rain, acid precipitation and dry deposition*): Rain, snow or fog with a pH of less than 5.6 Acid deposition is often caused by air-borne sulphur (SO_2) and nitrogen oxides (NO_x) reacting with moisture, to eventually form sulphuric and nitric acids. These acid causing compounds may fall as rain, snow, or fog or they may be deposited in the dry form. Acid deposition can harm aquatic ecosystems and kill freshwater fish. As well, it can damage trees and plants, and gradually erode stone, metal and other surfaces.

acidification: An increase in the degree of acidity (hydrogen ions) of an ecosystem (such as a lake, stream or soil) which can be caused by natural processes, acid deposition and acid fertilizers.

adsorbable organically-bound halogens (AOX): Represents the total quantity of organically-bound chlorine (i.e. halogens) in pulp mill effluent. It is a measure of organochlorine content (e.g. dioxins and furans) used to regulate discharges of these compounds in pulp mill effluents.

ambient air or water quality: Refers to the overall or general condition of air or water in a region outside the zone of influence of discharges in contrast to local condition which may be related to a specific source of contamination.

anadromous: Ascending rivers from the sea to spawn (e.g. salmon).

antisapstain: A fungicide used to treat lumber to prevent staining from fungi during storage and shipment.

aquaculture: The husbandry/cultivation of aquatic animals and plants in a restricted environment, generally for profit. Aquaculture has become a significant, growing sector of the B.C. economy in the last ten years. Oysters, trout and salmon are the mainstay of the industry. However, scallops, clams, mussels, abalone, arctic char, sturgeon and marine plants present good opportunities for future diversification.

aquifer: An underground zone or stratum of permeable rock or loose material where water accumulates and which can produce useful quantities of water when tapped by a well. It can be contaminated by improper disposal of waste.

assimilate: The ability of water to accept wastes without impairing uses of the water.

benthos: The plant and animal life whose habitat is the bottom of the sea. (**Benthic** is the adjective).

bioaccumulation: The increase in levels of toxic substances in an organism over time due to continued exposure. This can only happen if the substances do not break down quickly and are essentially stored in some part of the organism. Sometimes referred to as bioconcentration.

biochemical oxygen demand (BOD): The amount of dissolved oxygen required for the bacterial decomposition of *organic* waste in water. Large amounts of organic waste use up large amounts of dissolved oxygen, thus the greater the degree of pollution, the greater the *BOD*.

bioconcentration: See bioaccumulation, biomagnification.

biodegradable: Capable of decomposing quickly through natural biological processes.

biodiversity (*biological diversity*): A broad term referring to the variety of life in an area - from small areas such as a pond to the whole biosphere. Biodiversity encompasses four main considerations: landscape diversity, ecosystem diversity, species diversity and genetic diversity. It also involves the countless, complex ways in which living things function and interact.

biogeoclimatic: The complex interaction of climate, terrain, soil, plants and animals. The term is used in resource classification, mapping and land use management.

biomagnification: The increase in the concentration of contaminants as they move up the food chain. A predator unknowingly "collects" whatever toxic substances happen to be in the food that it consumes. Sometimes known as bioconcentration.

biomass: The amount of living matter in an area - most of it is plant material and a small quantity is animal matter. In general, biomass (wood, vegetation and crop residue) is burned either for disposal or to produce energy or it is left on the site to decompose.

biosphere (*ecosphere*): The total area of Planet Earth where life can survive - such as the soil, water and lower atmosphere.

biota: Collectively, the plants, micro-organisms, and animals of a certain area or region.

carbon dioxide (CO_2): An odourless and nontoxic gas normally present in the ambient air and also produced when any substance containing carbon (such as fossil fuels and wood) is burned in the presence of adequate oxygen. Carbon dioxide is the most important greenhouse gas. Human-caused emissions of CO_2 are largely responsible for the enhanced greenhouse effect.

carbon monoxide (CO): An odourless, colourless but toxic gas produced as a result of the incomplete combustion of fuels containing carbon. Carbon monoxide is a common air pollutant, mainly released by motor vehicles. At low concentrations, CO can impair vision, cause dizziness and trigger angina. It is lethal at high concentrations.

carcinogen: Any substance capable of causing cancer in animal or human tissues.

CCME: Canadian Council of Ministers of the Environment. The council provides an important opportunity for all Canada's environment ministers to discuss crucial environmental problems of national scope and impact, and to take cooperative action to resolve them. The CCME also promotes the sharing of information and skills by the federal, provincial and territorial environment ministries.

CFCs (*chlorofluorocarbons*): A family of manufactured gases composed of chlorine, fluorine, and carbon which, along with halons, are the main cause of stratospheric ozone depletion. CFCs (and halons) are inert, nontoxic and environmentally safe in the lower atmosphere. However, once they have made their slow journey to the ozone layer, they destroy ozone at an alarming rate. Their long lifetime in the atmosphere (up to several centuries) makes CFCs especially powerful players in ozone layer depletion. CFCs are also contributing to the enhanced greenhouse effect.

CFCs are used in refrigerators, freezers and air conditioners; industrial solvents, dry cleaning agents and hospital sterilants; and foam products such as cushions, mattresses and insulation. The compounds are part of the product in some aerosols. CFCs are no longer used as the propellant in aerosols, though, because of a Canadian ban in 1980, and similar bans in the U.S. and parts of Europe (see also halons).

chlorophenols: *(chlorinated phenols)* A group of toxic chemicals used as preservatives in paints, drilling muds, photographic solutions, hides and leathers, and insecticides and, most commonly, for wood preservative.

clearcutting: The complete removal of all commercially desirable trees in one area, at one time.

cogeneration: The generation of electricity in conjunction with the production of useful heat, usually steam.

CORE: Commission on Resources and Environment. This is an independent commission established by the provincial government in January 1992 to help resolve "valley-by-valley" conflicts over land use. CORE's mandate is to develop and implement a process that will create a comprehensive land use plan for British Columbia. The commission is also charged with initiating a regional process to resolve resource use disputes.

CORE's key goals are to sustain our environment, economy and communities; to inform and involve the public; and to replace confrontation with consensus in making resource management decisions. The commission will draw on the work of other important agencies dealing with resource use, such as the Round Table on the Environment and the Economy.

criteria: Exposures of selected contaminants that mark the onset of specific effects on health or the environment. These criteria form the basis for setting environmental objectives for a specific area. Criteria are often used in the management of water and air.

cross-contamination: Unlined or improperly lined wells may contaminate higher quality water in shallower aquifers with lower quality water (e.g. high salinity) from deeper aquifers.

dioxins and furans: Popular names for two classes of chlorinated organic compounds, known as polychlorinated dibenzo-p-dioxins (**PCDDs**) and polychlorinated dibenzofurans(**PCDFs**). Only a few of the 75 PCDDs and 135 PCDFs are highly toxic. The most toxic dioxin is 2,3,7,8-tetrachlorodibenzo-p-dioxin (**2,3,7,8-TCDD**), although tolerance to this compound varies considerably among species. Dioxins and furans are formed either as by-products during some types of chemical production that involve chlorine and high temperatures or during combustion where a source of chlorine is present. Elevated levels of 2,3,7,8-TCDD in the environment are linked to effluents from previous 2,4,5-trichlorophenol manufacturing, such as in the Love Canal area. Dioxins, including 2,3,7,8-TCDD, can also occur in airborne particulate material from incinerators that burn trash containing chlorinated compounds and in exhaust from diesel engines. Chlorine bleaching of kraft wood pulp is another source of 2,3,7,8-TCDD.

driftnet fishing: A fishing method that uses a series of connected nets hanging vertically in the ocean. The series of nets can range from 16 to 50 kilometres in length. Driftnets are used to catch (in their mesh) such species as salmon, squid, marlin and albacore tuna. The problem is that the driftnets also trap, and kill, many other species. These include large numbers of nontargeted fish, dolphins, porpoises, fur seals, turtles and seabirds.

ecological classification: A process of classifying ecologically distinctive areas of the earth's surface. Each area can be viewed as a discrete system which has resulted from the inter-play of the geologic, land form, soil vegetation, climate, wildlife, water and human factors which may be present. The relative importance of each factor varies from one area to another. This wholistic approach to classification can be applied incrementally from very specific ecosystems to very broad ecosystems. Ecoprovinces represent the large and very generalized ecologically unit for British Columbia. Progressively more detailed units (i.e. ecoregions and ecosections) are nested within the respective ecoprovinces.

ecology: The science concerned with the interrelationships of organisms and their environments. The word comes from the Greek term meaning "the study of the home".

ecoprovince: An area of the earth's surface characterized by very broad ecological interactions between the four major environmental components of the ecosystem: air, water, land and biota.

ecoregion: A part of an ecoprovince characterized by regional ecological interactions between the four major environmental components of the ecosystem: air, water, land and biota.

ecosection: A part of an ecoregion characterized by sub-regional ecological interations between the four major environmental components of the ecosystem: air, water, land and biota.

ecosystem: Organisms of a natural community together with their physical, chemical and biological environment ("ecological" + "system").

effluent: Liquids that contain contaminating waste material, released into the environment.

estuary: An area where fresh water meets salt water (bays, mouths of rivers, salt marshes, lagoons).

Eurasian watermilfoil: An aquatic plant native to Europe and Asia which was introduced to B.C. waters about 1970. Due to its aggressive growth habit it out competes native species interfering with shoreline recreation and can impede waterflow and deplete fish habitat.

eutrophication: The process by which bodies of water become better nourished by fertilization. This natural process is often accelerated by nutrient-rich discharges from agriculture or sewage, leading to a rapid and excessive growth of algae and water plants and undesirable changes in water quality.

fecal coliform: Bacteria usually present in the large intestinal tract of humans and other warm-blooded animals and therefore useful as an indicator of sanitary quality in water. Exposure to fecal coliforms in drinking water may cause diseases such as cholera and hepatitis.

food chain: A series of steps in which one group of plants or animals serves as food for another and these, in turn, for another.

food web: The complex interactions of several food chains. The term "food web" is more accurate than "food chain," which sounds like a simple one-to-one connection. Caterpillars, for instance, eat many different plants. They are the food for many different birds - and these birds, in turn, can be the prey of several different predators.

fossil fuels: Combustible fuels, such as coal, oil and natural gas, which are derived from the remains of ancient plants and animals.

global climate change: Major alterations in the climate of the earth, which most scientists predict will be the result of global warming. An increase in global temperature (due to the enhanced greenhouse effect) could lead to substantial changes in climate all over the world, including altered precipitation patterns and a rise in global sea level. Climate change is expected to be most pronounced in the polar regions, followed by the mid-latitudes (including Canada), with significant regional variations.

global warming: The warming of the earth and its atmosphere by the enhanced greenhouse effect. Global warming is expected to lead to global climate change. The Intergovernmental Panel on Climate Change predicts that by 2025 the planet will be about 1°C warmer than it is now, and 3°C higher by the end of the 21st century. To put these figures into perspective, the earth's average temperature during the last ice age was only 5°C colder than at present.

greenhouse effect: The heating effect of the atmosphere upon the earth. Light waves from the sun pass through the atmosphere and are absorbed by the earth. The earth then reradiates this energy as heat waves which are absorbed by greenhouse gases in the lower atmosphere (see below). Thus the atmosphere behaves like the glass in a greenhouse, allowing the passage of light, but not of heat. The greenhouse effect has been a property of earth's atmosphere for millions of years. Today, because humans are affecting the proportions of greenhouse gases in the atmosphere, an enhanced greenhouse effect (see global warming) is believed to be causing a rise in average global temperatures.

greenhouse gases: The gases that play a part in the greenhouse effect: carbon dioxide (the most important greenhouse gas), methane, nitrous oxide, ozone, water vapour, CFCs and other trace gases.

ground-level ozone: Ozone (O_3) found near the earth's surface, as opposed to the ozone found in the stratosphere (the ozone layer). Some ground-level ozone occurs naturally. However, concentrations are increased by human activities. Ground-level ozone is formed by the reaction of volatile organic compounds (VOCs) and nitrogen oxides (NO_x) in the presence of sunlight and warm temperatures. A stagnant air mass keeps the pollution from being dispersed. Motor vehicles are the major manmade source of VOC and NO_x emissions.

High concentrations of ground-level ozone can produce a decrease in lung function. In addition, ground-level ozone can reduce the productivity and damage the growth of vegetation, and accelerate the deterioration of such materials as rubber, fibres and plastics.

groundwater: Water in the saturated zone of an aquifer. Groundwater is often a source of surface water (i.e. a spring or stream) and well water.

groundwater mining: Refers to a situation where extraction exceeds aquifer recharge from surface water sources, causing a regional lowering of the water table. This phenomenon has been observed in the southern United States.

habitat: The place in which an animal or plant lives. The sum of environmental circumstances in the place inhabited by an organism, population or community.

halons (*brominated fluorocarbons*): Manufactured chemicals that play a major role in ozone layer depletion, along with CFCs. Halons can destroy up to 16 times as much ozone as CFCs can. For this reason, halons are the most serious ozone-depleting group of chemicals emitted in British Columbia. Halons are used in specialized fire extinguishers - for equipment and articles that would be destroyed by water or other fire extinguisher chemicals.

hazardous (special) waste: Substances covered by the Special Waste regulation and which require special disposal techniques. Examples include discarded PCBs, pesticides, used oils, spent solvents and paints.

heavy metals: Metals with a high molecular weight, such as mercury, lead, cadmium and chromium. Heavy metals are generally toxic to plants and animals even in low concentrations. Some are also essential to life i.e. copper, zinc. They are widely used and discharged by industry.

herbicides: A pesticide chemical that kills unwanted vegetation.

hydrogen sulphide (*H_2S*): A colourless, flammable gas with an odour of rotten eggs, which is a constituent of industrial emissions. At relatively low levels, H_2S can cause headaches, nausea and irritation of the eyes.

Under high temperatures (burning), H_2S reacts with oxygen to form sulphur dioxide (SO_2) which reacts with water to form $SO_4^=$, a major contributor to acid rain. H_2S also reacts with Oxygen and water to form $SO_4^=$. In B.C., the major sources of H_2S are pulp mills and natural gas processing plants.

in-stream use: Uses of water which do not require its removal from streams or lakes (e.g. hydroelectric power generation, navigation, recreation, fish, and wildlife). In-stream uses require minimum flow rates, water levels, and a certain level of water quantity.

indigenous species: Plants or animals that occur naturally in British Columbia. The term excludes those species that have been introduced into B.C. directly, as well as species that have been introduced into adjacent jurisdictions and then have migrated into the province.

integrated resource management: Land management that considers all resource values and allows for the operation of more than one resource use in the same land area. Integrated resource management considers both competing and complementary resource values in a comprehensive manner. The goal is to maximize social, environmental and economic benefits with no undue harm to any one resource sector.

inversion: Temperature normally declines with altitude. An inversion is an atmospheric condition caused by a layer of warm air above cool air. The inversion holds down pollutants that might otherwise be dispersed, and is therefore a contributing factor in the creation of photochemical smog.

kraft pulp mill: Produces coarse brown paper of great strength from wood pulp using the sulphite pulping process. Bleached kraft pulp mills typically use chlorine to produce whiter paper.

nitrate: An essential plant nutrient. It is found in fertilizers and may be produced in the breakdown of organic wastes. Excessive fertilizer application, improper agricultural waste management or underground septic tanks may increase nitrate levels in groundwater. Nitrates reduce the ability of blood to carry oxygen. Infants under six months are particularly at risk from drinking well-water containing excessive nitrates.

nitrogen oxides (*NO_x*): Gases formed when nitrogen combines with oxygen. NO_x consist of nitric oxide (NO), nitrous oxide (N_2O) and nitrogen dioxide (NO_2). At low concentrations, NO_x can trigger bronchial congestion in asthmatics and children. At higher concentrations, they can cause fluid buildup in the lungs and fibrotic changes. NO_x contribute to ground-level ozone, acid rain, the enhanced greenhouse effect and stratospheric ozone depletion.

Not Satisfactorily Restocked (NSR): This is a forestry term describing land that is not growing trees to its full potential. The stocking status of an area (i.e., is it satisfactorily restocked?) is evaluated on the basis of acceptable tree species (is the species economic to harvest and use?) and stocking levels for each ecosystem. Areas that are classified as NSR are considered as not contributing to the forest's growing stock from a forestry point of view, although they may still contribute to other forest values.

objectives: Specific minimal exposure levels of selected substances (for example, in water or air), which are set to protect the most sensitive uses. These objectives establish a standard against which the environmental quality at a particular site can be measured, and used to guide environmental management to protect the users and the environment.

old-growth forest: After a natural disturbance, such as a fire, or after being harvested, forests develop through a series of stages in a process called "succession". The last stage in forest succession is called old-growth. Depending on the type of forest, it may take anywhere from 100 to 250 years for a forest to enter the old-growth stage of development. In coastal British Columbia, old-growth forests range in age from 200 years to well over 1000 years. Once a forest has become old growth it is usually still changing in species composition and structure. Small-scale natural disturbances which result in the death and replacement of individual trees are key processes influencing the structure of old-growth forests. Old-growth forests are characterized by a large variety of tree sizes and ages, a great diversity in species of plants and animals, the presence of standing and fallen dead trees (which provide habitat for plants and animals), and an uneven canopy which allows light to penetrate to the forest floor in small openings.

ozone layer: A fragile band of gases ranging from about 15 to 40 kilometres above the earth, in the stratosphere. The ozone layer acts as the planet's natural sunscreen: it shields life on earth from much of the sun's potentially damaging ultraviolet radiation.

PAHs (*polynuclear aromatic hydrocarbons*): A family of chemical compounds found in a variety of natural and manmade sources. Some of the compounds are strongly mutagenic and carcinogenic. Sources include thermal power plants, coke ovens, sewage, wood smoke, and used lubricating oils.

particulate matter (*PM*): Fine liquid or solid particles - such as dust, smoke, mist fumes or smog - found in the air or emissions. Also known as **particulates**.

PCBs (*polychlorinated biphenyls*): A group of 209 chemical compounds, a small number of which are toxic, that are widely used as fire retardants in insulating and heat exchange fluids in electrical transformers and capacitors, as plasticizers, as waterproofing agents, and in inking processes to produce carbonless copy paper. PCBs resist biodegradation, accumulate in the food chain and are suspected carcinogens.

pesticide: Any chemical used to kill pests, such as insects and rodents. It also includes "herbicides," which are chemicals that kill plants.

pH: A measure of the acidity or alkalinity of a material, liquid or solid. pH is represented on a scale of 0 to 14, with 7 being a neutral state, 0 the most acid and 14 the most alkaline.

photochemical smog: An atmospheric haze sometimes found above large industrial and urban areas. Photochemical smog occurs in the lower portion of our atmosphere, known as the troposphere. Its main unhealthy component is "ground-level ozone". Carbon monoxide and particulates are other harmful ingredients of smog.

plankton: Tiny organisms living in the surface layer of an ocean or lake. They consist of plant organisms (**phytoplankton**) and animal organisms (**zooplankton**) which feed mainly on phytoplankton. Plankton are the vital first step in many aquatic food chains.

prescribed burning: A controlled burn in a designated area. The fire is ignited intentionally and allowed to proceed within well-defined boundaries. Prescribed burning is mainly used to remove vegetation which competes with tree crops, to make it easier to plant tree seedlings, to expose mineral soil for tree seedlings (in forestry and land development), and to reduce fire danger or to enhance wildlife habitat and cattle range.

Round Table on the Environment and the Economy (British Columbia): A 32-member advisory group representing a wide range of resource use interests in this province. It was set up in January 1990 to assist the government in achieving sustainable development and to work towards consensus among the competing land use interests. The Round Table is working to resolve land use debates, as well as other environmental and economic conflicts. (See **sustainable development**)

runoff: A term referring to that part of precipitation (rainfall or snowmelt) which runs off the land surface into streams and/or lakes. This is in contrast to those parts which either evaporate or soak into the ground.

saltwater intrusion: Can occur in coastal localities where drawdown of the water table allows saltwater to enter wells.

second growth forest: When an old growth forest is destroyed by a natural disturbance or by forest harvesting, the forest that develops to replace it is called a second growth forest. Second growth forests are the earlier stages of forest succession which precede the development of old-growth (see entry under "old growth"). Second growth forests, especially those managed for timber production, are usually more uniform in structure, species composition and age than old growth forests - they are simplified in structure relative to old growth. Some species do well in second growth forests but others require particular structural attributes found in old-growth (e.g. large snags and logs). Given enough time, second growth forests develop into old growth forests - all old growth forests were second growth earlier on their development - but it may take hundreds of years to do so. An older second growth forest often looks very similar to a young old-growth forest, but is very different

from that same old-growth forest after several hundred more years of development. The second growth forests that we are creating through forest management today, with timber as their main management objective, are very different structurally from the second growth forests created by natural disturbances in the past.

sediment: Soil particles and rock fragments transported and deposited by the action of river, glaciers, sea and wind.

selection cutting: An "uneven-aged" silvicultural system in which trees are harvested individually or in small groups at relatively short intervals. Selection systems of forestry require a thorough understanding of the ecology of the forest being managed, tree species which can regenerate in smaller openings than clearcuts, and careful long-term planning and monitoring. Without these, it can degenerate into "high-grading" where only the "best" trees are taken, leaving a forest with little remaining commercial value.

sensitive species: Those species for which population viability is a concern, as indicated by significant downward trends in numbers in the population or density, and/or habitat changes.

silviculture: The management, care and culture of forest trees; forestry.

solid waste: Discarded material that does not have enough liquid to be free flowing.

stratosphere: The layer of the atmosphere that lies between the troposphere and the upper atmosphere (mesosphere and thermosphere). It includes the ozone layer. The stratosphere begins at 9-16 km above the earth, depending on the latitude.

stratospheric ozone depletion: The thinning of the planet's protective ozone layer, which lies in the stratosphere. The major causes of stratospheric ozone depletion are manufactured chemicals called chlorofluorocarbons (CFCs) and halons (brominated fluorocarbons). The latest scientific evidence indicates that the ozone layer over the Antarctic is about 50-60% thinner than normal, during the polar spring, and as large in area as North America. Over the Arctic, the springtime ozone depletion is about 40%. At the northern and southern mid-latitudes the springtime depletion is between 2-6%.

sulphur dioxide *(SO$_2$)*: A colourless gas formed primarily by the combustion of fossil fuels that is one of the major contributors to acid rain. Sulphur dioxide and its atmospheric by-products can also cause respiratory ailments and cardiac problems. Sources of SO$_2$ in B.C. include pulp mills, smelters, natural gas processing plants and the combustion of high-sulphur fuels, such as coal and petroleum.

sustainable development: Economic and social development within the limits required to sustain long-term environmental well-being. Such development ensures that our use of the environment and natural resources today does not harm the prospects for their use in the future.

This concept gained worldwide attention and support following the 1987 release of the report by the World Commission on Environment and Development (*Our Common Future*).

threatened species: Any indigenous species of fauna or flora that is likely to become endangered in British Columbia if the factors affecting its vulnerability are not reversed.

toxicity: The potential or capacity of a material of being harmful to the health of a living organism.

troposphere: The lowest portion of the earth's atmosphere, it extends about 6 to 17 km upwards from the earth depending on latitude and season. Almost all of the earth's weather phenomena, as well as most pollution, occur in the troposphere.

ungulates: Mammals with hooves, including sheep, goats, horses, deer, caribou, elk and moose.

volatile organic compounds *(VOCs)*: Chemicals which contain hydrogen and carbon, and which evaporate easily. Hundreds of these compounds are present in the atmosphere and many come from natural sources (e.g. volcanoes, trees, vegetation, bacteria and fossil fuel deposits). The main human sources of VOCs are the fossil fuels burned in motor vehicles, as well as solvents and oil-based paints.

vulnerable species: Any indigenous species of flora or fauna which is not classified as a threatened species, but is particularly at risk - because of low or declining numbers; occurrence at the fringe of its range or in restricted areas; or some other reason.

water cycle: *(hydrologic cycle)* The endless circulation of water from the atmosphere to the earth and its return to the atmosphere through condensation, precipitation, evaporation and transpiration.

watershed: *(water basin)* The entire area drained by a waterway, or which drains into a lake or reservoir.

well interference: The process whereby a large well locally draws down the water table causing water levels in surrounding smaller wells to fall. This is a localized phenomenon and does not necessarily indicate regional drawdown of the groundwater resource (i.e. groundwater mining).

wildlife: In 1990, all native species of animals in the province were designated as wildlife, giving them full protection under provisions of the Wildlife Act. Invertebrates and fish are excluded from this designation.

withdrawal use: Uses of water which require its removal from lakes or streams (e.g. many residential, agricultural, and industrial uses). Not all withdrawn water is actually "consumed" (i.e. incorporated into final products or redistributed to other components of the water cycle). A portion (non-consumptive use) is typically returned to streams or lakes as wastewater, frequently of lower quality than when it was removed.

Index

127